The Rebel Den of Nùng Trí Cao

Image of Nùng Trí Cao's father Nùng Tôn Phúc among his clansmen and followers

The Rebel Den of Nùng Trí Cao

Loyalty and Identity Along the
Sino-Vietnamese Frontier

JAMES ANDERSON

UNIVERSITY OF WASHINGTON PRESS
Seattle

in association with

NUS PRESS
Singapore

Publication of this book is made possible with the assistance of a grant from the Charles and Jane Keyes Endowment for Books on Southeast Asia, established through the generosity of Charles and Jane Keyes; and by the Jackson School Publications Fund, established through the generous support of the Henry M. Jackson Foundation and other donors, in cooperation with the Henry M. Jackson School of International Studies and the University of Washington Press.

Copyright © 2007 by the University of Washington Press
Printed in Singapore

All rights reserved. No part of this publication may be reproduced or transmitted in any form or by any means, electronic or mechanical, including photocopy, recording, or any information storage or retrieval system, without permission in writing from the publisher.

Published simultaneously in Singapore and the United States.

University of Washington Press
PO Box 50096
Seattle, WA 98145, USA
www.washington.edu/uwpress

NUS Press
National University of Singapore
AS3-01-02. 3 Arts Link
Singapore 117569
www.nus.edu.sg/npu

ISBN 978-9971-69-367-1 (Paper)

Library of Congress Cataloging-in-Publication Data

Anderson, James, 1963–
　The rebel den of Nùng Trí Cao : loyalty and identity along the Sino-Vietnamese frontier / James Anderson.
　　p. cm.
　Includes bibliographical references and index.
　ISBN-13: 978-0-295-98689-0 (pbk.: alk. paper)
　ISBN-10: 0-295-98689-1 (pbk.: alk. paper)

　1. Vietnam—History—939–1428.　2. Nùng Trí Cao, ca. 1025–ca. 1055.
　3. China—History—Sung dynasty, 960–1279.　4. Vietnam—Boundaries—China.
　5. China—Boundaries—Vietnam.　6. Vietnam—Relations—China.
　7. China—Relations—Vietnam.
　　I. Title.

DS556.6.A54 2007
959.7'02—dc22　　　　　　　　　　　　　　　　　　　　　　　　　2006037840

Cover by Elvin Chng

The paper used in this publication is acid-free and 90 percent recycled from at least 50 percent post-consumer waste. It meets the minimum requirements of American National Standard for Information Sciences—Permanence of Paper for Printed Library Materials, ANSI Z39.48–1984.

Contents

List of Maps	vii
List of Figures	viii
List of Appendix Figures	ix
Preface and Acknowledgments	x
Conventions	xv

1. The Great King Nùng Trí Cao: A Rebel's Role in Shaping Regional Identity along the Modern Sino-Vietnamese Border — 3

2. The Legacy of the Chinese Imperial Tribute System in the South: Balancing Ritual Harmony with Frontier Stability — 15

3. Examples of Negotiated Autonomy: Sino-Vietnamese Relations Before the Eleventh Century — 33

4. Gaining Legitimacy at the Empire's Edge: Indigenous Tai-Speaking Communities along the Sino-Vietnamese Frontier through the Early Song Period — 68

5. The Specter of Southern Power: Nùng Trí Cao's Insurrection, Court Reaction, and the Legacy of Nam Việt — 88

6. Tempting "Treacherous Factions": The Manipulation of Frontier Alliances on the Eve of the 1075 Sino-Vietnamese Borderlands War — 119

7. Monumental Pride: Sino-Vietnamese Cross-Border Commemorations of Nùng Trí Cao — 152

8. Conclusion — 183

Appendix 1: Inscriptions from the Kỳ Sầm Temple   186
Appendix 2: Inscriptions from the Nùng Trí Cao Temple   189

Notes   193
Glossary   221
Bibliography   244
Index   265

List of Maps

Map 1. Modern Political Map of Sino-Vietnamese Border   5

Map 2. Lingnan Frontier Region Before the Eleventh Century   36

Map 3. Home Region of Tai Communities   70

Map 4. Nùng Trí Cao's Third Rebellion   99

Map 5. The 1075 Song-Lý Frontier War   141

Map 6. Temple Sites in the Modern Sino-Vietnamese Border Region   180

List of Figures

Title Page:	Image of Nùng Trí Cao's father Nùng Tôn Phúc among his clansmen and followers	ii
Figure 1.1.	View from the border region at Sóc Hà Commune, Hà Quảng County, Cao Bằng, Vietnam	4
Figure 2.1.	The Rites of Zhou Map of Tributary Domains	21
Figure 6.1.	An Illustration of Prefectures and Commandaries Beyond the Influence of Our Dynasty	147
Figure 7.1.	Commemorative stele to Nùng Trí Cao at Xia Lei, Guangxi, China, 1997	162
Figure 7.2.	Kỳ Sầm Temple, Cao Bằng city, 1997	166
Figure 7.3.	Stele from destroyed temple at Sóc Hà Commune, Hà Quảng County, Cao Bằng, Vietnam, 1997	174
Figure 7.4.	Temple at Quảng Hoà Commune, historically considered the home prefecture of Nùng Trí Cao, 1997	175
Figure 7.5.	Site of Nùng Tồn Phúc's citadel with more recent Mạc garrison and Nã Lư Temple structures, 1997	175
Figure 7.6.	Suburban Cao Bằng city temple devoted to A Nùng, 1997	176
Figure 7.7.	Kỳ Sầm Temple, 2001	178

List of Appendix Figures

Figure A. Inscriptions from the Kỳ Sầm Temple,   186
           Cao Bằng, Vietnam, purported to be the site of
           Nùng Trí Cao's tomb

Figure B. Left-hand altar inscriptions from the Nùng Trí Cao   189
           Temple, Quảng Hoà Commune, Quảng Uyên County,
           Cao Bằng, Vietnam

Figure C. Center altar inscription from the Nùng Trí Cao   190
           Temple, Quảng Hoà Commune, Quảng Uyên County,
           Cao Bằng, Vietnam

Figure D. Right-hand altar inscription from the Nùng Trí Cao   191
           Temple, Quảng Hoà Commune, Quảng Uyên County,
           Cao Bằng, Vietnam

Preface and Acknowledgments

My own interest in Nùng Trí Cao is three-fold. First, early on I found his life story to be an intriguing narrative. In the course of my studies on the evolution of post-Tang Sino-Vietnamese tribute relations, the bold and perhaps "devil-may-care" attempts of Trí Cao and his clan to carve out a political place between two powerful overlords stood out starkly in the reams of materials I pored over in my research. I have always been drawn to tales of marginalized characters and communities in all walks of life, and Nùng Trí Cao appeared to be a valiant but hopeless character struggling to find his place on the edges of recorded history. The more I read, the more I became fascinated by his short-lived achievements. Trí Cao's initial limited reliance on kinship and lineage alliances gave way briefly to the chieftain's dream of establishing a region-wide kingdom encompassing a much more diverse population along the entire South China coast. My curiosity was stirred not by his failure to establish such a realm but instead by Trí Cao's belief that such a kingdom might actually prevail against all odds.

Second, after some examination, I discovered that the Nùng Trí Cao rebellions fit a pattern of political behavior that emerged in what is often called the "Classical Period" of Southeast Asian history. This period, from roughly the ninth century until the fourteenth century, witnessed the appearance of a group of traditional states that would, in turn, play either territorial or symbolic roles in the establishment of modern nation-states in Southeast Asia, including Pagan (Burma/Myanmar), Sukhothai (Thailand), Angkor (Cambodia), Đại Việt (Vietnam), Sri Vijaya (Malaysia), and Majapahit (Indonesia). The actual periodization and historical importance of this era is not without controversy among Southeast Asia scholars.* However, the Classical Period does represent for many scholars a significant transitional phase between the era of relatively small and self-sufficient kingdoms that existed before this time and the age of larger, trade-oriented, multi-ethnic imperial orders that emerged after it.

Preface and Acknowledgments xi

Lastly, once I had completed my initial textual study of Trí Cao's revolts and had had the opportunity to visit the Sino-Vietnamese border region, I began to see similarities between events "on the ground" along the eleventh-century frontier and certain social and cultural changes occurring in the present age of globalization. Trí Cao, in his day, appealed to the Vietnamese and Chinese courts for patronage, but he also sought local support by evoking indigenous symbols of political identity. In recent years a variety of cultural events have also been conducted in the Sino-Vietnamese border region to express a local attachment to the legacy of Nùng Trí Cao. New scholarly and folkloric studies have been published, and conferences have been held both in China and in Vietnam to discuss and broadcast to a wider audience the endeavors of this historical figure. As I will discuss in my final chapter, temples and public memorials are two important aspects of this renewed cultural activity. However, one ought also to take into consideration international changes to explain the surfacing of such pursuits.

Along the route to completing this book, I received help from a large number of scholars, colleagues, and friends. I very much wish to acknowledge the intellectual debt that I owe so many. Every project has a beginning, and mine started at the University of Washington with a suggestion from Hok-lam Chan that I explore a foreign relations topic from China's imperial period. Under Professor Chan's guidance I first looked at the court debates that swirled about during the Ming's invasion and aborted occupation of the Vietnamese kingdom in the early fifteenth century. Because my interest in Middle Period China gravitated toward the Northern Song period, I explored the possibility that similar tensions existed between China and Vietnam at that time as well. Little did I know then that these tensions were two millennia in the making and that the Sino-Vietnamese relationship was a defining feature of multiple states founded by rulers in this region with varying degrees of success!

As a graduate student at the University of Washington, I benefited from my interaction with so many wonderfully talented people. I especially wish to acknowledge R. Kent Guy, Laurie Sears, Alan Wood, Gary Hamilton, Robert Stacey, Kenneth Pyle, William Boltz,

John Pemberton, and Patricia Ebrey for all their advice and help. I also wish to thank my classmates Michele Thompson, Li Yi, Steve Miles, Steve Udry, Jennifer Rudolf, Tom Reilly, and George Dutton, and my good friends Scott and Laura Heinlein, for all their help and suggestions. Li Yi deserves special thanks for reading and commenting on my translations of imperial edicts in the days when I was first getting accustomed to the particular style of Song-period bureaucrats. Michele Thompson must also be singled out for her assistance during the summer of 2003, when she read a full-length draft of the manuscript and then offered editorial suggestions over several rounds of coffee at the Broadway Au Bon Pain in New Haven, Connecticut.

I would also like to thank Professors Paul J. Smith, Don Wyatt, John Whitmore, and all my friends and colleagues at the University of North Carolina at Greensboro who have read all or parts of the manuscript. This project has benefited immensely from their comments and criticisms. Elizabeth Nelson, my UNCG colleague from the Department of Geography, deserves special thanks for the wonderful set of maps she created for this project. My original hand-drawn approximations of the frontier terrain lacked the precise detail that Liz presents so clearly in her maps. Working with Liz also revealed to me how much more one can accomplish in an interdisciplinary partnership.

Research for this book also took me overseas on numerous occasions, and I must thank all those persons who made these trips so profitable. Huang Kuanchong, before, during, and after his tenure as director of Academia Sinica's Institute of History and Philology, the current director, Wang Fan-sen, Liu Li-yen, and Chen Kuo-tung offered me a great deal of guidance at various stages in this project. Chen Zhichao at the Chinese Academy of Social Sciences in Beijing, Dai Kelai of Zhengzhou University, Zhao Heman at the Guangxi Academy of Social Sciences, and Nong Bing from the southern Guangxi village of Xialei all assisted me beyond measure.

In 2001 I spent eight months on a Luce-funded fellowship at the Australian National University's Research School of Pacific and Asian Studies in Canberra and at the Sino-Nom Institute in Hanoi. In Australia, Professors David Marr, Craig Reynolds, and the fellowship's coordinator, Ben Kerkvliet, were extremely helpful and supportive. I also wish to give Professor Phan Huy Lê, former director of the Sino-Nom Institute Phan Văn Các, the late Trần Quốc Vượng, and the late Hoàng Văn Lâu special thanks for their time, advice, and professional assistance, which allowed me the opportunity to gather notes, photocopies, and photographs of archeological and epigraphic materials unavailable in the United States.

Various organizations provided the funding necessary to complete this project, including Fulbright-Hays Doctoral Dissertation Research Abroad Fellowship, Ford Small Research Grant in Southeast Asian Studies, and the ACLS/Chiang Ching-kuo Foundation Fellowship. I also would like to make special mention of the Pacific Cultural Foundation Research Grant in Taipei for funding support during my overseas research in graduate school. More recently, I benefited from six months as a fellow in the John W. Kluge Center for International Studies at the Library of Congress in Washington, D.C. I made extensive use of the Library of Congress's collections of gazetteer materials for southern China, and I received very helpful comments on this project from my fellow Kluge scholars throughout my stay in Washington. For this opportunity I am grateful for the research assistance offered by so many members of the Library research staff, including Frank Wang, Judy Lu, and Lien Fielder in the Asian Reading Room. The Kluge Center's director, Prosser Gifford, deserves special recognition and thanks for all the support he offered to visiting scholars.

Regarding the editing and production of this book, I wish to thank my two anonymous readers commissioned by the University of Washington Press for their valuable comments, as well as Laura Iwasaki for her assistance in editing and polishing the manuscript. I also want to thank my editor Mary Ribesky and my executive editor Michael Duckworth at the Press. Their support for this first-time author was greatly appreciated.

Finally, I wish to thank my parents, Frederic and Anita Anderson, my siblings, Haideen and John, my wife, Yueh-miao, and our daughters, Claire Elisabeth and Svea Haideen for putting up with a "lifetime" student and distracted father for so long. Without their support and encouragement I could not have begun, let alone completed, this project.

I have published an early version of chapter 4 as "Man of Prowess or Errant Vassal: Nùng Tŏn Phúc's 11th Century Bid for Autonomy," *Southeast Review of Asian Studies* 22 (2002) and a section of chapter 7 as a research note titled "Monumental Pride: Sino-Vietnamese Cross-border Commemorations of Nùng Trí Cao" in the *Thai-Yunnan Project Bulletin*, no. 1 (July 2001): 1–2. I wish to thank the editorial boards of these publications for permission to include material from these articles here.

---

* For recent studies of this scholarly controversy, see Michael Aung-Thwin, "The 'Classical' in Southeast Asia: The Present in the Past," *Journal of Southeast Asian Studies* 26, no. 1 (March 1995): 75–92. See also Craig J. Reynolds, "A New Look at Old Southeast Asia (Early Southeast Asian Historiography)," *The Journal of Asian Studies* 54, no. 2 (May 1995): 419–47.

Conventions

I have attempted to remain as historically precise as possible when naming kingdoms and periods through various time periods and political shifts. However, some of the language I have used may not satisfy every reader. Prior to the twentieth century, modern names for the countries examined in this book and modern names for their inhabitants would not be relevant. In his recent study of East Asia to the tenth century, Charles Holcombe noted, "It is critical to a clear understanding of the origins of East Asia to realize that none of the modern nation-states of the region existed yet as such — not even "China" in a modern sense, although the limitations of our vocabulary may at times force us to use the modern English names."[†] Mindful of Professor Holcombe's prudent admonition, I have used the following modern English terms in this study.

I have chosen "Vietnamese" and "Vietnam" as terms to describe persons and places associated with political power situated in the vicinity of the Red (Hồng) River delta. I have rendered the Chinese characters for these persons and places in their Vietnamese (quốc ngữ) readings. Moreover, I have used the term "Chinese" to describe persons and places associated with courts and political centers north of the Red River delta, and I have rendered the characters for these persons and places in their modern (Mandarin) Chinese readings. This practice circumvents the issue of Tai names, but I do not mean for these terms necessarily to indicate modern ethnic identity. The terms "Tai" and "Tai-speaking" are used primarily as linguistic distinctions to mark the Sino-Tibetan language family spoken by the communities of indigenous people who claim descent from the powerful frontier clans in the period under study.

Wherever possible, I have used dynastic terms to indicate a person's political affiliation.

[†] Charles Holcombe, *The Genesis of East Asia: 221 B.C.–A.D. 907* (Honolulu: University of Hawaii Press, 2001), 166.

The Rebel Den of Nùng Trí Cao

1

The Great King Nùng Trí Cao: A Rebel's Role in Shaping Regional Identity along the Modern Sino-Vietnamese Border

Why should we in the early twenty-first century pay particular attention to the collective identity of and historical relationship between the regions now ruled as the People's Republic of China and the Socialist Republic of Vietnam? I once asked myself this question while standing in a valley near the commune of Hà Quảng on the Sino-Vietnamese frontier, where Chinese tanks had rolled through as recently as 1979, retracing the well-trodden paths of cavalry and foot soldiers from centuries earlier. Identities forged in the eleventh-century borderlands remain surprisingly salient today, reminding us of more volatile examples from other regions of the world, such as the Basques, the Kosovars, and the Kurds. Transnational bonds are an important aspect of these groups' collective identities and are often a source of tension in their relations with their respective national governments.

One important reason for paying attention to the Sino-Vietnamese borderlands is the modern reemergence of China as a regional power. Southeast Asian countries, once under the thumb of colonial masters, gained their independence just in time to face the effects of China's growing influence. Southeast Asia, Vietnam included, shows great

Figure 1.1. View from the border region at Sóc Hà Commune, Hà Quảng County, Cao Bằng, Vietnam (James Anderson)

potential for vigorous growth and innovation, supporting the development of an integrated, transnational economic power. Nevertheless, widespread confidence in the economic autonomy of this region, which suffered a financial crisis at the end of the twentieth century and the economic slump induced by severe acute respiratory syndrome at the beginning of the twenty-first century, may have been overstated.

In this destabilized economic environment, China became more involved in Southeast Asian affairs, and the large northern neighbor's influence on the region could surpass that of the United States in the near future. However, the historical record reveals that the Vietnamese and other Southeast Asian peoples have resisted northern pressures for ages, even as they borrowed institutions and practices with which to create and perpetuate their own regimes of local control. To understand this complex north-south relationship, we must develop a stronger sense of its genealogy. If we also take a closer look at the communities that reside along the political border separating modern-day Vietnam and China, we find numerous upland hillside- and plateau-dwelling ethnic groups that historically have resisted total incorporation by their politically and economically more powerful neighbors. Moreover, leaders of the Kinh Vietnamese, riverine-valley and delta dwellers, were not alone in their dreams of territorial autonomy apart from the region's dominant power, China. Looking back through history, we see that the emergence of an independent Vietnamese polity in 968 created a Sino-Vietnamese frontier region over which the Vietnamese court maintained limited administrative control. Under these political conditions, upland leaders who resided north of the Red River and south of the most densely settled population centers of South China (Ling Piao) also envisioned separate domains of authority. By the late tenth century, some local leaders from this region had succeeded in establishing such domains, while others attempted to do so in the ensuing years.

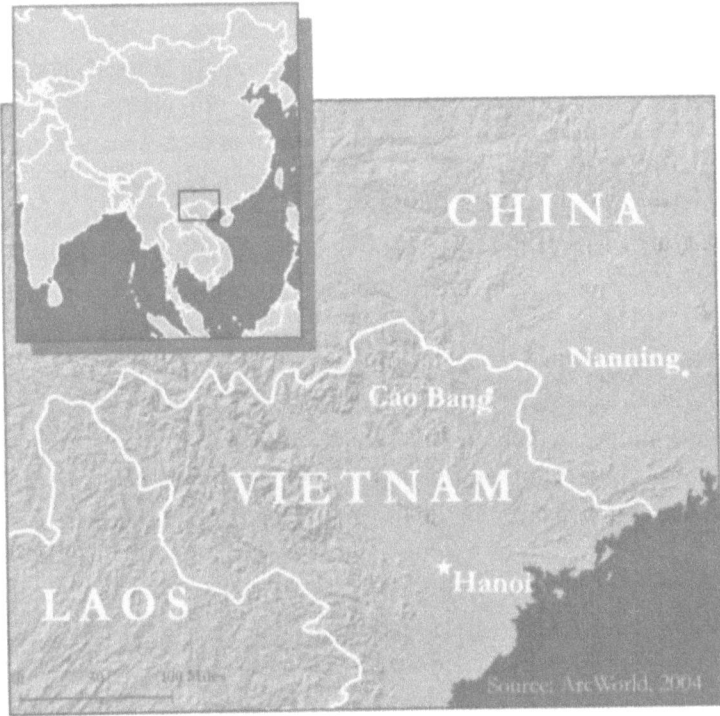

Map 1. Modern Political Map of Sino-Vietnamese Border (Elizabeth Nelson)

In terms of methodology, the general approach to frontier studies in Western scholarship has shifted direction in recent years, and this study has been influenced by that shift. Amy Turner Bushnell contends in a recent conference volume that both the "paradigm of power" and the related "paradigm of the victim" have given way to the "paradigm of negotiation" as an effective explanatory model in the study of relations between premodern core and peripheral communities. She writes that "the paradigm of negotiation examines the mechanisms other than force that deliver balance to relationships and keep disparate societies in equilibrium."[1] The paradigm of power, with its focus on agents of political, economic, and cultural hegemony, is only inverted by the paradigm of the victim, which accepts that power defined the terms of all essential core-periphery relationships. In this book, I note the importance of political and military power in certain situations, but I also note cultural and ritualistic power and highlight ritual practices and symbolic acts as essential tools in the brokering of relations between the core leadership and the peripheral communities, where acceptance of any terms of hegemony was shaped by local circumstances.

In the mountainous region separating Vietnam and China, far from the central governments in Hanoi and Beijing, there are a scattered handful of temples and memorials dedicated to the life and deeds of the eleventh-century Tai-speaking leader Nùng Trí Cao (ca. 1025–1055). Trí Cao, a rebellious local chieftain and would-be founder of an independent kingdom at the frontier between the Chinese Song (968–1279) empire and the emerging Vietnamese Đại Cồ Việt (Great Việt) kingdom (968–1054) achieved an influence on this region that has shifted from issues of political identity to those of community-defining "identity politics" since his final failed rebellion in 1052. Moreover, Trí Cao produced titles of authority and legitimacy when he created Chinese character–based names for his various attempted kingdoms and reign periods and for the noble titles he awarded himself and his followers. In his struggle to form independent kingdoms, Nùng Trí Cao engaged in the type of "finding of the middle ground" suggested by Bushnell's paradigm of negotiation. He fought for political differentiation with a set of titles that spoke two languages of power, indigenous terms of authority understood among his own upland neighbors and Confucian-patterned terms understood in the distant courts of Kaifeng and Thăng Long (modern-day Hanoi).

The Chinese-script titles adopted by the rebellious Trí Cao translated a claim to power grounded in local traditions into terms understood by the power brokers of his region. In his study of mid-twentieth-century Kachin chiefs and their relations with the Chinese court and the lowland Shan state, anthropologist Edmund Leach notes a similar balance of cultural symbols employed to enhance the political prestige of local leaders.[2] The rulers of the Song empire and the Đại Cồ Việt kingdom would certainly have grasped the Confucian messages of political legitimization implied in Trí Cao's actions, while border communities would have responded to signs of local prowess and leadership.[3] So strong is the legacy of Nùng Trí Cao's claims to independence that twentieth-century Marxist-trained Chinese scholars, following predominantly nationalist concerns, denigrated these titles in order to fit Trí Cao's identity into a more contained category of "local feudal authority."[4] Today, Trí Cao's ancient effort to shape a distinct political identity along the Sino-Vietnamese border continues to contribute to a modern sense of collective ethnic identity that links communities straddling the border between Chinese and Vietnamese states.

Perhaps due to the continuing peripheral status of the Sino-Vietnamese border region, the historic example of Nùng Trí Cao holds a very real attraction for modern-day indigenous inhabitants. The current source of regional pride in the eleventh-century chieftain may be found in tales of his three ambitious attempts to establish a border kingdom. In 1042, at the age of seventeen, Trí Cao established his first kingdom with the title Kingdom of the Great Succession (Dali Guo). For his efforts, Trí Cao was captured by Vietnamese troops and held at Thăng Long for several years. After his release in 1048, Trí Cao announced the founding of the Kingdom of the Southern Heavens (Nantian Guo).[5] Following this announcement, the Đại Cồ Việt court launched an attack on Trí Cao's stronghold, succeeding only in relocating the rebel leader and his closest followers farther north into Song territory. During his third attempt to gain regional recognition in 1052, Trí Cao not only proclaimed the establishment of the Kingdom of the Great South (Danan Guo) but also granted himself the title Benevolent and Kind Emperor (Renhui Huangdi). Finally, in the spring of 1052, Nùng Trí Cao ordered the burning of villages under his control and led five thousand of his subjects in a revolt that soon gained momentum and swept across the South China coast to the city of Guangzhou. Within the year, Song imperial troops had routed the rebels, and Trí Cao fled to the nearest independent kingdom founded by another Tai-speaking society, the Dali kingdom (937–1253), located in modern-day Yunnan. In official Chinese accounts, a wary Dali ruler reportedly executed Nùng Trí Cao and presented the rebel's severed head to Chinese authorities. According to popular accounts, however, the rebel was offered escort into northern Thailand, where his descendants continue to thrive today.

Officially, both Chinese and Vietnamese court historians have long labeled Nùng Trí Cao an insurgent and a troublemaker. In the shared vernacular of court-centered historiography, the image of Trí Cao became a trope for "trouble," and official handling of his rebellion provided a litmus test for judging proper conduct among the Chinese and Vietnamese court representatives who had the misfortune to be involved. Trí Cao's official image was not rehabilitated until Marxist regimes took power in these countries. He is now remembered on both sides of the border as an officially sanctioned "hero of the people," although the identity of "the people" remains curiously unclear.

This book examines how eleventh-century Sino-Vietnamese tributary relations shaped frontier administration in the southwest. The influences of local politics and regional trade during the tenth and eleventh centuries led to a transformation of Sino-Vietnamese relations, granting the Vietnamese leadership a much greater degree of autonomy and establishing points of contact beyond the control of a central Chinese authority. Eventually, conflict between the Song and Đại Việt courts shifted from concerns of royal succession and political legitimacy to focus on a strict reckoning of territorial administration along the two states' shared frontier.[6] Song rulers unquestionably placed the Vietnamese kingdom at the top of a hierarchical system of relationships with leaders along the southern frontier. Local Vietnamese leaders negotiated their status within the Chinese tribute system in such a way as to establish regional independence while maintaining a check on Chinese incursions.

If relations between the Song and the Đại Việt changed with nearly every tributary encounter, the same could be said of other local polities, such as that of Nùng Trí Cao, in their exchanges with Chinese and Vietnamese centers of power. Other frontier leaders also negotiated their positions between the Chinese and Vietnamese courts through tributary ties and thereby occasionally found support for their efforts to expand and challenge their neighbors. David Kertzer notes that "creating a symbol or, more commonly, identifying oneself with a popular symbol can be a potent means of gaining and keeping power, for the hallmark of power is the construction of reality."[7] For Tai-speaking leaders, given the brutal environment of political struggle in the early eleventh century along the frontier region, the option of a political reality constructed around the Chinese imperial order encountered locally through tributary practices certainly must have appeared appealing. Part of the story I tell here involves the process by which the local leadership of the frontier region could present the symbols of imperial submission as an act of reclaiming regional independence.

Chapter 2 offers a broad overview of the prevailing Chinese court notion of world order through the first years of the Song dynasty. The early Song rulers imagined a world order shaped by a latticework of "ritual practices" (*li*) that joined all polities, large and small. Through these rituals, there soon developed a system of titles and practices, centered on the emperor's person, which produced a hierarchical ordering of foreign courts and outlying chieftains. This new order retained its legitimacy only as long as its existence contributed to regional peace and tranquility. The Song ruler was himself constrained by this framework, because his status as emperor relied on the active participation of tributary "vassals" much as China's smaller neighbors depended on the Song court's sanction of authority.

In the same chapter, I also examine the development of the Chinese court's *jimi* (loose reins) system of frontier management as an extension of tributary relations. Japanese scholarship on the *jimi* system makes reference to a pacification policy of "appeasement control" in the early Song court's approach to managing its southern frontier giving way to Wang Anshi's (1021–1086) "positive policy" by the mid-eleventh century. One of my related arguments is that while the Song court may have developed a "multistate" system of relations with its military equals along the northern frontier, Song rulers sought to impose a strictly hierarchical framework of tributary relations on their less powerful southern neighbors, including the small frontier communities. These southern polities posed no direct military threat to the Song leadership, and so the Song court was not compelled to offer southern leaders the same "appeasement" it offered northern leaders, as was the case in the delicate relations it maintained with the Khitan leadership of the Liao kingdom (907–1125).

Chapter 3 briefly reviews the period of Sino-Vietnamese relations from earliest times to the early eleventh century. Important episodes in the development of Sino-Vietnamese court relations before the Song period may be divided into four related categories, each of which provided both Vietnamese rulers and upland local chieftains with different patterns of interaction with the Chinese leadership. The distinctive nature of cultural exchange amid contestations for political power distinguishes the revival of Sino-Vietnamese ties in the early Song period from both the Song court's relationships with northern nomadic kingdoms and the Sino-centric tribute relations that other Southeast Asian kingdoms would establish with the Song court.

Chapter 4 focuses on the frontier region and its inhabitants, looking closely at local competition for political control. Specifically, I examine the motives behind the brash actions taken by Nùng Trí Cao's father, the frontier chieftain Nùng Tôn Phúc, and his followers. Did he act as a rebellious vassal, who had abandoned his responsibilities to his direct superior, the Vietnamese ruler? Or did Tôn Phúc draw on political currents that found their origins beyond the court politics of Kaifeng or Thăng Long? A careful examination of these same events from an indigenous perspective reveals a complex balancing of local and interregional concerns, targeting multiple audiences.

Chapter 5 studies events leading to the Nùng Trí Cao rebellions and their immediate aftermath. In a network of collective and individual associations, the Nùng Trí Cao rebellions may be viewed as violent outbursts at the center of several sets of regional tensions. Trí Cao's rebellions meant different things to contestants for authority in the region, the local inhabitants as well as the Song and Vietnamese courts. These differences are explored within the context of the frontier's unstable political topology.

Chapter 6 looks at the pacification campaign launched against Nùng Trí Cao's followers in the 1050s, examining how the subsequent submission to the direct control of the Song court on the part of strategic Tai-speaking frontier communities contributed to the outbreak of the Sino-Vietnamese border war of 1075–77. In this chapter, I investigate both Chinese and Vietnamese accounts of specific conflicts—episodes involving disputes over the policing of local bandits, frontier revolts, and border disagreements—that led to military action. This study demonstrates how conflict between the Song and Đại Việt courts shifted from a context defined by the ideological aspects of the tributary relationship to one focused more on spatial relations between two neighboring states. I take a closer look at the indigenous communities that inhabited the frontier between the Song empire and the Đại Việt kingdom and examine shifts in the physical border between the two through the end of the eleventh century.

Chapter 7 explores the historical implications of cross-border difference in public commemorations of Nùng Trí Cao from the imperial period through the modern age, examining where the figure of ancient "local hero turned local deity" fits in today's cross-border community affiliations in the Guangxi–Cao Bằng region. These commemorations have been closely linked to differing Chinese and Vietnamese frontier- and, later, border-management policies as well as to differing local responses from communities living on both sides of the border. These communities still share a common thread of identity, preserved in part by devotion to the figure of Nùng Trí Cao. Their reverence for this eleventh-century rebel leader is a sentiment that transcends modern political demarcation.

Many frontier inhabitants in the eleventh century would today be characterized as Tai. This ethnic group was certainly not the only one present. Although there has been considerable interregional migration over the ages, we find great ethnic diversity in the Sino-Vietnamese border region, even in the earliest historical sources. As mentioned above, the dominant ethnic groups of this region today are Tai speakers, a broadly defined group found from the central Malay

Peninsula to the easternmost edge of the South China coast. The current on-line edition of the *Encyclopedia Britannica* estimates the population of Tai speakers in the region to be 75,760,00. *Britannica* divides this into 45,060,000 people in Thailand, 3,020,000 in Laos, 3,710,000 in Myanmar (formerly Burma), 21,180,000 in China, and approximately 2,790,000 in Vietnam.[8] Among the Tai speakers of Vietnam are the Tày, Nùng, and Thái peoples. The Tày make up the largest of these groups, with a 1999 population of 1,574,822, and the Nùng is the smallest, with 933,653.[9] The Tày were once generally known by the Sino-Vietnamese term "Thổ" ([people of the] soil), and they were considered the most Vietnamized of Tai-speaking groups in northern Vietnam.[10] The Nùng, in contrast, have long been regarded as the most sinicized of the Tai speakers in this region. The Nùng reside mainly in Cao Bằng and Lạng Sơn provinces along the border with China's Guangxi province. The Tày live in communities stretching from Quảng Ninh province on Vietnam's northeastern border with China to Lai Châu province, which borders on northern Laos. The various Thái subgroups, totaling 1,376,646, have been recognized as separate ethnic groups by the Vietnamese government only since the early 1960s. The Tày, Nùng, and Thái groups are very similar in customs and dress to the Zhuang of southern China and other Tai communities in the highlands of Burma, Laos, and Thailand, and they speak Tai languages as well as the national languages of their home regions.

In southwestern China, the Zhuang outnumber all other Tai speakers, with around 14.5 million in Guangxi province alone, which makes them the largest non-Han population of this region.[11] In fact, the Zhuang are the largest ethnic-minority group in the People's Republic of China today.[12] Predominantly Zhuang communities are found primarily in the southern Chinese provinces of Guangdong, Guangxi, Guizhou, Hunan, and Yunnan. There are also many other Tai-speaking groups, including Ai-Cham, Bouyei (Tai Yoi), Chu, Dai, Dian, Gelao, Hlai (Li), Kam (Dong), Laqua, Lati, Lue, Mak, Maonan, Mulam (Mulao), Ong-be (Lin-gao), Saek, Shan, Sui (Shui), Tai Ahom, and Then. Moreover, numerous communities of Tai-speaking Akha and Hani are spread throughout the region, with a total population of 2.5 million people by some accounts.

In addition, a variety of upland communities live above the riverine and lowland areas inhabited by the Tai. In Vietnam, there are upland communities of Tai speakers (Sán Chay) and non-Tai speakers (Hmông, Dao, Mường), among others. These communities traditionally have lived apart from the lowland Kinh Vietnamese villages and maintained a separate system of local administration as well. Finally, there are many other non-Han peoples in the border region, including the non-Tai-speaking Hui, Miao, Yao, and Yi. Han and Kinh Vietnamese communities are also found on each side of the modern political boundary. There are also reportedly several thousand ethnic Kinh Vietnamese living in Guangxi province. Periodic Han settlement in the Red River delta once brought a large overseas Chinese population to northern Vietnam. Modern events, particularly the border fighting of the early 1980s, resulted in the permanent displacement of much of this ethnic group.

The ethnonyms "Nùng," "Tày," and "Zhuang" are, of course, all products of the modern age and were not employed in most of the period under study in this book. The Vietnamese terms were, as Keith Taylor states, "[categories] of French colonial knowledge."[13] Such terms were used to differentiate upland peoples from their lowland neighbors in a systematic arrangement of discrete spheres of colonial administration. The term "Zhuang" was the product of the "ethnic identification project" (*minzu shibie*), which the Chinese Communist government pursued in the 1950s in order to distinguish a clear set of "national minorities" contained within the multiethnic post-Liberation "New China."[14] This effort, following guidelines shaped by Stalinist categories of ethnicity, produced a list of fifty-four separate ethnic groups, to which two more have been added.[15]

Humankind today maintains an unwavering obsession with its own division and categorization by physical appearance, habit, and political affiliation. As Stevan Harrell notes, "People in the modern world of nation-states are members of nationally- and often internationally-defined ethnic collectivities of which their local communities are a part, and the dialectical interaction between local, national, and cosmopolitan discourses is what shapes their lives as ethnic citizens of modern nations."[16] Inhabitants of the Asia Pacific region have long defined themselves and their communities through their contact and interaction with neighboring peoples and, later, with newcomers from outside the region. In this sense, a study of how a Chinese empire, an independent Vietnamese polity, and a scattered collection of upland chiefdoms sought to come to terms with one another between the tenth and eleventh centuries has certain implications for the global community today. The great historiographical gulf between the official histories of the People's Republic of China and the Socialist Republic of Vietnam with regard to their shared border provides striking evidence of continued differences. The persistent nature of transnational ethnicity throughout the modern world suggests that studies of the Sino-Vietnamese border regions could teach us valuable lessons about similar communities worldwide. Finally, China and Vietnam, the remaining Communist powers of the Pacific Rim, continue to build on their special relationship. The origins of this relationship might indeed tell us something of its future course.

2

The Legacy of the Chinese Imperial Tribute System in the South: Balancing Ritual Harmony with Frontier Stability

In 1034, a local non-Han leader, Trần Cồng Vĩnh (dates unknown), along with more than six hundred followers, crossed the frontier into Song territory. Cồng Vĩnh had earlier announced that his home region should become a *neifu* (interior dependency) of the Song court. *Neifu* status placed a region under the direct protection of the Chinese court. After doing so, any disturbance in that region would be viewed by the Chinese ruler as an intervention into his domain. A frontier community that received this designation was treated administratively as a *jimi*, or "loose reins," district, giving it peripheral but legitimate standing within the network of polities supporting the Chinese court's venerable system of regional ties, later known in the West as the "tribute system" (*chaogong zhidu*). Acquiring *neifu* status implied that the region's local leaders had accepted China's ritual supremacy and the Chinese emperor's "exemplary power" (*de*), and that these leaders would be held responsible for the presentation of tribute to the central court.

Cồng Vĩnh's efforts did not pass by unnoticed by the sovereign ruler, to whom the border chieftain nominally still owed loyalty. The Đại Cồ Việt ruler Lý Phật Mã (Lý Thái Tông [r. 1028–54]) concluded that such a move was not in his best interests. When the Vietnamese ruler assembled more than one thousand soldiers in the frontier region to challenge Cồng Vĩnh's move, the Song emperor Renzong (r. 1023–1063) ordered Cồng Vĩnh's group to return home.[1] The Chinese emperor then sent an official warning to Phật Mã, instructing the ruler not to act rashly when dealing with the insurgents.[2] It appears that although the Chinese emperor could not condone the rebellious behavior of Cồng Vĩnh's followers, he did not hide his pleasure upon hearing of their willingness to become his direct subjects. The Song ruler's order for leniency was the extent of direct Chinese action in this matter. Since the founding of the dynasty, the Song court had seldom directly addressed the affairs of the indigenous communities located along the southern frontier. Such communities were expected to police themselves, while the vassal Đại Cồ Việt court at Thăng Long normally handled the larger problems alone.

Other Chinese court officials looked favorably on these requests from the borderlands, believing that the "defections" resulted from China's positive influence on the region. After hearing of Trần Cồng Vĩnh's request for an alliance with the Song court, the "military affairs commissioner" (*shumishi*) Cai Qi (988–1037) wrote in a court memorial that "the southern barbarians (Man) had turned away from their cruel ways and had returned to virtue" when they requested that the Song state annex them. Qi also suggested that the group be given land in Jinghu circuit (*Jinghu lu*) (in modern-day Hunan) in which to settle and to manage themselves.[3] The image of a southern frontier community attracted by the superior culture of the Central Plains (Zhongyuan) brought with it reminders of Tang period (618–907) imperial glory. The request for resettlement within the Song empire was also a clear reference to a *jimi* system of frontier management in full working order. However, Cai warned, "if we now allow them to leave, they must not return to their old home. If these people spread out into the mountains and ravines, will not there be trouble?"[4]

Cai Qi described the chieftain's request for Song dependency as a sign of the Song's civilizing attraction, and his mild criticism of the emperor's rejection of this request reveals Cai's familiarity with the fragile nature of power sharing in this region. The emperor, in any case, saw no reason to change the existing arrangement in which the

Vietnamese leadership had been given a free hand in managing frontier matters. However, this arrangement did not adequately address the issue of growing regional instability, and greater disturbances along the Sino-Vietnamese borderlands soon brought the region to the immediate attention of both Vietnamese and Chinese authorities.

Throughout the first half of the eleventh century, the Vietnamese court gradually spread its influence throughout the region, while the Chinese court made very few attempts to exercise its own authority in more than the most populous areas of the Guangnan West circuit (*Guangnan xilu*), located today in China's Guangxi Zhuang Autonomous Region. This seeming indifference on the part of the Chinese court soon changed. By the 1050s, in the aftermath of the Nùng Trí Cao Rebellions, Chinese officials from as far off as today's Shandong province relocated to prefectures at the edges of the Sino-Vietnamese frontier, as discussed in chapter 6. The community of transplanted Han settlers soon began to challenge in size the numbers of locally born inhabitants. A change in Chinese administrative policy, along with the demographic shift, raised tensions between Song and Vietnamese authorities. These changes eventually contributed to the frontier war of 1075–77, which resulted in a fixed border between the two territories and brought the Vietnamese court a heightened status in its association with the Song empire. The problems of frontier management that began with scattered incursions by bands of local inhabitants did, in due course, transform the nature of the Sino-Vietnamese relationship.

The Sino-Vietnamese Frontier As Tributary Gateway

Early developments along China's and Vietnam's shared frontier were deeply influenced by relations fostered by the leadership of these two polities. Therefore, this study first examines court-to-court interaction in the political context of the tribute system before turning to developments among the frontier communities themselves. The tributary relationship long remained an important element in securing and legitimizing power for all militarily less powerful but politically flexible local leaders located on the Chinese empire's southern frontier. Those leaders who secured a lasting relationship with a northern (Chinese) court and its representatives had a better chance of surviving threats to their rule or of recovering control when driven from positions of power. By the early tenth century, relations with Chinese rulers could follow two principal patterns of interaction, either tributary relations or a system of localized ties termed *jimi*, or "loose reins." These two systems were closely related even as the idealized system of tribute relations differed from the practical and continually changing administration of the network of *jimi* prefectures.

When both the Song and the Lý (1010–1225) dynastic rulers in the eleventh century sought to locate and interact with local chieftains inhabiting the peripheries of their realms, they did so through a political vocabulary developed by ancient Chinese scholars in their discussions of an ideal world order, known variously as the System of Five Zones of Service (Wufu Zhizhi) and the Nine Zones of Service (Jiufu).[5] David Schaberg describes the world known to the Zhou period (ca. 1122–256 BCE) authors of *Zuo's Commentary on Spring and Autumn Annals* (Zuozhuan) and *Record of the States* (Guoyu) as "a space cleared in the wilderness by culture ... bounded on one frontier by the spirit world and on the other by the non-Chinese world."[6] Culture, defined by Schaberg as "a system of prescriptions and the legitimizing account of their origins," took form in the descriptions and performance of court-sanctioned rituals. The five zones under the administration of the Zhou ruling house, as described by the court historian Sima Qian (ca. 145–ca. 86 BCE), radiated out from a ritually "orthodox" center to a "heterodox" periphery: *dianfu*, a zone under the administration of the royal family; *houfu*, a zone ruled by the nobility; *bingfu*, a militarized and pacified zone; *yaofu*, the strategic zone under the administration of friendly non-Han peoples; and *huangfu*, a zone of cultural and ritual desolation.[7] Vera Dorofeeva-Lichtman has defined these early terrestrial schematics as "cosmograms," describing such maps as "instruments for conveying conceptions of space dominated by closely interrelated political and religious meanings."[8] Dorofeeva-Lichtman's cosmogram also suggests the important role correlative cosmology played in delineating the outer limits of a world regulated by the ritual practices of the center. The hierarchical cartographical model representing degrees of "otherness" was tempered by the early Han period (206 BCE–220 CE)

Confucian conceptualization and promotion of the Great Unity (Datong), a period of ancient history during which all human beings shared a common concern for one another's well-being.[9] Therefore, the Five Zones world order was not a static model; instead, it suggested the recognition of cultural difference in preparation for the peaceful harmonization and acculturation of all peoples willing to accept the practices of the center.

Rituals as externalized indicators of appropriate behavior were the means for bringing about this process. Benjamin Schwartz notes that the ancient philosopher Xun Kuang (Xunzi [d. 238 BCE]) regarded the ancient sage-rulers to have, through rituals, made "manifest the overall pattern appropriate to the end of harmonizing the centrifugal tendencies found in the individual human organism."[10] David Schaberg writes that "what unites the many specific principles of human relations is a flexible and encompassing concept of ritual propriety (li)."[11] Such rituals checked the natural propensity of the Five Zones to remain separate and instead encouraged individuals on the ritually heterodox periphery to accept the guidance of the orthodox center. It is important to note that both Chinese and Vietnamese leaders relied on numerous strategies for engaging or subduing their immediate neighbors. The Five Zones world order remained an ideal, for which one strove, while problems that occurred with each encounter along the various states' frontiers required individual solutions. Nonetheless, ritualized action still often factored into these encounters as a way of formally initiating new ties or marking distinctive changes in existing relationships.

The ideal world order described above was expressed through a series of ritual performances known collectively in Western scholarship as the "tribute system." Imperial Chinese and Vietnamese political, economic, and cultural exchanges with neighboring polities eventually revolved around tribute relations, or gift giving, as a court-centered activity. The size and nature of offerings were of special significance in the tribute relationship, as was the proper observance of protocol. The acts of offering and receiving tribute, the performances of roles assigned to both guests and hosts, and the processions of tribute embassies were all part of the tribute institution.[12] Even activities that existed in the shadows of the tribute system, opportunities for unofficial trade and official information gathering, should be factored into the evaluation of particular tribute missions.

The leading principles of world order and tributary relations known to Chinese and Vietnamese leaders in the eleventh century were, in turn, based on an early Han period understanding of legendary ties fostered between the Zhou ruling house and its vassal states during the Spring and Autumn Period (771–476 BCE).[13] The tribute system in its earliest applied form has been described as the successor to the "peace through intimacy" (*heqin*) system employed in the Former Han (206 BCE–8 CE) to define relations with the Xiongnu nomadic peoples along the northern and northwestern frontiers. In order to address the general problems the empire faced in engaging the world beyond the Han empire, the eminent Confucian theorist Dong Zhongshu (195–115 BCE) proposed a modified system of tribute and oaths that incorporated a moral dimension into the terms of the relationship. For subsequent Chinese dynasties, as well as for rulers in other areas of East Asia, this relationship had come to represent a perfected state of balance between inner (*nei*) and outer (*wai*) subjects of the central court. The greater duties of the ruler, the Son of Heaven (Tianzi), are introduced in the following manner in the *Rites of Zhou* (Zhou li):

> [The early Zhou ruler] controlled the arrangement of All under Heaven so that he could control the lands of All under Heaven. He studied and differentiated between the peoples of his vassal states, cities and remote towns, including the four eastern tribes (Yi), eight southwestern tribes (Man), seven southeastern tribes (Min), nine northern tribes (Mo), five western tribes (Rong), and six northern tribes (Di). Along with their riches, [the ruler] made use of their great quantities of the Nine Grains [millet, panicled millet, glutinous millet, paddy rice, hemp, lentils, and wheat] and the Six Domesticated Beasts [horses, oxen, goats, pigs, dogs, and poultry]. The Zhou ruler knew the benefits and dangers of each region. He understood well the states and leading clans within the Nine Provinces (Jiuzhou), and his subordinates united the resources and services of the peoples in this region [under the Zhou ruler's control].[14]

According to this ideal version of imperial administration, the ruler viewed his empire through the setting of the Nine Domains, emanating out from his personal residence (see Fig. 2.1). As a means of maintaining his realm of authority, the ruler awarded fiefs of land to all of his subordinates according to their hierarchical rankings. In return, the ruler expected regular presentations of tribute from all quarters. Local resources from each region, called "native tribute" (*tugong*), dictated the quality and quantity of these gifts. Several works in the Confucian

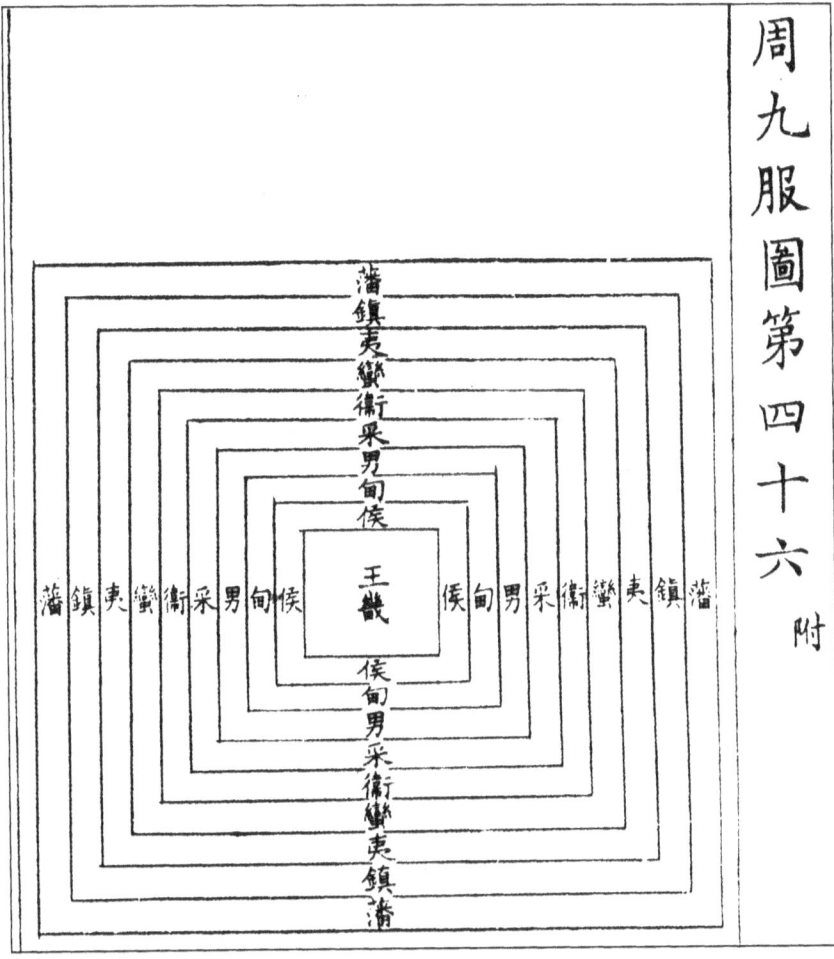

Figure 2.1. The Rites of Zhou Map of Tributary Domains (Shanghai Guji Pub., 1996)

canon, including the *Rites of Zhou* and the *Tribute of Yu* (Yugong), describe the spatial arrangement of tributary states beyond the Zhou royal house as well as the positioning of these states' emissaries in ceremonies involving the Zhou rulers.[15]

The *Rites of Zhou* describes this system of domainal relations in the following passage:

> [The ruler] distinguished between the nine domains or areas of service [*fu*] among the vassal states. The area covering one thousand *li* [from the emperor] is called the Royal Capital Domain [Wangji]. The area five hundred *li* beyond the Royal Capital Domain is the area called the Marquis Area of Service [Houfu]. The area five hundred *li* beyond the Marquis Area of Service is the area called the Master of the Hinterland Area of Service [Dianfu]. The area five hundred *li* beyond the Master of the Hinterland Area of Service is the area called the Baron Area of Service [Nanfu]. The area five hundred *li* beyond the Baron Area of Service is the area called the Pledged Official Area of Service [Caifu]. The area five hundred *li* beyond the Pledged Official Area of Service is the area called the Guard Area of Service [Weifu]. The area five hundred *li* beyond the Guard Area of Service is the area called the Man Barbarian Official Area of Service [Manfu]. The area five hundred *li* beyond the Man Barbarian Official Area of Service is the area called the Yi Barbarian Official Area of Service [Yifu]. The area five hundred *li* beyond the Yi Barbarian Official Area of Service is the area called the Defense Commander Area of Service [Zhenfu]. Lastly, the area five hundred *li* beyond the Defense Commander Area of Service is the Barbarian Border Official Area of Service [Fanfu].
>
> When granting vassal states as fiefs, each will be one thousand square *li* in size. If the ruler grants fiefs of five hundred square *li* to his dukes, the ruler may reward four dukes. If the ruler grants fiefs of four hundred square *li* to his marquises, the ruler may award six marquises. If the ruler grants fiefs of three hundred square *li* to his earls, the ruler may award seven earls. If the ruler grants fiefs of two hundred square *li* to his viscounts, the ruler may award twenty-five viscounts. Lastly, if the ruler grants fiefs of one hundred square *li* to his barons, the ruler may award one hundred barons. So that the Zhou ruler might control All under Heaven, officials

of all vassal states, small and large, must complement one another and be united. The ruler establishes his governance and orders his administration, employing each official according to his ability. The ruler regulates his officials' presentations of tribute, asking from each official according to his [local] resources.[16]

The successful reign of a Son of Heaven as envisioned by the authors of the *Rites of Zhou*, required political unity under the legitimate leadership of the royal house. This was a ruler whose every action had a direct effect on his subjects. Only when all peoples had recognized the legitimacy of the Son of Heaven would this designated ruler have the power to bring harmony to the forces governing Heaven and Earth. Early political treatises, such as the *Tribute of Yu*, the *Record of the States*, the *Rites of Zhou*, and *The Works of Master Xun* (Xunzi), all detail behavior for the Son of Heaven and his subjects, including non-Chinese subjects beyond the nine central provinces, in their encounters with one another.[17]

This pivotal role of the Chinese emperor was certainly not unique to the early Chinese imperial system. Considering early state development worldwide, Henri Claessen and Jarich Oosten note that in many societies, "the central position of the ruler is usually based upon a mythical charter and a genealogy which connects him to gods, ancestors, or spirits." They contend that the legitimacy of these early states was often "based upon a notion of reciprocity," by which subjects provided the sovereign with gifts and services and the ruler responded with promises of an orderly society and "the bestowal of benevolence."[18] In the Chinese imperial practice, gift giving in increasingly elaborate ceremonies became an integral part of these encounters. Although these early descriptions of tribute giving were highly idealized, the implied relationship between an absolute ruler from the Central Plains region of North China and his non-Chinese subjects continued to appeal to subsequent generations of Chinese emperors.

Ideally, the imperial practices of the Guest Ritual (Binli) lay at the center of relationships between the emperor in premodern China and the rulers of foreign kingdoms. James Hevia describes these practices in detail in his study of the Qing period Macartney mission and the famous incident in which the British envoy refused to kowtow before the Qianlong emperor (r. 1736–96). Although Macartney's audience with the Chinese emperor took place some eight hundred years after the events examined here, some general observations by Hevia hold true for the early Song performance of the Guest Ritual as well. As Hevia notes, the court perpetuated an imperial cult that placed the Chinese emperor at the center of an ordering of Heaven, Earth, and humanity. The emperor employed the exemplary power of his heightened position to perform this task, and he maintained this position through the execution of the appropriate ritual cycle.[19] Following the protocol dictated by the Guest Ritual, a lesser lord, drawn to the center, was required to request permission to enter the domain of the supreme lord, the Chinese emperor. The imperial audience, which would bring the lesser lord to the center of the imperial order, the emperor's own residence, followed certain procedural steps and modes of behavior. The conclusion of each visit by a lesser lord completed the process set in motion by the exemplary acts of the emperor, and each encounter between the emperor and his vassal constituted yet another full expression of the emperor's successful execution of his role in orienting world order. While the details of the Guest Ritual by no means remained the same through the centuries, Chinese rulers as far back as the early Han were influenced by this ideal in their conduct of foreign relations.

The imperial institutions of universal leadership, embodied by the emperor, espoused principles of harmony and hegemony in equal measure. Expressions of harmony stemmed from ancient political theories that described a network of subordinate states around a central court; hegemony was expressed in military action taken by the central court for the purpose of reimposing balance in "proper" relations between the subordinate states. Such action often also fitted into a ritual context. Chinese rulers were bound by the axioms of imperial institutional standards to address issues of harmony and hegemony in order to complete their duties as Sons of Heaven. Although ambitious leaders may have been piqued by limitations placed on their rule, their high moral position curtailed much variation from historically sanctioned behavior.

Chinese rulers rarely administered their empires solely on the basis of ideological purity. Imperial courts considered both ideological and nonideological factors in their foreign policy decision making. Pan Yihong describes the interaction of these factors as one between "ideological purity and practicality."[20] Although this notion is less controversial today, a flexible approach to foreign relations runs counter to traditional notions of a rigid Sino-centric "Middle Kingdom" world order best known to many Western readers.[21] Following this adaptable pattern of relations, the court adhered to a perception of the emperor as the Son of Heaven, maintaining a universal political authority, when such a view could be effectively articulated to willing foreign or domestic audiences.

The ritual order of the tribute system was based on the assumption that the emperor wielded universal authority. As Pan notes, "Such an ideology imposed political pressures on the Chinese rulers not only to maintain security on the frontiers but also to exert their influence over the areas beyond the frontiers."[22] In this ideological setting, the emperor, due to his position at the apex of this world order, was justified in nearly every edict he issued. Geoff Wade states that "the emperor as representative of Heaven obviously provided a pretext for any action by a Chinese emperor, as all actions were, by definition, divinely sanctioned."[23] Based on ideology alone, the Chinese ruler could demand total submission from his neighbors. Then again, militarily powerful or physically distant kingdoms seldom heeded such demands, and the Chinese court required a different approach in these cases.

The Chinese imperial leadership could also ignore the particulars of ideological purity so as to adopt a more flexible approach in specific foreign policy and frontier management decisions. Some scholars now suggest that Song rulers and their officials were required to overlook the tangled state of Realpolitik so that they could allow room for the ideal Chinese world order implied in the tribute system.[24] Beyond the greatest military threats China faced along the northern frontier, Chinese adherence to a universalistic notion of rulership actually required hegemonic expression, even during the early Song period. Peace in the region could last only if the potential for forceful and effective intervention backed it up. Harmony could justify both military conquest and subjugation for the sake of border defense as well as territorial expansion for the sake of regional pacification.[25] Coercion and hegemony could be considered tools of harmony and order, and in the intersection of purposes, a Chinese emperor found the means to project both political power and moral authority. In this case, virtue and coercion were essential components of a Chinese emperor's authority. However, when the situation dictated withdrawal from a position of universal superiority and even acceptance of bilateral equality, the Chinese court could make these accommodations in policy without permanently subverting adherence to the conventional world order.

The *Jimi* System in Chinese Frontier Management

This court-based version of tributary exchange worked well in managing relations with larger or more distant neighbors, and a related system was eventually introduced that organized ties with China's smaller frontier communities. The Tang dynasty had brought the *jimi* system to frontier prefectures and districts. Tang Taizong's chief minister Wen Yanbo (573–636) proposed the system as a means of gradually acculturating the nomadic northern peoples to Chinese customs and ways of life. Wen advocated Chinese control throughout the region, but he believed that direct military intervention was too risky. Speaking specifically of the Turkic peoples on the Tang frontier, Wen argued that the most stable and effective way to gain the loyalty of the barbarians was to allow them to settle within China and still retain their own customs and local leadership.[26] Later, the court could use these loyal communities to defend the Tang empire from threats even farther from the borderlands. Wen Yanbo contended that the Chinese emperor, as the Son of Heaven, should show pity to frontier inhabitants who approached the court in submission and should employ these foreigners who had submitted to his rule so that they would not rebel.[27]

The *jimi* system also played an important role in shaping regional political developments on the Sino-Vietnamese frontier. Local leaders who were granted special authority by the court passed the mantle on to their descendants. Second- or third-generation leaders often sought to consolidate and expand their powers. As Tang rulers progressively lost centralized control over their frontier to court-appointed "military commissioners" (*jiedushi*), these local leaders appropriated for themselves both civil and military powers within their domains before proceeding to challenge the authority of the central government. In the aftermath of the Huang Chao Rebellion (875–84), the strained allegiances of these regional leaders shattered into hundreds of contesting factions.

The *jimi* system fit into the traditional Chinese frontier policy of "using barbarians to control barbarians" (*yi man zhi man*), although the general stability of the southwestern frontier during the Tang certainly played a role in implementing such a lenient policy. Under this system, the Tang court appointed leaders of local ethnic groups to exercise authority at the "military prefecture" (*fu*), "civil prefecture" (*zhou*), "county" (*xian*), and "mountain grotto" (*dong*) levels. The official rank of these local leaders varied; some were granted the appellation "area commander-in-chief" (*dudu fu*), a military designation, while leaders at the civil levels, such as the prefecture and county, often received irregular hereditary titles such as "regional chief" (*cishi*), "commandery prince" (*junwang*), "princedom administrator" (*zhangshi*), and "equestrian sentinel" (*sima*). The Tang court charged these local leaders with the collection of native tribute, the organization of corvée labor, and the pacification of banditry. Although this system collapsed with the fall of the Tang, the founders of the Song dynasty immediately restored the institutions as a part of their own borderlands policy, even granting titles to clans that could provide evidence of their service to Tang rulers.

Once the Song court had gained control of the south and southwest, it established three hundred *jimi* prefectures throughout the area, including modern-day Guangdong, Guangxi, Hunan, and Sichuan.[28] In the region of southern Guangxi between the Left River (Zuojiang) and the Right River (Youjiang), the court eventually established forty-four *jimi* prefectures, five counties, and eleven mountain grottoes.[29] Han leaders of influential clans that claimed to have entered the frontier region during the Tang, including Long Yanyao (d. 971) and his family in Yongzhou (Nanning, Guangxi's modern-day provincial capital), began to request titles from Kaifeng almost as soon as the Song founders had taken power.[30] Soon, local upland leaders who approached the Song court with requests for *neifu* status were awarded with a variety of honorific titles. As mentioned at the beginning of this chapter, when a previously unincorporated region became a *neifu*, it was placed under the direct protection of the Chinese court, and the Song's apparent military superiority inspired loyalty among these local chieftains. Jeffrey Barlow writes that "The [Song] campaigns against the Southern Han were so swift and well-managed that they must have seemed, to the Zhuang, irresistible. We also suppose that many Zhuang lords, like many Han people, had missed strong centralized rule with its many opportunities for enrichment."[31] In this context, the example of the Tai-speaking frontier chieftain Mo Hongyan (dates unknown) illustrates the Song court's desire to exercise control along its southern frontier. During the summer of 974, Mo Hongyan, an "upland militia leader" (*xidong qiushuai*) of Nandan Aboriginal Prefecture (near the modern-day city of Nandan, in northern Guangxi), sought *neifu* status from the Song court.[32] Chinese sources suggest that Mo first proclaimed himself "military governor" (*jiedushi*) of his region and then sent his "lieutenant" (*yajiao*) Chen Shaogui to establish tribute relations with the Chinese court.[33] The first Song emperor Taizu (r. 960–76) reportedly granted Mo the title of regional chief.[34] The Mo clan continued to receive this title for several generations, maintaining its position of leadership in the region. Leaders of the frontier region saw security and stability in the establishment of tributary ties with the Chinese court, placating a powerful potential adversary while securing support for their own local expansion. Meanwhile, Song officials measured the depth and breadth of the empire's influence by the number of tributary titles granted and the number of tribute missions received at court.

In 976, at a time when the recalcitrant Southern Tang (Nantang) (937–76) armies had just fallen to Song forces, the newly enthroned Song Taizong (r. 976–97) announced that the frontier policy would continue to follow ancient precedents. In a court debate in his first days of rule, Song Taizong addressed his "grand councilor" (*zaixiang*) Bi Juzheng (912–981), saying, "Border defense is important, and many issues have become increasingly grave. We ought to understand the matters according to the precepts of former emperors, as these methods cannot be easily changed."[35] Mo's son thereafter sent another envoy with tribute and a request for an imperial seal to confirm his appointment. The emperor ordered that this seal be carved and given to the tribute mission.[36] Mo's position was thus made hereditary, marking the beginning of the Mo clan's administration of Nandan prefecture for future generations.

With court patronage, the Mo clan expanded its territorial reach and economic control as cattle herdsmen and even commanded a local militia of sixty men. While Mo gained stature and power through his appointment, he also was beholden to the Song court. Mo's indebtedness was clearly marked by his offering of one hundred *liang* of silver in 980; he was probably a member of a group of 734 local leaders from the south who brought tribute and prized horses to the Chinese on the eve of an attempted invasion of the Đại Cồ Việt kingdom. Ample textual evidence provides a clear picture of the Mo clan's rise to local prominence through Song court patronage in Guangxi. However, the Mo clan's case was not exceptional; the Nùng clan took a similar path to power, as noted in chapter 3.

The Vietnamese Approach to *Jimi*

Although the Vietnamese leadership of the early eleventh century also described relations with its neighbors, particularly China, in tributary terms, the Đại Cồ Việt court's method of controlling the peoples along its northern borderlands initially differed considerably from the Chinese model. First of all, the Đại Cồ Việt ruler maintained personal bonds with his frontier officials, all of whom were allied to the central court through yearly oaths of loyalty.[37] Second, the Lý court leadership, after quelling the civil warfare that followed the collapse of the short-lived Former Lê dynasty (980–1009), faced very little domestic unrest, and the early Lý emperors could turn their attention to the direct control of Vietnam's southern and northern frontiers. However, the northern frontier was shared with many independent ethnic groups, who lived on their respective sides of the imprecise borderline in the rugged mountain region that separated the Đại Cồ Việt kingdom from the Song empire communities. For these reasons, control of the northern frontier involved more than simply promoting trade or flexing military muscle.

The Lý leadership considered a number of options in its effort to consolidate its control of the northern frontier. For example, the ruler Lý Phật Mã married his daughter, the princess Bình Dương (dates unknown), to a powerful border official in an effort to support good relations.

Marriage alliances between emperors and foreign rulers were practiced in the past in China as well. The Vietnamese court, however, was not firming up ties with neighboring kingdoms; rather, it was strengthening domestic stability by personalizing ties between the central court and its appointed borderlands representatives. While the Chinese court granted titles and extended institutions as a way of laying claim to frontier authority, the Đại Cồ Việt court at the beginning of the Lý dynasty was elaborating on a more personal, more engaged policy of frontier relations.

Conclusion

The Sino-Vietnamese frontier has seldom been the site of concentrated political power. Scattered Han and Kinh communities aside, the premodern groups of Tai-speaking upland peoples described in this study fit Stevan Harrell's definition of "peripheral peoples," located as they were "far from the centers of institutional and economic power and of dense population concentrations."[38] As "peripheral peoples," they were subject to particular freedoms and institutional neglect that the lowland subjects of the Chinese and Vietnamese courts did not experience. The leaders within these communities were essentially unincorporated (at the state level) and unprotected under the existing administrative arrangements of the central courts. They were free to govern their populations according to local practices as long as their rule did not disrupt communities outside their own regions. When a leader emerged to challenge this arrangement, he was summarily punished, while those leaders who followed the courts' wishes would in the main benefit mostly from being ignored.

Throughout the premodern history of the Sino-Vietnamese frontier region, various factors, such as demographic shifts and patterns of economic development, have caused ethnic divisions to multiply and change. However, the tributary relationship between Vietnamese and Chinese courts often played a central role in governing the patterns of interaction among these frontier communities. Frontier management in the early Song period remained closely linked to the imperial tribute system. For this reason, frontier relations at this time must first be viewed from the court's perspective before taking into consideration the facts on the ground among the communities residing in these areas. As discussed later, the Song court followed its suppression of the Nùng rebellions with an increasingly expansionist frontier policy. The Chinese leadership gradually disregarded the traditional bounds of authority accorded to the Vietnamese rulers in an effort to monopolize the resources found in the region. During the early years of the dynasty, Song emperors had required only that native leaders submit token tribute. The court had based levels of tribute on each region's agricultural output. As the state developed costly economic interests, the region's tax burden grew heavier. By the 1070s, the court, following the spirit of Wang Anshi's "new policies" (*xinfa*) reforms, pushed for direct control of its borderlands, including the military suppression of local dissent. The Chinese court eventually moved from a policy of allowing the Vietnamese court to manage affairs to a policy of requiring more active Chinese intervention, and this trend toward direct control in frontier management had a dramatic impact on Sino-Vietnamese relations.

By the time the new interventionist frontier policy had taken effect, some officials within the Song court had already begun to call for a revival of the *jimi* system. Song rulers had originally encouraged strong leadership from their local representatives. Yet critics of this policy were well aware of instances in the past when powerful chieftains had chosen to establish independent kingdoms, challenging the Tang court's regional control and eluding Chinese sovereign might, as was the case with the founding of the southwestern Nanzhao kingdom. The Song scholar Fan Zuyu (1041–1098), a critic of Wang Anshi who entered government service with his *jinshi* degree in 1063, commented indirectly on his court's experience with the *jimi* system in his private chronicle of the Tang dynasty *Mirror for Aid in Government of the Tang* (Tangjian). Fan did not shy away from the inherent problems in an administrative institution that granted local leaders considerable autonomy: "Since the founding of the Tang, in activities requiring leadership in the south, [Chinese] rulers all have turned to border officials who grab up positions with an eye toward personal gain. They begin by gathering together local Man people, and then come to our country to pillage and rob. This situation has become a great concern to the country."[39] Despite this genuine problem in the system, Fan maintained that no strong alternative to the *jimi* system yet existed. Moreover, he was critical of Tang Taizong's attempts to accelerate imperial expansion and control all along China's frontier, a policy that aggravated existing tensions and brought no lasting peace to the empire.[40] In this context, whatever difficulties were encountered in the implementation of the *jimi* system of frontier management, Fan saw such solutions as preferable to outright annexation and direct control of peoples who did not share the central court's ritual values.

By the time that Fan Zuyu served at court, many other supporters of Wang Anshi's changes instead felt great reservations, regarding the efficacy of this traditional system of frontier management that depended on a delicate balancing of tributary and related *jimi* connections. In many instances, these officials equated problems with frontier communities with flaws in the existing relationship between the Chinese empire and the Vietnamese kingdom. The revolts along the frontier indicated that the Vietnamese leadership was not strong enough to control matters properly. The comments of these officials implied the need for more direct Chinese involvement. The long-standing frontier arrangements, based largely on pacification and fostered by tributary convention, no longer seemed adequate to these court administrators, who sought to exert direct control in the region. To achieve this control, the Chinese court necessarily bypassed its former tributary vassal and frontier partner the Vietnamese leadership. However, the same notion had likely crossed the minds of local leaders south of the frontier as well. In order to understand better how changes in the regional existing arrangement of frontier authority had evolved by the time the Song made its move toward direct control, we first must gain a better understanding of the Sino-Vietnamese relationship as it had developed by that same period.

3

Examples of Negotiated Autonomy: Sino-Vietnamese Relations Before the Eleventh Century

Chinese court relations with the nomadic peoples to the north always differed from the types of arrangements rulers made with the non-Han peoples inhabiting China's shifting southern frontier. Specifically, from the founding of the Song dynasty in 968, the court at Kaifeng treated the Vietnamese people of the Red River delta differently from other neighboring societies that supported or competed with the new Chinese leadership. Sino-Vietnamese relations were necessarily a complicated affair. For the historically minded Chinese officialdom, An Nam (Pacified South), which constituted northern Vietnam, had been an integral part of the Chinese political and cultural empire for nearly one thousand years. The system of Sino-Vietnamese relations prior to the Song had been one of a central government directly linked to a web of subordinate local governments. However, the influences of local politics and regional trade during the tenth and eleventh centuries led to a transformation of Sino-Vietnamese relations, establishing points of contact beyond the control of a central Chinese authority. Eventually, the Song court itself would draw on the precedent of Zhou dynasty (ca. 1122–256 BCE) feudalism or Five Dynasties (Wudai) period (907–60) frontier management, and not Tang (618–907) dynasty hegemony, to produce the new terms of interaction.[1] Sino-Vietnamese relations of the

Song period should therefore be distinguished from the relationships of the northern kingdoms within the multistate Chinese empire and from the Sino-centric tribute relations that other Southeast Asian kingdoms would establish with the Song court.

The Sino-Vietnamese relationship had also long sought its foundation in good trade relations. Kenneth Hall notes that "early Chinese political interest in Vietnam was a consequence of the desire among China's rulers to secure southern trade routes and to gain access to southern luxury goods, which included pearls, incense, drugs, elephant tusk, rhinoceros horn, tortoiseshell, coral, parrots, kingfishers [and] peacocks."[2] For their part, Alexander Woodside writes, Vietnamese leaders "quite sensibly did not want to deprive themselves of access to Chinese innovations, and used the cultural bridges which had already been built between the two countries to continue to participate in the Chinese world."[3] An important point to consider here is the distinction between tribute and trade in Sino-Vietnamese relations. The tribute missions themselves were, most importantly, opportunities to negotiate the balance of status and authority between Chinese and Vietnamese rulers and not thinly veiled attempts to promote trade. Nonetheless, there were trade opportunities present during the ritual performance of tributary protocol.

First, tribute missions to the Chinese court were commonly granted periods of "free trade," often lasting several weeks, following a particular court visit. At this time, certain members of the foreign mission, which usually outnumbered the delegates who had been granted the imperial audience, would bargain and trade in the markets near the court and along the route to and from the metropolitan capital. Second, many kingdoms engaged the Chinese court in formal tribute relations, following a schedule set by court protocol, through which to open informal trade contact with the empire's representatives at other times. Stronger trade relations appear to have been the desired goal of many maritime kingdoms that participated in the Chinese tribute system, and the Chinese court's policies toward these kingdoms by the late eleventh century indicates that the rulers were likely also aware of their tributary partners' unstated objectives.

The relationship that existed between Vietnam and China by the beginning of the eleventh century was a long time in the making, and important episodes in the development of Sino-Vietnamese court relations before the Song period may be divided into five periods of encounters. The first involved the emergence of autonomous polities that grew out of political arrangements initially established by a distant Chinese court. This period is exemplified by the Nam Việt (Nanyue) kingdom (207–111 BCE) along the southern frontier of the Qin (221–206 BCE) and early Han (206 BCE–220 CE) empires. The strength of the Nam Việt kingdom, although short-lived in comparison to Chinese dynastic power, provided an example for subsequent generations of Vietnamese and other local leaders who sought confirmation for their own political legitimacy. The first ruler of the Nam Việt kingdom, Triệu Đà (Zhao Tuo [r. 207–137 BCE]), had been a delegate of the Qin court; however, he is said to have soon gained local support for his administration. When Triệu Đà first named himself the "martial king of Nam Việt" (*Nanyue wuwang*), and later emperor of the territory, he did so without the approval of the northern court.[4] Triệu Đà's autonomous state could not survive the transfer of power to his son in the face of the Han court's concerted effort to bring the region back under central control. However, the short-lived existence of an autonomous polity stretching from the Red River along the South China coast to the Pearl River remained an element in the political imagination of anyone involved in contests for political control in the region. The territorial objectives involved in the eleventh-century revolt of Nùng Trí Cao and his followers, examined in chapter 4, further illustrate how frontier communities without imperial sanction could still find inspiration in the Nam Việt legacy.

A second period of interaction involved local leaders' largely unsuccessful attempts to establish local political order without seeking accommodation within the framework of China's developing tribute system. During periods of strong northern administrations, overwhelming military might from the north eventually defeated southern leaders who relied only on indigenous support to challenge imperial representatives. During periods of imperial decline, local leaders could briefly carve out independent polities, but these spheres of power only lasted as long as the vacuum of military strength from the north remained unfilled. An example of such a revolt is the one led by Lý Bí (544–602), the son of settler aristocracy that had arrived in the northern Vietnamese region

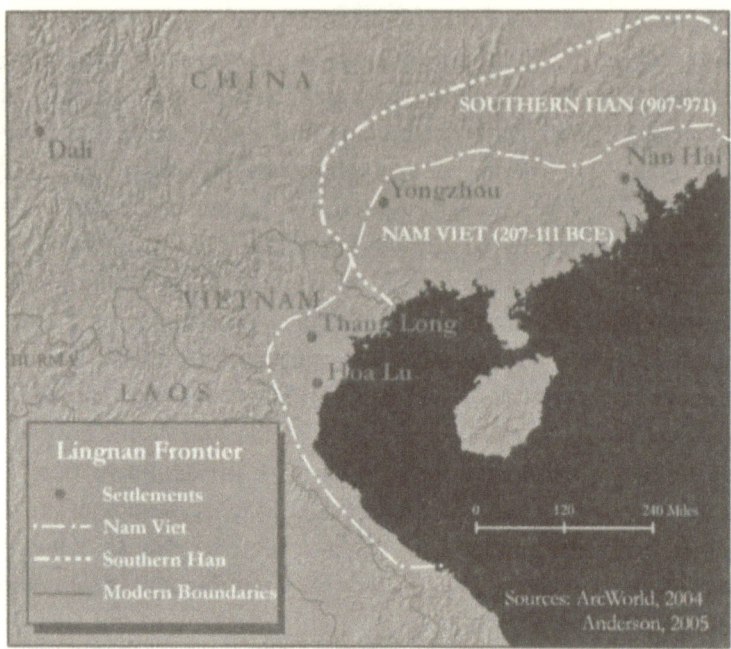

Map 2. Lingnan Frontier Region Before the Eleventh Century (Elizabeth Nelson)

upon the breakup of the Han dynasty. By the early sixth century, growing contradictions had appeared between administrators dispatched from the north and the Sino-Vietnamese elite, and the tipping point came when the Southern Liang (Nanliang) (502–557) court imposed on the region a tighter local network of control and a greater tax burden. In 542, Lý Bí resigned from official service when a local administrator frustrated his chances for advancement. He and another local official whose talents had also gone unappreciated returned to their home village and rallied support for a rebellion.[5] In the spring of the same year, Lý Bí overthrew the local government and forced the governor Xiao Zi, nephew of the emperor Wudi (r. 502–49), to flee. Following this initial success, Lý Bí drew on the region's political past to strengthen his local rule.

In the winter of 544, Lý Bí announced the founding of the Văn Xuân (Eternal Spring) kingdom and brought attention to the legacy of the Nam Việt kingdom. He proclaimed himself "Nam Việt emperor" (*Nam Việt dế*) and took the title Lý Nam Dế. He also adopted the reign name Thiên Đức (Heavenly Virtue).⁶ He established a new calendar and ordered the construction of a pagoda named Khai Quốc (Setting Up the State). Lý Bí's kingdom was unified for a short period and stretched from the Cham frontier to the white Thai communities in the northern highlands. The Liang court counterattacked with thirty thousand men, and in 545, Lý Bí fled his kingdom. He died while fighting at the Khuất Liệu aboriginal community in the Hung Hoa Mountains in 548. The period of resistance continued as Lý clan members and associates fought off the Southern Liang advances. In 583, the Lý clan under Lý Hữu Vinh dispatched a tribute mission to the ailing Chen (557–89) court presenting tame elephants as tribute.⁷ At this time, the Lý and another clan, the Triệu, had partitioned the kingdom, and perhaps the mission was a bid to gain support for Lý interests. Yet the court from which the southern leaders sought patronage was in no position to grant it. In 587, the Sui (581–618) dynastic founders crushed all opposition, including the Chen court, and reunified China. Not until 602 did a Lý descendant, Lý Phật Tử, finally submit to the new Chinese emperor, and Phật Tử eventually died in a Sui prison. Although Lý Bí's southern base of power could not be sustained, a political order with imperial adornment had emerged to revive the notion of an independent Nam Việt kingdom. In general, however, local leaders from the Red River region before the tenth century sought accommodation with neighboring northern courts because they did not control the resources or organized military force required to resist the immediate influences of these centers of power.

A third period began in the late Tang period with the transformation of a frontier administrative institution, the military commissioner or *jiedushi*, together with changes in titles and accompanying responsibilities that the Tang court assigned to its representatives in the south. This important administrative change occurred in conjunction with the abolition of the An Nam Protectorate (Annan Duhufu) in late 866.⁸ Throughout much of the Tang dynasty, the An Nam Protectorate had been an integral part of the Chinese empire, and military appointees to this protectorate from the central court ruled the region with varying degrees of independence. The ruler Tang Xuanzong (r. 712–56) marked a new phase in frontier administration with the rise of regional area commands led by military commissioners. Xuanzong was reportedly more adventurous in his rule, and he often agreed with expansionist proposals brought to his attention by certain military advisers.[9] His court launched a greater number of expeditions along the Tang empire's border region, and there was significant non-Han involvement in these expeditions. Problems with Xuanzong's more aggressive policies became starkly evident with the outbreak of frontier disturbances that culminated in the An Lushan Rebellion (755–63). The rebellion was finally suppressed, but the Tang never was as strong again.

The Nanzhao War (862–66) had an even more dramatic impact on the frontier. The early Tang had initially established the Nanzhao kingdom in southwestern China as a *jimi*, or "loose reins," frontier administration. Tang rulers were seeking allies to fend off powerful leaders coming from the region of Tibet. In 738, Tang emperor Xuanzong granted the Nanzhao ruler the title "king of Yunnan." As the Nanzhao court gained power through regional alliances, it began to challenge Tang insistence on tributary ties. Eventually, the Nanzhao court became a vassal of the Tibetan court. At this point, Nanzhao armies began to threaten Tang allies in the region. Many mountain chieftains, and the anti-Tang element among the Vietnamese region's population, had expressed loyalties to the Nanzhao leadership. Fighting broke out between the Tang and Nanzhao courts when Nanzhao armies advanced on the capital of the An Nam Protectorate. The Tang court, already weakened by internal strife and frontier disputes to the northwest, took two and a half years to locate a capable military commander, Gao Pian (d. 887), and a force large enough to drive out the Nanzhao occupying armies.

In the early winter of 866, the Tang emperor announced a general amnesty and called on the armies stationed in An Nam, Xizhou, and Yongzhou to secure their borderlands. At the same time, the An Nam Protectorate administrative region was replaced with a new "defense command" (*jiezhen*) called the "Army of the Peaceful Sea" (Jinghaijun). Gao Pian, who at that time served as the region's military commissioner, was appointed to lead the new defense command.[10] Gao also received the honorific title "king of the southern pacified region" (*nanping wang*). The Tang emperor was careful to insist that no further attacks be launched on Nanzhao forces, wishing instead to revive harmonious relations among the parties involved. The Tang court could hardly have desired anything else, given its weakened position in the region. A proposed bulwark of regional stability, the Army of the Peaceful Sea, would remain the administrative title for the region through the early Song period.[11] Its architect, the Tang court, however, was several decades from extinction.

The enhanced authority of local administration under the military-commissioner system gave rise to a new type of local leader, one who could serve a court properly while consolidating the military means to pursue his own political ambitions. The slow decline and fracturing of the Tang imperial order eventually produced the need for quick-witted leaders who functioned on two levels, as agile military strategists and as astute court-oriented political figures. Only leaders who could successfully navigate the shoals in both realms emerged in a secure and strong enough position to maintain local control.

The Song Restoration of a Tributary Framework on the Sino-Vietnamese Frontier

The fourth period of interaction, which built directly on the third, occurred in the period from the fall of the Tang in 907 through the founding of the Song dynasty in 968, during which time conditions became right for an independent polity to emerge under local leadership from the Red River region. The Song dynasty's first rulers initially sought to project an image of sweeping territorial dominance before actually achieving it. For example, they included the Vietnamese kingdom rhetorically in the category designated for tributary kingdoms while granting official titles that suggested a greater amount of political independence. Meanwhile, Vietnamese rulers used the evolving relationship with China to set the foundation for their own indigenous power base. The emerging Vietnamese political order was shaped by interplay between Chinese signs of authority expressed through the tribute system and local Vietnamese responses to and adaptations of these signs. Three successive Vietnamese ruling families — the Đinh (r. 968–980), the Lê (r. 980–1009), and the

Lý (1010–1225) — expanded their regional control within this tributary framework, while leaders of these clans competed with others, even their own kinsmen, for local dominance.

The Đinh, Lê, and Lý clans all entered into tributary relations with the Chinese court, but each clan approached this relationship somewhat differently. The Đinh clan used its tributary relationship to structure the local court's bifurcated authority, setting forth the loyal son Đinh Liễn as the vassal ruler in the Song court's eyes, while the father, Đinh Bộ Lĩnh, ruled as an autonomous king at home. The Lê clan, beginning with Lê Hoàn (r. 980–1005), used the rituals of tributary protocol to seek legitimacy for his usurpation of Đinh authority when that clan failed to produce an effective political heir apparent. Finally, the Lý clan, beginning with Lý Công Uẩn (r. 1010–28), employed the titles and political associations of the tribute system to establish local institutions of political control. As the recipients of a long, varied history of political interaction with northern powers, these leaders from the northern Vietnamese region all understood the variety of roles available to satisfy the expectations of distant emperors. Yet when all options within the tributary relationship were exhausted, Vietnamese leaders would ultimately amass forces for adequate military responses.

The relationship between the areas now known as China and Vietnam went through great changes during the early tenth century. As Paul Smith argues, the early Song court benefited from the state-building experiences of various northern regimes, with Tang period roots, that came into their own during the Five Dynasties period.[12] In particular, as Smith notes, the Song founder Zhao Kuangyin (r. 960–76) paid close attention to the reunification and state-building efforts of his former lord Chai Rong (r. 954–59), of the Later Zhou (Hou Zhou) dynasty (951–60), and Chai's adoptive father Guo Wei (r. 951–54).[13] Once Zhao himself took power and proclaimed the founding of the Song, he carried on his predecessors' efforts to reunify and pacify China's northern region before attempting any further territorial expansion. Therefore, the Song court paid very little attention to political change south of Lingnan (modern-day Guangdong and Guangxi) until well after the period during which a core of indigenous leadership developed in the Red River delta region.

The recentralizing of the Chinese empire began in the north, and leaders of this effort came from the ranks of military governors who had served the Tang court in its last years. However, local leaders representing a different type, as Paul Smith writes, of "military entrepreneurs," local militia leaders from outside of the former Tang bureaucracy, would rule the area of southern China that eventually came under Song authority.[14] These strongmen seized political control in the midst of regional chaos and maintained their power by regulating the trade volume and agricultural capacity of their domains and enlisting the support of local elites. In South China, such a strongman, Liu Yan (r. 917–42), the founder of the Southern Han (Nan Han) kingdom (907–71), employed this method of mustering political power, and his effort would be followed closely by lowland Vietnamese militia leaders who emerged in northern Vietnam and eventually established an independent kingdom in the region. Upland chieftains from the frontier region also took notice and employed the same tactics when establishing local authority.

The Five Dynasties period was marked by the struggle between a number of regimes, not only for regional dominance but also for the legitimacy to reestablish the authority the Tang rulers once held. The leaders of these competing kingdoms understood world order as a system that contained at its political and cultural center a regime located in, or in control of, the Central Plains region, the wellspring of Han ritual orthodoxy. Leaders of states closer to the imperial court allied themselves as "inner vassals" (*nei chen*) of the new central authority, while states farther away revived the practice of presenting tribute as the expression of their submission. As the Five Dynasties period progressed, and hopes for a rapid reunification of the region faded, rulers focused on their own military and political experiences as they searched for solutions to the establishment of a strong central authority and loyal administration at the borders. In this search, the position of military commissioner, or *jiedushi*, received much of the attention. Historian Wang Gungwu wrote that "the [Five Dynasties period] led to a central government which succeeded not because it rejected the *jiedushi* system and returned to Tang institutions, but because it had incorporated the basic features of the *jiedushi* system itself."[15] When the first Song emperor established a fully unified regime, he incorporated elements of the military-commissioner frontier system into the larger network of tributary relations.

The military-commissioner frontier system did not survive intact under the new Song court. By 977, Zhao Kuangyin's brother Zhao Gui (Taizong [r. 976–97]) eliminated the positions of the last eighteen military commissioners and installed in their place civilian officials under the direct authority of the central government.[16] Therefore, when military strongmen of the northern Vietnamese region approached the early Song court as tribute bearers and received honorific imperial titles related to a regional association with past military commissioners, these tributary envoys were not, in the eyes of their hosts, participating in regional power sharing. However, Vietnamese leaders and, eventually, other frontier chieftains considered that the title *jiedushi*, when granted by the Chinese court, still gave them a greater aura of legitimacy and authority to rule in the eyes of their followers. Only in 997 during the last year of Taizong's reign did the court complete the political reconfiguration of the Chinese empire by establishing the fifteen regional circuits and dividing the Lingnan region into the Guangnan East circuit (*Guangnan donglu*) (modern-day Guangdong) and the Guangnan West circuit (modern-day Guangxi). Until this time, the political status of leaders along the frontier had not yet lost all of its Tang period connotations.

In such a setting, there were a variety of strategies employed by local leaders to seize or expand power. Tactics relevant to this study include (1) local leaders providing feasts and public presentation, (2) leaders using outright force, (3) leaders forging external ties, (4) leaders expanding the number of households under their direct control, (5) leaders obtaining existing principles of legitimacy, (6) leaders creating new principles of legitimacy, and (7) leaders taking control of external sources of wealth.[17] The Vietnamese rulers and frontier leaders we examine in this book employed a combination of all these strategies to reach their goals, and they did so largely through participation in tributary relations with the Song court.

The Chinese court during the early Song focused on the consolidation of civil authority. To this end, the Song court followed General Pan Mei's (925–991) subjugation in 971 of its last southern rival, the Southern Han kingdom, with efforts to recognize and secure the loyalty of local leaders along the southwestern frontier. In the second month of 971, Zhao Kuangyin announced a general amnesty for regions that had once resisted his rule. He also produced his version of the Emancipation Proclamation for the southern frontier. During the following month, Zhao announced that all persons male or female who had once been considered slaves were to receive the status of servants.[18] This change was likely to undermine the economic power of local clans and draw the region more tightly under central control. Northernmost Vietnam, still called Giao Chỉ (Jiaozhi) in all discussions at the Song court, was among the regions to respond to its call.[19] Subsequently, both Song Taizu and his brother Taizong attempted to configure relations with the Vietnamese kingdom in a manner that would simultaneously resonate with historical precedence and follow the territorial ambitions of the Chinese empire's newest rulers.

Upon closer examination, the course of events does not appear to be so clear-cut. As noted earlier in this chapter, South China passed through the hands of many leaders throughout the Five Dynasties period. During these political maneuvers, the various lords fighting for territory in the Vietnamese region had chosen a political course that would leave the orbit of the Song empire. The first post-Tang Vietnamese leader to claim an independent identity for the region was Ngô Quyền (r. 939–44). He did so without cultivating tributary ties, but he had been able to achieve enough political unity and military force to repel opposition to his autonomous control. During this period, the Southern Han leadership showed a renewed interest in controlling the Việt region directly. In the autumn of 938, Liu Hongcao (d. 938), son of the ruler Liu Gong (r. 917–42), led the unsuccessful Southern Han expedition against Ngô Quyền's forces. Ngô Quyền defeated the Southern Han troops at the now famous Battle of Bạch Đằng River, drowning half of the Chinese soldiers, including Liu Hongcao himself.[20] This famous battle, and the military strategy of sinking stakes into the river at low tide that impaled the Southern Han vessels, brought Ngô Quyền into the pantheon of Vietnamese national heroes. Following his victory against the Southern Han forces, Ngô Quyền dropped references to the title "military commissioner." Instead, he took the title "king" (vương) and established his court at the Cổ Loa citadel, which was built in the modern-day Đông Anh district on the outskirts of Hanoi. Cổ Loa had been the ancient capital of the Âu Lạc kingdom (257–207 BCE), founded by An Dương Vương in the lower Red River delta. This choice of court location reinforced the notion that Quyền was a Vietnamese leader who was independent from northern control.[21] Ngô Quyền reigned for five years from Cổ Loa, establishing the semblance of a Chinese-style court with specific administrative functions. The Ngô clan continued to maintain its control of the region from 939 to 965, although the final years were tumultuous, known in Vietnamese sources as the anarchic Twelve Lords (Thập Nhị Sứ Quân) period.

In the midst of this struggle for regional control, Đinh Bộ Lĩnh (923–980), the son of a local military leader, defeated the last of Ngô Quyền's clansmen. In 965, Bộ Lĩnh established his own court at Hoa Lư, declaring himself to be the "Great Victorious King" (Đại Thắng Vương).[22] Bộ Lĩnh chose this title to indicate only his local authority, demonstrated by the fact that he initially sought political confirmation for himself and his son Đinh Liễn (d. 980) from the Southern Han court at Guangzhou. Bộ Lĩnh soon indicated that he intended to establish himself as the sole ruler of the Vietnamese region. In 966, he adopted the supreme title of "emperor" and dropped any reference to the Chinese-coined toponym "Giao Chỉ" in favor of the Vietnamese title "The Great Việt Kingdom" (Đại Cồ Việt).[23] Bộ Lĩnh also granted Đinh Liễn the title "king of Nam Việt" (*Nanyue wang*), a strong indication that multiple sources of authority carried weight for leaders in this region. Although he soon sent tribute missions to the Song court, Bộ Lĩnh had first set about establishing his kingdom's self-government. It would appear that the Chinese leadership did not fully realize the importance of this change at the time, as the emperor continued to grant Vietnamese officials titles that had once gone to Tang military commissioners.

Bộ Lĩnh and his son consolidated their control of the region around Hoa Lư for a period of seven years, during which time the Vietnamese court made tentative moves toward establishing relations with the Chinese court at Kaifeng. During this period, the son, rather than the father, may have been most interested in fostering ties with the Chinese. In the spring of 970, Đinh Bộ Lĩnh reportedly sent envoys to China "to foster good relations," after the Song court ordered General Pan Mei to pacify South China.²⁴ Vietnamese sources also refer to a mission led by Đinh Liễn himself in 972.²⁵ Historian Robert Hartwell argues that this trip was an advance reconnaissance mission to the edges of Song territory and not a tribute mission to the Song court. He suggests that Đinh Liễn seems more likely to have ordered the 972 trip but didn't actually participate himself.²⁶ From the account given in *The Complete History of the Great Viet* (Đại Việt sử ký toan thư), it appears that Đinh Bộ Lĩnh, and not Đinh Liễn, was responsible for the order to present tribute. Regardless of which leader made the initial decision, the order to engage the court at Kaifeng was clearly a response to the arrival of the Song general Pan Mei's army in South China.

When Đinh leaders learned in 973 that most of South China had been pacified by Song forces, they likely realized that a direct encounter with Chinese court representatives was rapidly approaching and that the outcome remained uncertain. Therefore, they quickly sent envoys to China to present tribute, requesting *neifu* status from the Song emperor.²⁷ The Song court was quite willing to receive Vietnamese messengers as the first step in securing tributary ties with that kingdom. During this mission to Kaifeng, the emperor decreed that both attending Vietnamese envoys, Trịnh Tú and Vương Thiệu Tộ, be given honorific titles. Zhao Kuangyin also ordered that Đinh Liễn be given the title "grand preceptor" (*taishi*) as well as the late Tang period titles "Army of the Peaceful Sea military commissioner" (*Jinghaijun jiedushi*) and An Nam protector-general (*Annan duhu*). With the granting of these titles, the Song emperor was harking back to the Tang era of southern frontier management while also furthering the long-standing relationship on his own terms by including additional titles for his southern visitors. At some point later in 973, Đinh Liễn's mission returned to Hoa Lư, accompanied by a Song delegation. This delegation was under orders from Zhao Kuangyin to enfeoff Đinh Liễn's father, Đinh Bộ Lĩnh, and by doing so, to make the necessary connections between the two courts that would complete this first round of tributary protocol. The Chinese likely believed that they had made an equally important connection with the Vietnamese leadership when the emperor entrusted Đinh Liễn with the job of military commissioner. The revival of Vietnam as a subordinate frontier region was most certainly the Song's ultimate plan.

In these exchanges, the Song leadership appears to be concerned primarily with the political aspects of these early tribute missions from the leaders of their former protectorate. However, Đinh Bộ Lĩnh and Đinh Liễn were not the only rulers from the Southeast Asian region to engage the Song court in such activities. In early 961, within a year of the Song dynasty's founding, a mission from Champa (Zhancheng) arrived in Kaifeng to convey the greetings of their ruler, Jaya Indravarman I (Shili Yintaman) (r. 959–ca. 965). The emissaries brought as tribute rhinoceros horn, ivory, "Borneo camphor" (*longnao*), various medicinal herbs, four peacocks, and twelve "Arab" (*dashi*) bowls.[28] In 966, and subsequently every year from 970 to 974, Cham missions came to the Song court with a variety of tribute, including trained elephants, ox tails, ivory, and bolts of fine white silk known as *baidi*, among other items.[29] The 974 mission was particularly substantial and represented the largest gift from any southern kingdom to the Chinese court to that point in the dynasty.

This flurry of tributary activity is unprecedented in Sino-Cham relations and likely reflected the Cham rulers' increasing concern over the growing strength of their newly independent northern neighbor, the Đại Cồ Việt kingdom. The Cham request includes a petition for *neifu* status. However, there was another strong reason for the Cham visitors' generosity and persistence. The Southeast Asian insular kingdom Sri Vijaya (Sanfoqi), an important trading power, had sent a mission to the Chinese in 971 and sent another substantial mission in 974.[30] The result would be a steady stream of tribute from Champa and Sri Vijaya, which, next to the Vietnamese, were the most active Southeast Asian participants in China's tribute system throughout the early Song. The early Song court may have accepted each of these missions equally, but the missing pieces, that is, information regarding the level of informal trade between each of these kingdoms and the South China coast, could determine the commercial gains that were made by this ritual display of local products.

In the summer of 975, the Vietnamese court initiated another cycle of tributary protocol by sending envoys to the Chinese court with a number of rhinoceroses and elephants and a quantity of medicinal herbs. *The Complete History of the Great Viet* notes that earlier in the spring, Đinh Bộ Lĩnh decided on the caps and gowns to be worn by civil and military officials at his court, elaborating on his own imperial institutions, and later sent Trịnh Tú again with gold, silk, rhinoceroses, and elephants to the Song court.[31] Differences between the Chinese and Vietnamese accounts indicate some confusion on the part of Kaifeng as to the true nature of authority at the Đinh court.

In the autumn of 975, the Song court sent Wang Yanfu to present the letter describing titles for the Vietnamese ruler, and, according to *The Complete History of the Great Viet*, "after this exchange, when the court sent envoys to the Song, the Chinese regarded Đinh Liễn to be the master of the Vietnamese region."[32] The *Official History of the Song Dynasty* (Songshi) notes that the Song court wished to glorify the elder Đinh Bộ Lĩnh and to co-opt his realm. On September 14, 975, Kaifeng drafted the following edict for Bộ Lĩnh, which was presented at the court in Hoa Lư in early 976:

> Because you have led your local people to our leadership, we will respond with benevolence. To appreciate your entire lineage and assimilate [you into the tribute system], it is fitting [for us] to grant honorific titles to our subordinates. Officials at large [*waichen*][33] who bow deeply [before the throne] with hands reverently clasped bring honor to their forebears with this superb performance of ceremony. Your clan, Bộ Lĩnh, has for generations been a prominent local family. You have the strength to protect your distant lands, while you also display an appreciation for Chinese customs by not forgetting to request "interior dependency" status from our court. As a result, the Nine Regions have been unified and the Five Peaks are at peace.[34] This area is limitless and huge, and its people wish to offer their treasures as gifts.[35] I complimented your son and awarded him the rank of my *fan* border officer.[36] Doing this, I reward his individual talents and upright behavior, and single him out as a role model for the common people to know of his loyalty. Moreover, you, as the senior family member, may at this time wear on your clothing a special insignia. You may accept the titles of "commander unequaled in honor" and "acting grand preceptor." You may also take the name "commandery prince of Giao Chỉ" [*Jiaozhi junwang*].[37]

The Song emperor Taizu recognized that Đinh Bộ Lĩnh exercised a certain amount of authority along the southern frontier, although Bộ Lĩnh's son had advanced himself as the point man for the region by accepting the title of military commissioner. Within the framework of tributary relations, the Chinese ruler made efforts to acknowledge this local authority. The Song rulers also wished to take advantage of the "treasures" now being presented as local products from the region, including articles of trade passing through the Red River delta region from other parts of Southeast and southwestern Asia. However, these articles were not yet the primary reason for engaging the Vietnamese in tributary relations. According to the Song's evolving system of frontier administration within a framework of political consolidation, the Đinh clan provided an important political link between the central court and its peripheral representative. Trade through the frontier region was already common, but the Song court did not yet regard this activity to be of any great importance.

Tribute and Trade during the Reign of Lê Hoàn, 980–1005

Song Taizu's brother and successor Song Taizong was more ambitious and expansionist in his approach to official relations with Vietnamese rulers. However, his court met its match in Lê Hoàn, a former military commander who seized the throne from the heir apparent Đinh Tuệ (974–1001), the younger son of Đinh Bộ Lĩnh. According to the *Official History of the Song Dynasty*, the powerful general Lê Hoàn assumed dictatorial powers following the assassinations of Bộ Lĩnh and his elder son; Lê Hoàn then turned for support to a sympathetic faction in the Đại Cồ Việt court that likely included the fallen Đinh ruler's queen. Chinese sources report that Lê Hoàn ultimately removed Đinh Tuệ from the throne, placing all remaining Đinh family members under house arrest.[38] Vietnamese sources suggest that Lê Hoàn took power by popular fiat. In any case, Song Taizong and his court did not wish to accept such a flagrant flouting of authority, and the Chinese soon mounted a punitive military expedition. Unfortunately for the Song court, the military expedition ended in abysmal failure in the spring of 981. The Song armies were eventually forced into a disgraceful retreat, for which their leaders were punished with summary execution in Kaifeng. The harsh punishments meted out to these disgraced Song generals were not uncommon as an imperial response to military failure. For Taizong, the Song emperor who was responsible for the loss of an earlier opportunity to retrieve border territory from the Khitans, this inability to dominate militarily in a territory that had once been an extension of the Tang empire must have caused particular bitterness.

Lê Hoàn, for his part, soon consolidated political control and defined the extent of the territory formerly under Đinh rule. Not only did Lê Hoàn force Kaifeng to accept his usurpation of the Đinh throne by soundly defeating the Song invasion, but he also struck a decisive blow in the continuing regional competition with the Chams along the Đại Cồ Việt kingdom's southern frontier. In late 982, the Lê court reportedly attempted to present ninety-three Cham war captives to the Song court. In making this offer, Lê Hoàn likely wished to provide further evidence of his military successes to the Song leadership at the same time that he made overtures to repair the tributary relationship.

However, the Chinese emperor was not interested at that point in engaging the Vietnamese in official relations, and he ordered Song officials at Guangzhou to prevent the transportation of these captives beyond the frontier. Local officials then provided the Cham prisoners with clothing and other supplies and ordered that the group be returned to Champa. In an act that must have irked the thwarted Vietnamese envoys, Song Taizong also ordered that his officials pass along an imperial greeting to the Chams' ruling prince. Thereupon, the Cham court sent envoys mounted on elephants to bear tribute to the Song court. The Chinese emperor eventually ordered that these elephants be left in Guangzhou.[39] Perhaps Song Taizong saw the act of fostering tribute relations with Cham leaders to the south of the Đại Cồ Việt kingdom as another approach to limiting Lê Hoàn's ambitions to expand his own power.

Champa was certainly an economically strategic partner when it came to Chinese trade throughout tenth-century Southeast Asia. Anthony Reid notes that, "as the last port of call before this stream of shipping sailed across the Gulf of Tonkin to South China, Champa had to be heavily involved in the trade, tribute, and voyages of pilgrimage moving to and from China."[40] Unfortunately for Kaifeng, the Chams were not a unified political force on a par with the Việt leadership. In the spring of 983, Cham elephant and equine cavalry troops, following both sea and land routes, entered and plundered Giao Chỉ. Lê Hoàn led his troops in defeating and driving back the Cham forces, with approximately one thousand of the enemy captured or killed.[41] Lê Hoàn's decisive victory against the Chams was striking evidence of Vietnamese military superiority. Therefore, Song Taizong's court likely reasoned that renewing Sino-Việt tributary ties would prove to be the best solution to the frontier conflict. In mid-autumn of the same year, Lê Hoàn was given permission to present his first successful tribute mission to the Song court since the conclusion of hostilities between the two courts two years earlier.[42]

After the Vietnamese sacked the Cham capital Indrapura and executed its ruler, the Đại Cồ Việt kingdom appears to have taken control of many of the Gulf of Tonkin region's important natural resources and exerted a direct influence on the trade of products that originated outside the region. While the Đinh leadership had established an active entrepôt in the Red River delta at Po Hai in order to extend Hoa Lư trading activities to maritime contact, Lê Hoàn demanded greater loyalty from his frontier representatives and thereby found new sources of Vietnamese gold and silver to pay for and capitalize this trade.[43] This trend toward political and economic consolidation would continue at an even quicker pace during the subsequent Lý dynasty (1010–1225). Moreover, during the Lý period, Vietnamese leaders moved farther inland in search of mineral resources to supplement their state-building efforts, and by the 1040s, the Vietnamese court would make direct contact in the frontier region with the Tai-speaking Nùng communities at the center of this study.

In early 985, still capitalizing on his military contests with the Chams, Lê Hoàn sent his lieutenants Trường Thiệu Phùng and Nguyên Bá Trâm and other envoys to present tribute at the Chinese court. The Vietnamese mission also made a formal request for official sanction to administer the Đại Cồ Việt kingdom region as a defense command. Before the Song period, the term for this type of command, *jiezhen* or *jiezhengzhen*, indicated a frontier command led by a nearly autonomous military commissioner, effectively ruling the territory as an independent satrap. By the early Song, the court had specifically begun granting the title of military commander to non-Han chieftains who had properly demonstrated their submission to Song authority.[44] A modern observer could reasonably conclude that such titles held very little real political meaning for Lê Hoàn, because the Song court exercised almost no political control over the frontier region at this time and the Vietnamese leader was largely free to rule as he pleased. Lê Hoàn's request could well have had a greater economic than political benefit if taking such a title gave him any advantage over his chief economic rival, the Cham ruler at the court in Vijaya (the coastal Bình Định province in modern-day central Vietnam).

His Cham challengers were also aware of the benefits of allying themselves with the strengthening Song empire. In the autumn of 986, the Song prefect of Danzhou, on modern-day Hainan Island, reported that Pu Luo-e, a subject of Champa, was leading a group of more than one hundred followers. The group requested the protection of *neifu* status from China, citing harassment by the Đại Cồ Việt kingdom. The Song emperor made no response to this request. However, as a result of another tribute mission sent to Kaifeng by Lê Hoàn during the same period, Song Taizong issued a long edict in late 986, which concluded with these words, "Lê Hoàn will be expected to control and soothe the unrefined barbarians, and spread the grace of Heaven."[45] Surprisingly, the southern frontier between the Đại Cồ Việt kingdom and Champa remained relatively calm for a long period after the resolution of unrest. Several factors have been cited for this change.[46] First, the Kinh Vietnamese and Cham peoples were similar ethnically, and both societies were primarily agricultural. Second, the frontier was clearly defined, as it was located on a broad plain. Third, the large amount of trade between the two kingdoms mitigated tensions that might have led to greater borderland conflict.

Lê Hoàn's overall efforts to control the movement of people and goods through his region did not enhance his image as a model partner in the eyes of the Song leadership. With their historical insight, the compilers of the *Official History of the Song Dynasty* contended that it was during the period between 988 and 995 that Lê Hoàn gradually lost his adherence to the ideal of a *fan* border official.[47] During the spring of 995, the Guangnan fiscal commissioner Zhang Guan and Wei Zhaomei, supervisor of the Ruhong garrison (*Ruhongzhai*) near modern-day Qinzhou, jointly memorialized the Song emperor. According to their report, more than one hundred warships from the Lê kingdom attacked the Ruhong garrison and the township beyond its gates, assaulting the local people and stealing produce from the granaries before leaving.

In his memorial, Zhang noted that during the previous summer, Lê Hoàn's officials from Tô Mậu Châu prefecture led a village force of five thousand men to plunder Luzhou, which was a prefecture under the jurisdiction of Yongzhou (Guangxi's modern-day provincial capital of Nanning). The "chief military inspector" (*duxunjian*) Yang Wenjie defeated the attackers and drove them away. According to the *Official History of the Song Dynasty*, Emperor Taizong was determined to relieve tensions among the people of this distant land that served the Song empire, so he did not wish to ask who was at fault.[48] The Chinese leadership would instead adjust its own expectations for the relationship. More likely, the leadership in Kaifeng did not wish to disrupt officially regulated trade by launching a military intervention in the region, and separating legitimate from illegitimate trade in that period had become difficult. When Lê Hoàn soon thereafter sent an envoy Đỗ Hanh to lead an embassy to the Song court, the Song authorities were afraid that this embassy was another invading militia band.[49] Discriminating between friend and foe in this region was temporarily beyond the ability of the Song court from its vantage point in Kaifeng.

Relations with Lê Hoàn had become quite messy, but there were other troubles brewing along the frontier. These involved Lê Hoàn's competition, local strongmen who sought to control trade and local resources for their own benefit, and not distant Cham rulers. The Song sites of military control in Qinzhou prefecture — the Ruxi garrison (*Ruxizhai*), the Ruhong garrison, and the Duobu garrison (*Duobuzhai*) — all bordered on the coastline. When a local inhabitant, Bộ Văn Dũng, from the Vietnamese Triều Dương township committed a murder, he and his kinsmen all fled to Ruxi, where the local garrison commander Huang Lingde gave them shelter. Lê Hoàn ordered Triều Dương's defense

Examples of Negotiated Autonomy 53

commander Hoàng Thành Nhã to carry an official dispatch to Chinese authorities in China requesting the apprehension of the fugitives. Huang Lingde, however, declined to surrender them.

In 996, the Chinese emperor appointed Chen Yaosou to the position of fiscal commissioner and sent him with an imperial edict to Lê Hoàn's court. When Chen arrived in South China, he sent Li Jianzhong, a local militia leader from Leizhou's Haikang garrison (*Haikangzhai*), to question Lê Hoàn about the situation and present the Chinese court's message. If Chen himself had entered the Đại Cồ Việt court with this message, he would have contravened tributary protocol; sending an underling to perform such an ad hoc task, however, did not interrupt normal relations.

Chen instead traveled to the Ruxi garrison, where he found Bộ Văn Dũng still in hiding. Chen captured Bộ Văn Dũng and 130 of his kin, including women and children. The Kaifeng delegate then requested that Vietnamese officials from Triều Dương take custody of the captives, but he warned them not to inflict any cruel punishments.[50] Hoàng Thành Nhã took custody of the prisoners and formally thanked Chen Yaosou for his help. Subsequently, Lê Hoàn sent a message of gratitude to the Song emperor. At the same time, the *Official History of the Song Dynasty* records, Lê Hoàn had twenty-five pirates captured and presented to Chen Yaosou. Moreover, Lê Hoàn reported to Chen that Vietnamese officials had already met with native leaders, who had given reassurances that they would not cause disturbances.[51] This meeting could very well refer to Lê Hoàn's 996 springtime attack on four aboriginal settlements in the Đại Phát, Đan Ba, and Ma Hoàng regions. The account in *The Complete History of the Great Viet* suggests that only after learning of this attack did the Song ruler wish to punish Zhang Guan and others for spreading their inaccurate rumors.[52]

During July of that year, Song Taizong sent Li Ruozhuo, a high-ranking court official who had participated in the post–980 war trip to the Vietnamese court in 983, to recognize Lê Hoàn's new authority. Acting as state courier and envoy, Li planned to present the gift of a beautiful jade belt to Lê Hoàn. The exchange of dialogue between the Vietnamese ruler and the Song envoy, as recorded in Chinese sources, is remarkably similar in tone to the much earlier exchange between the

Han envoy Lu Jia and Triệu Đà, the defiant southern ruler of the Nam Việt kingdom. In both cases, the imperial envoy encounters an imperial vassal who appears set on flaunting his "barbarian" nature.

When Li Ruozhuo arrived at the Đại Cồ Việt court, Lê Hoàn came out to the outskirts of the city to welcome the envoy. The *Official History of the Song Dynasty* notes that Lê Hoàn's manner was particularly rude and overbearing, and he said to Li:

> Those who plundered Ruhong garrison were, in fact, Man barbarian bandits from beyond our borders. Does the emperor know that these were not troops from Giao Châu [Vietnam], or not? If I truly gave Giao Châu the order to rebel, I would first attack Panyu [Guangzhou], and then attack Min [Fujian region] and Yue [Jiangnan]. Why would I only stop at Ruhong!

To Lê Hoàn's heated outburst Li Ruozhuo calmly replied:

> When the emperor first heard about the attack on Ruhong, he didn't know where the attackers came from. However, you, sir, were promoted to the position of Giao Châu's military commander and are bound to the obligations of the appointment. Therefore, you should be loyal and honest as repayment. With your handling of the search for those pirates, the outcome was very clear. Yet, Chinese high officials have made recommendations that the Chinese court build up its military forces to calm the sea-lanes in the southern region. Today, there is the issue involving the pillaging of the Man barbarian bandits. This matter is due to the fact that Giao Châu is not capable of controlling the situation by itself. So, leading officials have proposed that the Chinese court send several tens of thousands of crack troops to join Giao Châu soldiers in destroying the bandit forces, to spare both Giao Châu and the Guangnan regions this disastrous situation. However, the Song emperor said to me, "Do not put this plan into practice without thinking carefully about it. I worry that Giao Châu's leader cannot understand our court's edicts, and that such an action will frighten them. Why not just authorize Lê Hoàn to send an expedition to attack the pirates. Their force should be sufficient to calm down the region gradually." Therefore, we are not going to send troops at this time.

When Lê Hoàn heard this news, he was stunned by the message and, standing upright, exclaimed:

> The pirates attacked our border; the fault lay with the acting official [Lê Hoàn himself]. August Lord, you are lenient and merciful, and your compassion is greater than that of my own parents, as you will not execute me as a result of my liability. From today on, I will carefully follow the contract of my acting official duties, to protect Trương Hải [the South China Sea region] forever.[53]

The Vietnamese ruler allegedly then faced north and kowtowed in thanks to the Song emperor.

With this act, the lingering theme of ancient Nam Việt ambitions quickly subdued and tempered by signs of imperial compassion is played out once again in this description of Song events. Appeals to observe tributary obligations are coupled with military threats. The rude, uncultivated manner of the Vietnamese leader is contrasted with the calm and cultured responses of the court envoy. Although Lê Hoàn certainly held the upper hand in controlling trading activities in his own region, and Li Ruozhuo likely recognized that fact in his day, later historians reconstructed the exchange in such a way as to introduce the dynamics of past exchanges and thereby suggest the lasting value of imposing tributary norms on the relationship between the northern court and the Vietnamese region.

Formal tribute relations continued when Song Zhenzong (Zhao Dechang [r. 997–1022]) came to the throne. Notably, Vietnamese gifts of tribute had increased considerably in value. The new emperor granted Lê Hoàn the titles "prince of the Southern Pacification" and probationary "princely attendant." The Vietnamese ruler then sent Supreme Commander Nguyễn Thiệu Cung and Vice Commander Triệu Hoài Đức to present as tribute to the Chinese court one gold-and-silver chair encrusted with the "seven jewels" (*qi bao*); ten silver bowls; ten rhinoceros horns and elephant tusks; and fifty bolts of fine cloth.[54] The emperor ordered that these articles be displayed in the Longevity Pavilion (Wansuidian) at Taizong's shrine and allowed Nguyễn Thiệu Cung and the other Vietnamese envoys to approach the shrine in worship to pay their respects to the deceased emperor. When the envoys returned to court, the emperor gave them an armored horse for Lê Hoàn along with an edict praising the Vietnamese ruler.

In 1001, Lê Hoàn sent the adjutant Lê Thiệu and the vice adjutant Hà Khánh Thường to the Song court to offer as tribute one tamed rhinoceros, two elephants, and one "seven-jewel"-encrusted vase. During the same year, the Qinzhou administration reported that a group of people from Giao Châu's Hiệu Thành Tràng market town, including the leader of "the eight prefectures" (frontier territories in the Lê kingdom), Hoàng Khánh Tạp, and several hundred others, arrived at the borderlands to submit themselves to Song authority. Such movement of people across the frontier region would become more and more common, as both the Song and Đại Cồ Việt court reached farther into this region. Zhenzong did not wish to upset the balance of power at that time. He sent word that he sympathized with their desires, but he also ordered that they be sent back to their home territories.

In early 1006, Lê Hoàn died, and he was immediately succeeded by his middle son, Lê Long Việt (983–1005).[55] The Vietnamese court did not experience a smooth succession of power. Lê Long Việt's older brother, Lê Long Toàn (d. 1006), proceeded to plunder the royal reserve and soon disappeared from the capital. Long Việt managed to rule for only three days before he was assassinated by his younger brother, Lê Long Đĩnh (Lê Ngọc Triệu [r. 1006–9]). Lê Long Toàn launched an unsuccessful counterattack, after which he was forced to flee to Champa, where he was killed. Lê Long Đĩnh's other older brother, Lê Minh Hộ, led the troops stationed at Phù Lan Trại stockade into the ensuing military struggle. The sibling acting as official envoy, Lê Minh Đề, was unable to return home owing to the chaos in the region. The Song emperor sent out special orders instructing the local government at Guangzhou to offer the Vietnamese envoy unprecedented assistance. Guangzhou's prefect Ling Ce and other local officials made the following report:

> All of Lê Hoàn's sons are competing to take over as ruler, and the general populace will most certainly rebel. The local [Tai-speaking] leaders Hoàng Khánh Tạp and Hoàng Tú Man are among

several thousands of people who disobeyed the Vietnamese court's troops, and the Hoàng leaders were massacred by court troops for challenging Lê authority. Survivors have arrived at the frontier to surrender and pay allegiance to the prefectural government of Lianzhou. The Hoàng leaders petitioned the Lianzhou prefectural authorities to dispatch two thousand men to the Giao Châu to assuage the upheaval, while Hoàng Khánh Tạp and others showed their desire to be assigned to the vanguard of this force.[56]

Song Zhenzong announced to the court that Lê Hoàn had been loyal and obedient to the Chinese empire in the past, as evidenced by the Vietnamese leader's observance of tribute protocol. Although I have found no specific references to a change in trade policy, I suggest that, tributary protocol aside, Kaifeng also regarded regional stability to be in the court's economic interest. Zhenzong very quickly dispatched his envoy, the "Destiny Sea pacification commissioner" (*Yuanhai anfushi*) Shao Hua, to Hoa Lư, to convey the Song court's intentions to the Vietnamese. Shao Hua presented a letter to Lê Minh Hộ, instructing him to take heed of the Song's "awesome power" (*weide*). He noted that if the quarreling parties continued to stall in choosing a leader for the Vietnamese throne, the Chinese court would send a small force of troops to take the wrongdoers to task. Lê Minh Hộ appears to have been frightened by this news and made Lê Long Đĩnh one of his leading military leaders. Lê Long Đĩnh took the title "military commissioner" and then offered to send his own tribute mission to the Chinese court. Lê Minh Hộ also gave himself the honorific titles "acting defender-in-chief," which was typically offered to a senior military officer, and "enlightened prince."[57] When Shao Hua heard about these developments, he remarked, "the far-away and unrefined foreigners have different ways [*su*], and they don't understand the practice of ritual. How could this fact not be strange?"[58] Already, the desire to maintain proper tributary relations with Vietnamese leaders had become less important than keeping the peace.

The memorial quoted above indicates that a slight shift in Song court policy regarding frontier management had most certainly occurred. Shao Hua noted to the court that Hoàng Khánh Tạp, who had earlier approached Song authorities in 1001, had not participated in the rebellion but instead had "come to China to be transformed by Chinese culture [*laihua*]." Shao contended that Hoàng Khánh Tập's followers were still quite numerous, and if these people were to be sent back to their home region, they might face being massacred. The emperor ordered that Hoàng Khánh Tập be given the petty official position of grade three lictor and a post at Chenzhou, in modern-day southern Hunan province. He then permitted Hoàng Khánh Tập to enter the court to present tribute. Later frontier leaders beyond the Vietnamese court would attempt to foster similar tributary relationships with the northern court as a buffer against the aggression of Vietnamese leaders.

During this same period, Song Zhenzong faced a crisis in authority that resulted from a 1005 military defeat in a northern frontier conflict with the Khitan-led Liao kingdom. The Song's defeat caused a loss of both territory and prestige to the court, and advisers to the emperor suggested that he seek heavenly signs of his continuing mandate to rule.[59] In early 1008, the first of four "celestial orders" (*tianshu*) suddenly appeared in the imperial palace. These celestial orders referred to communications received by Zhenzong from the Daoist Primal Celestial Excellency (Yuanshi Tianzun) or the Jade Emperor. As reported by the emperor himself, on January 8, 1008 (or December 28, 1007, in some sources), a deity appeared before Zhenzong and spoke these words: "during the first month of the year, you must build a 'golden seal "purgatory" altar' (*huanglu daochang*) at the Pavilion of Orthodoxy (Zhengdian). To that altar I will deliver a celestial order, a 'great axial and auspicious charm' (*dazhong xiangfu*), which will be divided into three parts. You must not reveal these divine truths."[60] By most accounts, the "director of the bureau of military affairs" (*zhiqu miyuanshi*) and Zhenzong's closest adviser Wang Qinruo (962–1025) was the likely author of these celestial orders. Nonetheless, the Song emperor embarked on a flurry of court activity after reporting these heavenly visions. This event had an impact on the Sino-Vietnamese tributary relationship as well. When conducting the Eastern Fiefs (Dongfeng) ritual for the Jade Emperor at Taishan, the emperor requested that all tribute kingdoms dispatch envoys to the court for special awards.[61] Relations throughout the Song empire were recalibrated during this period, and the Vietnamese ruler must have noticed his regional status rise as a result.

At the same time, problems with regional stability increased as local people began to respond to the increasing presence of both Vietnamese and Chinese authorities on the frontier. In 1009, the Guangnan West circuit administrator reported that the Man barbarians of Qinzhou had robbed the Tanka boat people in the harbor. The Ruhong garrison commander Li Wenzhu (d. 1009) led a squad of seasoned troops to attack and pursue the bandits. In the midst of the fighting at sea, Li Wenzhu was shot dead by a stray arrow. Zhenzong immediately ordered the Vietnamese court to capture these bandits. A year later, in 1010, Vietnamese forces caught thirteen people of Địch Lão ethnicity and presented the captives to the Chinese court.[62] Lê Long Đĩnh subsequently sent Administrative Assistant Nguyễn Thû Cương on a tribute mission with gifts of rhinoceros horn, elephant tusks, gold and silver, and a striped bridal veil.

Later in the same year, Lê Long Đĩnh again sent envoys to the Song court. This time, the Vietnamese ruler had trade issues in mind. As soon as the Vietnamese envoy entered the Chinese territory, he issued a memorial requesting that officially sanctioned trade between the Song and Giao Chỉ be permitted at Yongzhou. When Yongzhou's fiscal commissioner made this request known to the emperor, Song Zhenzong replied: "Many of the people who live by the seaside have suffered from the plundering and raiding of Giao Châu. Therefore, I had earlier allowed only trade between Lianzhou and the Ruhong garrison, so that it would be possible to control this section of the borderlands. The region now in question involves territory right beside the Song interior. This change in trade would certainly not benefit us."

The emperor ordered that existing precedents remain in place. In fact, calling on the Vietnamese leadership to abide by its obligations as a tributary vassal made perfect sense to the Chinese leadership in terms of its developing trade policy. While expanded economic activity in this period had to be acknowledged, the potential for regional instability caused by even greater traffic through the region must have been a concern of the central court.

Political fortunes in the Vietnamese region were about to change once again. A longtime Lê military officer, Lý Công Uẩn (r. 1010–28), had been acting as Long Đĩnh's close adviser. Long Đĩnh had made Công Uẩn an honorary member of the Lê clan in an effort to secure his loyalty. In 1010, however, Lý Công Uẩn plotted against Lê Long Đĩnh and rose up against him. When the Lê clan retaliated, Lý Công Uẩn killed Lê Minh Đề, Lê Minh Sưởng, and others, declared himself to be their successor, and sent envoys to the Chinese court to present tribute. From Kaifeng's perspective, this was a frustrating sign that imperial sanction often had little effect on local events in Vietnam. The Song emperor Zhenzong reportedly commented, "Lê Hoàn was not righteous, but he was able to receive imperial sanction. Lý Công Uẩn has imitated Lê Hoàn in his wrongdoings. This is really to be detested!"[63] The emperor nevertheless chose to follow the existing tributary protocol when the Song court ultimately recognized Lê Hoàn. Zhenzong ordered that Lý Công Uẩn should receive all the prestigious titles once granted to Lê rulers. Lý Công Uẩn also asked for imperial writings in the hand of Song Taizong, and the Song emperor ordered that one hundred scrolls be delivered to the Vietnamese court.[64] And so began the longest-lasting Vietnamese dynastic power of the premodern period, the Lý dynasty.

Despite his outburst upon hearing of Lý Công Uẩn's rise to power, Zhenzong on several occasions demonstrated his acceptance of Lý dynastic authority. During the spring of 1011, the emperor Zhenzong, a great promoter of Daoist ritual at court, led an imperial procession in the performance of sacrificial rites at the Fenyin "temple of the earth goddess" (houtu) in Puzhou's Ronghe county (modern-day Shanxi). In 1007, with the support of close court advisers, Zhenzong had first emphasized the importance of this Western Han period (206 BCE–8 CE) ceremony, and in 1011 he ordered the renovation of the Fenyin temple.[65] The Vietnamese ruler Lý Công Uẩn marked the Song court's observation of rites by sending a tribute mission. Once the rituals had concluded, Song Zhenzong granted Lý Công Uẩn the title "manager of affairs and the secretariat-chancellery" (tongping zhangshi), along with a fief of one thousand households and a "substantive fief" (shi feng) of four hundred households. The Song court also recorded the official rank of the Vietnamese mission's envoys, including the "administrative assistant to the military commissioner" (jiedu panguan) Lương Nhâm Văn and a "surveillance commission inspector" (guancha xunguan) Lê Tái Nghiêm. Although Lương Nhâm Văn and the other envoys may have given only ad hoc titles to their Chinese hosts, Lý Công Uẩn's act of marking Zhenzong's Fenyin ceremony with the special tribute mission indicates the Vietnamese ruler's understanding of the Song court's ritual life and the role his participation could play in securing stronger ties with Kaifeng.[66]

Song Zhenzong's reign also marked the period in which the Song court sought to extend to local upland representatives of the Lý court its practice of granting titles to *jimi* chieftains on the Chinese side of the frontier. When Lý Công Uẩn sent a mission to Kaifeng in late spring of 1012, Zhenzong, among his official duties, appointed the "memorial transmitter-envoy" (*jinzoushi*) Lý Nhân Mỹ to the position of regional chief in Thành Châu frontier prefecture.[67] Thành Châu was located in territory under Lý authority, and Song rulers through this period had not claimed the right to grant even nominal titles for posts administered by their Vietnamese tributary vassals. At the same time, the Chinese court raised the profile of its relationship with increasingly grand titles for the Lý ruler. During the winter of 1013, Zhenzong called for a special observance of the Fengshan rites at Taishan (central Shandong) to honor the Yellow Emperor, who had revealed himself to Zhenzong in a vision as the Zhao clan's "august ancestor" (*shengzu*). Following the ceremony, Song Zhenzong gave Lý Công Uẩn the titles "commander unequaled in honor" (*kaifu yitong sansi*) and "venerated and successful official" (*yidai gongchen*). In 1014, Lý Công Uẩn received the additional honorific title "preserver of temperance, guardian of rectitude, and successful official" (*baojie shouzheng gongchen*), along with a fief of one thousand households and a substantive fief of four hundred households. That year, Zhenzong ordered that all the Song's tributary states should come to Kaifeng, with the Song court taking care of lodging and food for the envoys. Lý Công Uẩn chose his trusted "grand preceptor" (*đại bảo*), the Đường Châu regional chief Đào Thạc Phụ, to lead this tribute mission.[68] The Chinese emperor commanded that Đào Thạc be appointed regional chief of Thuận Châu. The emperor further offered the Vietnamese envoy a Southern Han title from the Five Dynasties period, "adjutant of An Nam's Army of the Peaceful Sea" (*xingjun sima Annan Jinghaijun*). Furthermore, Zhenzong instructed that Đào Thạc Phụ's "assistant" (*fushi*) Ngô Hoài Tự be appointed Trùng Châu regional chief, serving concurrently as "aide to the military commissioner" (*jiedufushi*). *The Complete History of the Great Viet* makes no mention of these extraordinary titles in its account, but Chinese sources likely emphasize this event to underscore the prestige these titles still held on both sides of the frontier.

Throughout the early Lý period, Sino-Vietnamese relations had remained focused on diplomacy and not trade issues, even when local events demanded direct action. Such events often involved indigenous frontier inhabitants and the court-appointed officials assigned to police their activity. Early in the Lý, the Địch Lão chieftain Trường Bà Khán fled to China in order to avoid punishment. The prefect of Qinzhou, Mu Zhongying, first summoned the Vietnamese fugitive to his post. En route to the prefectural seat, Bà Khán changed his mind and declined the summons. Guangnan's chief military inspector then ordered that the Ruhong garrison be offered a bounty reward of cattle and wine. Vietnamese officials had been secretly monitoring the situation, and in an effort to capture the Địch Lão fugitive, they bribed the officials at the Ruhong garrison, who then seized both people and animals in great numbers. The Chinese emperor ordered Lý Công Uẩn to investigate this matter. The Song court then ordered that from that point onward, Chinese border agents could not bait Man barbarian Địch Lão people into rekindling the disturbance. After this event, Lý Công Uẩn continued occasionally to bring tribute to the Chinese court, although such missions became less frequent. At the same time, missions from other Southeast Asian trading kingdoms and missions originating in the Arab world became more common.

During the winter of 1017, the Chinese emperor granted Lý Công Uẩn the title "prince of the southern pacified region" (*nanping wang*), adding a fief of one thousand households and a substantive fief of four hundred households. The following year, Zhenzong offered Lý Công Uẩn the added post of "acting defender-in-chief" (*jianjiao taiwei*), accompanied by a fief of one thousand households and a substantive fief of four hundred. With each offering of new titles, both sides sent envoys to their respective sides of the border, where the emperor gave Lý Công Uẩn sacrificial vessels and currency, imperial robes, a gold belt, and an armored horse.

When Zhao Zhen (Song Renzong) ascended to the throne in 1023, he granted Lý Công Uẩn the title "acting grand preceptor" (*jianjiao taishi*). Lý Công Uẩn sent the Trương Châu regional chief Lý Khoan Thái and the "aide to the protector-general" (*duhu fushi*) Nguyễn Thủ Cương to present tribute to the Song court. During the summer of 1028, Lý Công Uẩn sent the Hoan Châu (located on the boundary between Nghệ An and Hà Tĩnh) regional chief Lý Công Hiển to present tribute. Renzong had Lý Công Hiển appointed to the position of Tự Châu regional chief. Lý Công Hiển then sent some younger members of his clan, including his son-in-law Thàn Thừa Quý, to lead people into China to plunder the border territory. Thàn Thừa Quý was a chieftain in Lạng Châu (modern-day Lạng Sơn), with his base of power in the Giáp Dồng grotto settlement, and his son Thàn Thiệu Thái would become an important ally of the Lý court during the rebellions led by Nùng Trí Cao. The Chinese emperor ordered that the head of the Tax Transport Bureau (Zhuanyunsi) of the Guangnan West circuit assemble a militia of able-bodied men from the region's aboriginal settlements to attack and capture the offenders.

When Lý Công Uẩn passed away soon thereafter, his twenty-eight-year-old son Lý Phật Mã took the title "interim capital liaison representative" (*quanzhi liuhoushi*) and sent envoys to China to announce his father's death.[69] The Chinese emperor granted Lý Công Uẩn the posthumous appellation "most loyal" (*zhizhong*) and the title "prince of Nam Việt" (*Nanyue wang*). The Song ruler then ordered the "fiscal commissioner" (*zhuanyunshi*) of Guangnan West circuit, Wang Weizheng, to act as the "envoy for sacrifices and libations" (*jidianshi*). Wang was also given the position of "envoy for appointment verification" (*guangaoshi*). The emperor gave Lý Phật Mã the titles "acting defender-in-chief" (*jianjiao taiwei*), "Army of the Peaceful Sea military commissioner," "Annam protector-general," and "commandery prince of Giao Chỉ" (*Jiaozhi junwang*). During the autumn of 1031, Lý Phật Mã sent the Phong Châu (located in northern Hà Tây) regional chief Lý Ac Thuyên and the Aí Châu (modern-day Thanh Hóa) regional chief Xuất Nhật Tân, among others, to the Chinese court to express the Viet ruler's thanks. The Chinese emperor granted Lý Ac Thuyên the title of regional chief of Hoan Châu and granted Xuất Nhật Tân the title of Trân Châu regional chief. Titles granted by the Chinese to Vietnamese envoys continued to support a healthy tributary relationship, even as they reflected a growing Song interest in seeking allies in the frontier region.

Perhaps in response to these titles, local leaders began to seek the approval and outright protection of Chinese authorities in this period. As noted in chapter 2, the Lý and Song courts faced the first significant challenge to their developing relationship in 1034, when Trần Công Vĩnh and his six hundred followers crossed into Song territory and requested *neifu* status from the Song court. Lý Phật Mã sent a military force of more than one thousand men to the border region to capture and pursue Trần Công Vĩnh's followers. As noted earlier, the Song emperor ordered that Trần Công Vĩnh and his followers return to their home region, but the Chinese ruler warned Lý Phật Mã not to kill any of Trần Công Vĩnh's men. In an effort to defuse a tense situation, Lý Phật Mã soon dispatched a tribute mission to the Song under the leadership of Trần Ứng Ky and Vương Duy Khánh. The Chinese emperor granted Trần Ứng Ky the title "companion to the heir apparent" (*taizi zhongyun*) and granted the title "assistant minister to the court of judicial review" (*dali sicheng*) to Vương Duy Khánh. As a result of this mission, Lý Phật Mã received from the Song court the title "acting grand preceptor" (*jianjiao taishi*), one of the honorific titles once held by his father Lý Công Uẩn. Good relations seem to have been restored, and yet, after this period, the relationship continued to change in response to further efforts at territorial expansion among the upland inhabitants of the frontier.

By the time Lý Phật Mã took the throne at Thăng Long, the Lý desire for expansion and regional control was stronger than ever. Phật Mã again sent troops to conquer Champa in 1044. The invasion was hugely successful, and it strengthened the Vietnamese court both politically and economically.[70] The Song court suspected that the Vietnamese had a hidden plan in their campaign and for the first time took direct steps to counter Vietnamese movements. The court ordered that local officials check on all sixteen routes established between China and the Vietnamese region since the Tang. Furthermore, the Chinese emperor ordered the fiscal commissioner Du Qi to cross into this strategic region and erect defenses. The Vietnamese regiment did not try to attack the borderland area. Meanwhile, disturbances among the

Tai-speaking inhabitants of the frontier, in particular within the Nùng clan, had become quite severe.

Conclusion

The aforementioned narrative of Song period Sino-Vietnamese relations suggests that the Chinese court began with the issue of political authority as its primary source of anxiety. The Chinese leadership in the early Song was greatly concerned with succession as related to the maintenance of proper relations with its tributary neighbors. The transfer of power from one generation of hereditary leadership to the next lay at the heart of the tribute system. The Đinh clan had come to power in the mid-tenth century to the south of the Red River delta in northern Vietnam, and thus the clan's leaders stood apart from the traditional Sino-Vietnamese elite. Nevertheless, the Đinh clan's style of rule appeared from afar to fit the picture the Song central court envisioned for its southern frontier. When Song Taizong ascended to the throne in 976, Đinh Liễn fittingly sent envoys to the court at Kaifeng to present tribute and congratulate the new Chinese ruler.

The Song court later tried to take advantage of the chaos that ensued following the death of Đinh Bộ Lĩnh and his son, and the court further justified the invasion by insisting that a legitimate vassal king must be protected. When Song Taizong's forces failed in their attack on Lê Hoàn's army in 980–81, this military weakness undermined the Song's subsequent demands. However, Lê Hoàn quickly calmed the Song court, preserving the integrity of a newly revived tributary relationship. In most communications with Song representatives from the north, southern leaders continued to present themselves as compliant participants in Kaifeng's effort to create a web of tributary relations beyond its frontier, even after their military ability had been clearly demonstrated. In fact, local Vietnamese leaders looked differently at the role, if any, that the Chinese court ought to play in the power succession in the Đại Cồ Việt kingdom. In mainland Southeast Asian politics of this time, the ruler at the apex of the tributary hierarchy seldom interfered in successions within his subordinate kingdoms, whether or not the succession was hereditary or expropriated.[71] Đại Cồ Việt leaders, given the history of Sino-Vietnamese interaction, could have anticipated that the Song court would react to political instability south of the frontier. Nevertheless, local acceptance of such a power struggle did not depend on sanction from any power other than the Đại Cồ Việt leadership.

When the Song court eventually faced another usurper in the south, the Chinese acceded to the regional precedent they had established and instead welcomed the new leadership. This new leader and founder of the Lý dynasty, Lý Công Uẩn, initiated a very different style of rule. Lý rulers actively modeled their court on the Chinese imperial example, but they eventually named their kingdom without seeking Chinese approval, depending very heavily on local sources of power and authority. Recent scholarship argues that the state established in the Red River delta by the founders of the Lý dynasty was "eclectic, elitist and non-bureaucratic in a pattern similar to those of the other great Southeast Asian states of the classical age."[72] Local deities and Buddhist cults provided a rich source of support for the cultivation of Lý power. Moreover, this was the dynasty that produced an ambitious leadership with desires to expand and deepen its personal power well into the frontier region. Lý advisers, many of them Buddhist clergy who had counseled Lê Hoàn in his dealings with the Song, instructed their rulers on tenets of imperial behavior. When, in the late summer of 1010, Lý Công Uẩn established his new capital at Đại La, an ancient citadel renamed Thăng Long (on the site of modern-day Hanoi), the Vietnamese ruler signaled a shift in the center of power, away from the coastal focus of Hoa Lư in the lower delta region. Eventually, expanding dominion in the northern Vietnamese region led to closer contact with the people already residing in, and ruling, the frontier areas. These encounters would finally bring Chinese and Vietnamese interests into their greatest period of conflict by the mid-eleventh century.

Many aspects of Sino-Vietnamese tributary relations during the early Song changed with the outcome of each tribute mission sent north to Kaifeng by Vietnamese envoys. With few exceptions, the tribute missions themselves were important opportunities to negotiate the balance of status and authority existing between Chinese and Vietnamese rulers. The titles granted to Vietnamese rulers by Chinese emperors were cumulative, indicating the varying degrees of association the two courts had shared throughout their histories. The titles and fiefs offered with each visit by Vietnamese envoys affected the local standing of southern rulers among their southern neighbors. These gifts also influenced the degree to which Chinese courts attempted to interfere in the affairs of Vietnamese courts. Participants in any system of tribute relations along the Song's southern frontier negotiated their alliances through the giving and receiving of valuable assets.

In the Sino-Vietnamese relationship, these assets included both material commodities, such as rare plants, exotic animals, and precious manufactured goods, and nonmaterial commodities conveyed with honorific titles, imperial seals, and honorific land fiefs. The fact that these titles and fiefs often included long local pedigrees contributed to the local rulers' legitimacy. Many other frontier communities also accepted the power of such titles. Local Vietnamese leaders negotiated their status within the Chinese tribute system in such a way as to establish regional independence while maintaining a check on Chinese incursions. Other frontier leaders also negotiated their positions between the Chinese and Vietnamese courts through tributary ties and thereby occasionally found support for their efforts to expand and challenge their neighbors.

4

Gaining Legitimacy at the Empire's Edge: Indigenous Tai-Speaking Communities along the Sino-Vietnamese Frontier through the Early Song Period

In late 1038, the Tai-speaking Sino-Vietnamese frontier chieftain Nùng Tôn Phúc (or Toàn Phúc) (d. 1039) made his bid for kingship.[1] Tôn Phúc's grab for power was as bloody as it was sudden when, in late autumn, he allegedly murdered both his brother and his brother-in-law and seized their lands. Tôn Phúc gave his newly amalgamated realm the hopeful name Kingdom of Longevity (Trường Sanh Quốc) and took for himself the title Luminous and Sage Emperor (Chiêu Thánh Hoàng Đế) and for his wife A Nùng (d. 1054) the title Enlightened and Virtuous Empress Dowager (Minh Đức Hoàng Hậu).[2] Tôn Phúc then broke off all ties with the Vietnamese ruler Lý Phật Mã, his principal patron and leader of the expanding Đại Cồ Việt kingdom.

The suggestion that Tôn Phúc's family could be elevated in status to that of an imperial household brought the frontier chieftain into direct conflict with both the Chinese Song and Vietnamese Lý courts and constituted a direct challenge to their rule. Nevertheless, the Chinese authorities hesitated to take direct action. The Song statesman Sima

Guang would later comment that when the local prefect at Tianzhou (modern-day Tianyang county in northern Guangxi) requested assistance in dealing with Nùng Tôn Phúc's revolt, officials from the circuit seat of Yongzhou (modern-day Nanning) appeared afraid to become involved and declined to offer assistance.[3] Concern in Kaifeng with the emergence of the powerful Xi Xia kingdom (982–1227) along the western frontier in the same year could have been a factor as well. In contrast to Chinese indecision, Lý Phật Mã's response to Tôn Phúc's actions was swift and unwavering. In the spring of 1039, the Vietnamese ruler led an army into the northern upland region to capture Tôn Phúc, his oldest son Nùng Trí Thông, and their closest accomplices. The chieftain's wife and second son, Nùng Trí Cao, both managed to escape by fleeing to the Song side of the border. Meanwhile, the hapless captives were taken to the capital city of Thăng Long, where the Vietnamese court beheaded them all in a public execution.

At first glance, this event appears to be no more than a minor disturbance along the Sino-Vietnamese frontier. Moreover, it is difficult to determine the motive behind the brash actions taken by Tôn Phúc and his followers. Did he act as a rebellious vassal who had abandoned his responsibilities to his direct superior, the Vietnamese ruler? Or did Tôn Phúc draw on political currents that originated beyond the court politics of Kaifeng or Thăng Long? As events are described in the extant court chronicles, one could easily conclude that Tôn Phúc's behavior was influenced by the same forces that motivated many would-be founders of Chinese-style dynasties in the south, including even the Vietnamese rulers of the early tenth century. A careful examination of these same events from an indigenous perspective reveals a more complex balancing of local and interregional concerns, targeting multiple audiences.

Tai Clan Rivalry and the Frontier's Political Geography

To understand the local balance of power in the southern borderlands region, we must picture a social order that predated the imposition of Chinese imperial institutions. The frontier region inhabited by Tai-speaking indigenous peoples in the eleventh century extended from, in the west, Bảo Lạc prefecture to, in the east, Vĩnh An prefecture in the northern Vietnamese region and Qinzhou prefecture on the South China coast. Although both Vietnamese and Chinese authorities labeled all of the local inhabitants "barbarians of the South" (Man), there were many distinct communities throughout this region. The majority belonged to a single Tai-speaking ethnicity, the Chinese Zhuang (or Vietnamese Nùng) ethnic group.

Map 3. Home Region of Tai Communities (Elizabeth Nelson)

Cultural artifacts may assist us in determining precisely where these Tai-speaking communities lived in earlier times. The production and ritual use of elaborate bronze drums were distinctive characteristics of ancient Zhuang society. One must take some caution in exploring this field of research, because the study of the region's ancient bronze drum tradition is not without controversy, much of it fueled by the nationalist concerns of the modern Chinese and Vietnamese governments that sponsor the research.⁴ A study of motifs from the bronze drums themselves, identifying motifs used by specific communities in Southwest China and northern Vietnam, avoids the most controversial issue, which is determining the origins of the bronze technology itself. The Tai-speaking communities examined here appear to be unified in their use of the frog motif in their ritual bronzes, referring to the frog as their group's primary "totem" (*tuteng*). The frog motif appears on the bronze drums produced by many communities along the Sino-Vietnamese frontier for ritual use. "Third grade" (*bingxing*) bronze drums bearing frog motifs are found mainly in Tengxian county (located to the north of the Xun River), Pingnan, Xiangzhou, Guixian (located to the west of the Yu River), Hengxian, Binyang, Wuming, Longzhou (located near the modern Sino-Vietnamese border), and Daxin county, among other places. This area marked the lower limits of the Song empire during the Northern Song dynasty (960–1127).⁵ It also represents the northernmost region, where the Tai-speaking clans under discussion were active.

For a better understanding of the settlement of Tai-speaking communities in modern-day southern Guangxi and northern Cao Bằng, one must take a close look at the topography and natural resources of the region. Nanning, the modern provincial capital of Guangxi, was the prefectural seat of Yongzhou during the Song period. This settlement had been the southernmost site of official Chinese administration since 207 BCE, when the Qin empire incorporated it into Guilin prefecture.⁶ Located in the Nanning basin and surrounded to the north and west by the relatively low-elevation karst geomorphology, the city was situated on the northern banks of the Yong River, a section of the Yu River. The Yu River itself is a tributary of the much larger Pearl River (Zhujiang), which flows southeasterly from the Yunnan Guizhou plateau through southern Guangxi to the sea, south of Guangzhou, the modern-day provincial capital of Guangdong. Several miles upstream from Yongzhou, one finds the confluence of the Left and Right rivers, which fan out to the northwest to modern-day Bose and southwest to modern-day Longzhou and create the outer boundaries of the region that held the greatest concentration of Tai-speaking frontier communities by the early Song period. The lowland region between the Left and Right rivers was fertile, fed annually by the seasonal monsoon rains and protected by a temperate and dry winter season. As Ella Laffey notes, the topography of southern Guangxi is high and rugged, but even the smallest tributaries of larger rivers support green river valleys suitable for settlement.[7]

The Left River winds upstream through Longzhou and eventually meets the more mountainous landscape at the edge of the modern-day border between Vietnam and China. The river, at this point known as the Bằng River, heads northwesterly through Phục Hòa and the upland city of Cao Bằng. The headwaters for this river are located to the northwest of Cao Bằng near the modern-day hamlet of Hà Quảng. The "home region" of the Tai-speaking Nùng clan, including Nùng Tôn Phúc, was located along this stretch of the Bằng River between Cao Bằng and Hà Quảng. The Nùng collective community consisted of nine semiautonomous regions of various sizes, called *po* or *bu*. During the early eleventh century, these regions were named Slốc, Ngàn, Dái, Lài, Nuống, Má, Héc, Ngà, and Săng.[8] Their exact location cannot be easily determined. The Bằng River region's steep mountains and valleys, in which the Nùng clan lived, were known for gold and cinnabar, although the people lived primarily from agricultural production. Settlements were established in villages along the Bằng River, in connected valleys, and at higher altitudes along mountain slopes. Although the village settlements were secluded from one another, interaction with other native groups, and later with Han settlers, was common.

Historians of upland Tai-speaking societies on the premodern Southeast Asian mainland refer to such communities as *müang*.[9] As Ann Maxwell Hill notes, *müang* is not easily translated in English as "kingdom" or "state," because these terms suggest a unity that *müang* traditionally lacked.[10] The historian David Wyatt writes that the term "denotes as much personal as spatial relationships."[11] *Müang* grew and contracted as the result of capture, marriage alliances, and the cooperation of leaders from a single clan. As Hill writes, "such alliances created loose, shifting hierarchies of *müang* in which one domain and princely family would be recognized by the others as the political center."[12] Under such circumstances, control from the center of a *müang* depended heavily on the consensus of the leader's most powerful followers.

Local Tai-speaking leaders of these *müang* in the Sino-Vietnamese frontier region saw the lands that lay on the periphery of Chinese and Vietnamese imperial interests as central to their political authority. Most of the Sino-Vietnamese borderlands region was controlled by a small number of clans (or surname-groups). In the easternmost area of the frontier, the Hoàng (Huang) clan was predominant. During the Tang, when the "military commissioner" (*jinglueshi*) Xu Shen (737–806) administered the Yong frontier command (*Yongguan*), the Hoàng clan submitted to Tang court control. The clan leadership brought with them thirteen *po* amalgamated villages and twenty-nine "aboriginal prefectures" (*zhou*).[13] According to Chinese sources, local Vietnamese leaders soon thereafter took control of this territory, and from this time, the Hoàng clan and its followers owed their service to the Vietnamese. Although the Hoàng clan was relatively small, Vietnamese rulers often assigned its members leadership positions in An Vĩnh.[14]

By the early Song period, the Vi (Wei) clan had settled in Tô Mậu prefecture in the northern Vietnamese region and in Siling and Xiping prefectures on the Song side of the border. The Hoàng and Vi, along with the Nùng (Nong) and Chu (Zhou) clans, were by this time the principal occupants of a region between the Vietnamese and Han settlements in the Left River region. Leaders among these clans maintained strong personal, quasi-familial ties, through which they sustained their authority. Describing the indigenous border communities of sixteenth-century Guangxi, one historian writes, "while chieftains who shared the same family name did not necessarily share the same ancestry ... they often invoked the real or imagined ties to form alliances or to assert their influence."[15] The practice of fashioning a network of kinship-like relations, joined by particular surnames, predates even the time period under study here. This custom accounts for the considerable decline in the number of local inhabitants bearing the surname Nùng following the various Nùng rebellions and the increase in the number of people from the same region using the surname Triệu (Zhao), which was the surname of the Song ruling family.

Eventually, the influence of the Nùng would surpass that of the Hoàng clan. The Nùng clan also traditionally owed its loyalty to the Sino-Vietnamese elite who had governed An Nam (or northernmost Vietnam) during the Tang dynasty. By the early Song dynasty, Nùng leaders were in charge of four "administrative units" (*dao*) that had been part of the Tang's *jimi*, or "loose reins," system, the most important of which was the Temo *jimi* prefecture, which encompassed territory from modern-day Wenshan in eastern Yunnan to Jingxi in southern Guangxi.[16] Temo also included areas of northern Vietnam, such as modern-day Quảng Nguyên county (which included neighboring Vũ Lặc prefecture in the eleventh century) in Vietnam's northeastern Cao Bằng province.[17] With the decline of the Tang and the resulting dissolution of direct northern-court control in the region, the Nùng continued to accept the patronage of absent rulers, both from the north and from the Vietnamese region, who claimed nominal control of the borderland region. However, the bellicose nature of these communities was never in doubt for Chinese chroniclers. The compilers of the *Official History of the Song Dynasty* succinctly note that "[these people] love to fight, treat death lightly, and are prone to rebellion."[18]

The *Jimi* System by the Early Song Period and the Rise of the Nùng Clan

During the early Song period, the Chinese court divided the Left River region into at least twenty-six *jimi* prefectures and four smaller *jimi* districts.[19] Each of these administrative units was granted to a local clan leader, who was to accept, in theory, Song political sovereignty in the area. Given the strategic location of this region amid the mountains bordering on territory claimed by the Đại Cồ Việt kingdom, the Chinese emperor was wise to gain its leaders' loyalties. Moreover, the court's policy toward these communities by no means remained static throughout the Song dynasty. Although the Song court's early attention to the frontier leaders was largely symbolic, by the time of Song Shenzong (r. 1065–85), "local militia" (*tuding*) were being actively organized among the aboriginal villages so as to provide the first line of defense for the Chinese empire. Wang Anshi would comment in an essay on the administration of the Yong frontier command that the aboriginal communities of the Left and Right rivers should be relied upon for the security of both Guangxi and

Guangdong.[20] Before the reign of Zhezong, from 1086 to 1100, the Song authorities' efforts to organize these communities in some manner were not highly effective.[21] Nonetheless, the early Song court took a genuine, if less engaged, interest in the frontier when Song Taizong bestowed special favors on the Nùng leadership, acknowledging that, during Taizong's reign, this clan had succeeded the Hoàng clan as the dominant political presence in the Left River region.

The first member of the Nùng clan to gain official recognition was Nùng Tôn Phúc's father, Nùng Dân Phú (dates unknown). In early 977, a memorial from the Yongzhou garrison reported that the "aboriginal chieftain" (*manqiu*) of Quảng Nguyên prefecture, the "peaceful and generous" (*tanchuo*) leader Nùng Dân Phú, had already established himself as the leader of a *po* of ten neighboring villages after gaining the support of the Southern Han (907–71) court.[22] Dân Phú's title "peaceful and generous" was often granted to princes within the ruling clan of the Nanzhao kingdom (649–902). During the Five Dynasties period, the powerful Nanzhao military commissioner Duan Siping (893–945) conscripted troops for his army from upland areas on the outskirts of his command, which included Temo. After Duan took control of failing Nanzhao and established Dali, he rewarded upland supporters such as Nùng Dân Phú with titles. Duan Siping rewarded another Temo leader, Nùng Hạ Thanh, with the high-ranking Nanzhao title "*buxie*" to further solidify good relations with his leaders on his own state's periphery.[23] When Song authorities entered modern-day Guangxi, they discovered such evidence of a preexisting relationship between leaders from the Temo *jimi* prefecture and the rulers of Nanzhao and, later, the Dali kingdom. The task of the Chinese leadership then was to forge even more durable ties with these local leaders.

Imperial authorities in Yongzhou recommended that the Song court ask for Dân Phú's lands by imperial decree and grant the local leader *neifu* status in return for the payment of tribute and taxes. The emperor decreed that Dân Phú receive the titles "minister of works" (*sigong*) and "grand master of splendid happiness bearing the golden pocket with purple trimming" (*jinzi guanglu daifu*).[24] The court assigned Xu Dao, transport commissioner of Guangzhou, the task of traveling to Dân Phú's home region to confer the titles. These titles were much too grand to hold any specific meaning for the local leader; however, the Chinese court wished to make its mark in this far-flung territory. The Song leadership had granted nominal ranking to local leaders from the Right and Left rivers region who joined Chinese forces in the ultimately unsuccessful assault on Lê Hoàn's forces in 980. Granting lofty titles to this local leader may well have been an effort to instill allegiance to the Song throne in those who wielded authority in this distant region.

Dân Phú eventually passed his honors on to his son, and Nùng Tôn Phúc was granted the additional authority to rule Thảng Do prefecture in the southeastern corner of modern-day Jingxi county, in Guangxi.[25] His younger brother Toàn Lộc (d. 1039) controlled Vạn Nhai prefecture (near modern-day Na Rì county in Bắc Kạn province), while his wife A Nùng's younger brother Nùng Đanh Đạo (d. 1039) controlled Vũ Lặc prefecture, which was his family's traditional seat of power near Quảng Nguyên prefecture.[26] Nùng Tôn Phúc's local prominence was bolstered by both wealth and political influence. Quảng Nguyên prefecture was reportedly a great source of gold, and this natural wealth had made Nùng Tôn Phúc a rich man.[27] Tôn Phúc's local standing did attract the attention of potential rivals, such as the Western Nùng clan chieftain Ha Văn (dates unknown), who likely sided with the Vietnamese court in the final decision to subdue Tôn Phúc's revolt.[28] Despite these political challenges, the Nùng clan of Dân Phú and his descendants managed to dominate the region through a network of sturdy kinship ties.

Nùng Tôn Phúc also augmented his riches through local trade.[29] His citadel's location on the banks of the Bằng River suggests that he had managed to capitalize on his power base's placement along the region's main trading artery. Control of river traffic was likely Tôn Phúc's method for extracting the greatest material benefit from his political command. Tôn Phúc's behavior in this regard was not unique. The anthropologist Ann Maxwell Hill notes similar behavior in her work on Yunnanese Kachin and Haw Chinese traders. By the late Qing, "toll tribute" had become a regular feature of doing business along the caravan routes that reached from Burma into areas of northern Southeast Asia and southwestern China.[30] Equally important was Tôn Phúc's reputation in both courts for being a loyal and trusted vassal in a region that had seen considerable turmoil for more than one hundred years. At the time of his rebellion, he was the region's most powerful man. Political authority coupled with military might, and not the accumulation of material wealth, was the measure for individual success in Tôn Phúc's day.

The Lý Court's Activist Frontier Policy

Around the fall of the Lê dynasty in 1009, the Vietnamese leadership began to show growing interest in the people and resources of the upland region to the north of the Red River delta. The Lý court's grants of fiefs to clan members had increased considerably, and the need for new lands could not be satisfied with existing coastal territory. Therefore, an inland push began among the princes of the Lý court soon after the founding of the dynasty. Moreover, Vietnamese interest in controlling coastal trade had been satisfied with early military successes in containing economic competition from the court's southern Cham neighbors. Instead, the Lý leaders sought to exploit the resources found in their hinterland above the delta region. These included mineral resources found on land then occupied by the upland Tai-speaking communities, and it was these areas that Vietnamese leaders soon targeted.

Vietnamese Lý court excursions into Song territory in the period before Nùng Tôn Phúc's revolt were quite common. As Jeffrey Barlow writes, "Typical examples of Vietnamese raids include one ordered by Lý Công Uẩn (974–1028), the founder of the Lý dynasty in 1009, who in 1017 dispatched his brother-in-law to raid into Yong prefecture. The local administrators ordered local militia (*tuding*) from the mountain grotto settlement to pursue them."[31] The Lý court also established stable, lasting ties with leaders along Vietnam's northern frontier by means of marriage alliances with upland chieftains. In early 1029, Phật Mã attempted to pacify the border region with an arranged marriage between his daughter, the princess Bình Dương (dates unknown), and Thân Thiệu Thái (dates unknown), the head of the Thân clan and the hereditary head of frontier Lạng Châu prefecture (present-day Lạng Sơn).[32] Despite his efforts to establish strong local ties, the Vietnamese ruler was soon busy suppressing rebellions across the territory under his control.

Shortly after the marriage alliance was announced, Đãn Nãi Giáp, leader of the southern Ai Châu prefecture (present-day Thanh Hoà), revolted. Phật Mã personally led the expedition to put down the rebellion and capture its leader. When the southernmost Cham-Viet frontier prefecture of Hoan Châu (present-day Diễn Châu, in Nghệ An province) rebelled in early 1031, and the upland prefectures of Định Nguyên Châu and Trệ Nguyên Châu followed suit in the spring and autumn, respectively, of 1033, Phật Mã again led punitive campaigns to suppress these revolts.[33] In Hoan Châu, Phật Mã punished the local officials and dispatched a new court representative to carry out imperial orders in that prefecture. Phật Mã's son and heir apparent Lý Nhật Tôn (r. 1054–72), the Khai Hoàng prince, accompanied the ruler in Trệ Nguyên Châu. There and in Định Nguyên Châu, Phật Mã quelled the disturbances and, once order was restored, commanded court officials to take up their posts. In the summer of 1034, the local leaders of Hoan Châu presented the Lý court with a tributary gift of ivory as a sign of their continued submission.[34] All this activity indicated that the Đại Cồ Việt ruler paid close attention to both northern and southern frontiers of his kingdom as a gauge of the overall stability of his rule. The quick pacification of unrest was a sure sign that the Lý court continued to maintain legitimacy and the ability to rule effectively. This legitimacy was tested again shortly when the Vietnamese leadership increased the territory under its direct control throughout the kingdom.

By 1034, the Đại Cồ Việt ruler had decided to make a stronger display as a regional leader by assuming an imperial image. In the spring of 1034, Phật Mã adopted a new reign title, *Auspicious Leadership* (Thông Thụy), to acknowledge both his military victories and the appearance of various auspicious signs around the palace compound. He then issued an edict commanding all officials to present memorials formally before his throne and convene in a hall he designated the "imperial court" (*triêu đình*).[35] The Vietnamese ruler further tested his authority at court a year later by promoting a favorite concubine to imperial status as Empress Thiên Cảm. When dissent over this change in the imperial household erupted in the form of another rebellion in Ai Châu prefecture, Phật Mã swiftly crushed his opposition.

By late 1036, unrest in the vicinity of the Đại Cồ Việt kingdom came to the attention of Kaifeng when violence spilled across the frontier. In the fall of 1036, the revolt spread to Giáp Đồng in Lạng Châu, the northeastern prefecture Tô Mậu (within present-day Hải Ninh), Quảng Nguyên (northeast of municipal Cao Bằng), and Đan Ba district (south of present-day Lộc Bình) as well as to the Bình Nguyên, Đô Kim, and Thương Tân prefectures — all within the northwestern Lâm Tây administrative circuit. The insurrection eventually crossed into Song territory at the prefectures of Siling, Xiping, and Shixi, which were all quite close to Yongzhou. Rebels reportedly robbed both indigenous inhabitants and Chinese settlers of horses and cattle and burned their homes before returning to the Vietnamese side of the frontier. Upon hearing of these attacks, the Chinese court held the Vietnamese court responsible for a lack of regional supervision; the Song emperor officially admonished Lý Phật Mã, demanding that the perpetrators be attacked and captured.[36] Interestingly, the account in the 1993 *Complete History of the Great Viet* (Đại Việt sử ký toàn thư), which is based on the earliest available edition, makes no comment on the Song emperor's response to the rebellion or the Việt acceptance of responsibility and moves directly from an account of the unrest to a report on the Việt emperor's expedition.

The Vietnamese leader did not require much encouragement to extend his control into this borderland region. On February 17, 1037, Lý Phật Mã and his son the Phụng Kiền prince led a military expedition to Lâm Tây, leaving Lý Nhật Tôn, the Khai Hoàng prince, in charge of affairs at court. The court military quickly subdued the rebel force, and by the third month, the troops had returned to the capital. Turning south of the capital city, the Đại Cồ Việt ruler also ordered the imperial garrison at Nghệ An prefecture to establish fifty new local storehouses in areas that included Tư Thành, Lợi Nhân, and Vĩnh Phong.[37] In the process of responding to the Song edict, the Lý court did not hesitate to take control of the area's resources. This quest for power consolidation directly influenced the development of events in the next large-scale disturbance. In little more than a year, Nùng Tôn Phúc would launch his bid for power in the face of expanding Vietnamese authority.

The Vietnamese court's early attempts to spread its authority into the frontier went largely uncontested by the Chinese court. In fact, such efforts were likely appreciated; the Chinese emperor had other interests in the region. For example, on January 8, 1039, Emperor Renzong granted Phật Mã the title "king of the southern pacified region," among three other titles that the Chinese emperor granted that day.[38] The emperor did this as a way of rewarding loyal frontier officials, but his actions were motivated by specific events. One month earlier, he had ordered that the inhabitants of Yizhou (located to the south of Luocheng county in north-central Guangxi) and Rongzhou (modern-day Rongxian) prefectures be permitted to pay only half of their "summer tax" (*xiashui*) and that the indigenous inhabitants be wholly exempted.[39] The region had been plundered by a neighboring Man settlement, and the emperor was concerned about the economic stability of the affected communities. Emperor Renzong did not, however, send military aid on this occasion. The court likely regarded the title granted to Phật Mã as a reminder of the Vietnamese ruler's position within the network of tributary relations and also as a request that the Vietnamese leader keep a watchful eye on this weakened region and curtail the activities of any group who might wish to stir up trouble. Without a strong military presence along the southern frontier, the early Song court continued to turn defense and policing over to its local representative, presumed to be the vassal ruler in Thăng Long.

Lý Phật Mã's harsh response to Nùng Tôn Phúc's act of defiance fit his position as a tributary vassal of the Song court. Tributary protocol required that the Vietnamese leader take responsibility for all local disturbances in this Sino-centric world order. Perhaps more importantly in the eyes of his own subjects, Lý Phật Mã chose to interpret Tôn Phúc's act as a threat to the harmony of a world order that he alone maintained. Shortly before killing his prisoners, Phật Mã expressed his anger to his assembled court and restated the imperial scope of his own leadership in the short "Imperial Mandate to Pacify the Nùng" (Bình Nùng chiếu):

> Once I had come to possess All under Heaven (*thiên hạ*), all of my generals, ministers, and officials led a great celebration. From all foreign lands and special regions, there was no one who did not attend. Furthermore, according to precedent, the Nùng clan for generations has protected our frontier, and they have frequently

come to court bearing tribute. Today, Tôn Phúc is displaying a great arrogance by illicitly adopting a reign title and by issuing edicts. His followers are gathering like swarms of gadflies, and he has spread poisonous ideas among the borderlands people. With Heaven's authority, I will strike out and punish him. I have made five members of that group, Tôn Phúc among them, outlaws, and I will have them beheaded at the capital.[40]

This claim of a heavenly right to resort to hegemonic action for the greater good sounds much like the type of world order promoted by Chinese rulers. Since the founding of an independent Vietnamese state, the Lý rulers were the first local leaders to project this vision onto their realm. In claiming universal authority and Heaven's sanction for his actions, Lý Phật Mã placed himself at the same level of power as a Chinese emperor. In order to appeal to his own subjects, the Vietnamese ruler was prepared to reach beyond the Song's conferred tributary vassal status and claim imperial omnipotence.

Contemporaneous Chinese sources contain a very different understanding of this relationship. According to Sima Guang, Tôn Phúc owed his prosperity to China's benevolent rule, as did all the local people under him. Moreover, it was China's leadership and Nùng Tôn Phúc's prosperity that Giao Chỉ detested, and for those reasons, the Việt ruler sent troops to invade Tôn Phúc's territory and capture the chieftain. Sima Guang continued his sharp criticism of the Vietnamese leadership with this statement: "Giao Chỉ extracted taxes without satiation, and the people of the local prefectures suffered for it."[41] According to Sima Guang, the Vietnamese court's mismanagement of the communities entrusted to it by the Song ultimately led to the initial unrest.

For Lý Phật Mã, Nùng Tôn Phúc's claims to regional control over the Sino-Vietnamese frontier violated the bond of personal loyalty that connected him with the Lý ruling house. Moreover, Tôn Phúc's claim to the status of "king" (*guo wang*) and his use of a separate reign title echoed similar claims that had been made by the Đại Cồ Việt founder, Đinh Bộ Lĩnh (r. 968–80). Đinh Bô Lĩnh had himself risen politically from the status of a local chieftain under the Southern Han at the end of the Five Dynasties period. He eventually broke free from this arrangement with the establishment of the Đại Cồ Việt kingdom, which the Chinese refused to recognize, and the announcement of a new reign period titled Great Peace (Thái Bình). Such similarities certainly must have seemed disquieting to the leadership in Thăng Long.

Nùng Tôn Phúc's Revolt As a "Tai" Political Act

Nùng Tôn Phúc's defiance may well have been directed primarily toward the Lý ruling house. However, the significance of his revolt and the titles he adopted carried several levels of meaning, which would have stirred different reactions from his fellow chieftains in the upland frontier areas than from the lowland Vietnamese leadership. For this reason, we will look briefly at Tôn Phúc's revolt as a "Tai" political act, with the intention of uncovering another underlying motive for his behavior and revealing a new dimension in the complex network of relationships that tied local leaders to distant courts.

An important feature of political relations among the communities of the southern frontier was a nascent client-patron system of social intercourse. Thongchai Winichakul writes that, "in the indigenous Southeast Asian tradition, a subject was bound first and foremost to his lord rather than to a state."[42] This system has been described in the context of the early Thai kings, but it applies as well to relations among leading Tai-speaking clans in the Left and Right rivers region and the Song and Đại Cồ Việt courts. This patron-client system involved the presentation of gifts as the central feature of a request for protection and patronage.[43] David Wyatt writes, "Although *müang* society was hierarchical, it must be emphasized that the patron-client relationship, the ruler/ruled dichotomy, was not nearly as one-sided as it may appear."[44] Another Thai historian notes that "when a 'Phu Noi' [the Inferior] gave gifts [to] or performed services [for] a 'Phu Yai' [the Superior] and the [latter] gave favor, protection or assistance to him in return, then the 'Phu Noi' kept on doing so. If the 'Phu Yai' didn't do anything in return, the 'Phu Noi' could stop giving ... services."[45] This system of reciprocity differed from the Chinese system of tribute relations in that it was based on actions taken by each party and not on the relationship that existed between them.

Song Taizu, by accepting the tribute of the Nùng leader Nùng Dân Phú, saw the established relationship as hereditary and unconditional. This relationship was regulated with each presentation of tribute to the Chinese court, although its position within the overall tributary hierarchy was left unchanged. From the Nùng leadership's perspective, the presentation of tribute set up obligations for both parties. When the Nùng found themselves squeezed by an expanding Vietnamese dominion to the south, and without the direct support of their Song "patron" to the north, they felt no obligation to temper their own bids for power.

The traditions of political leadership differed somewhat between the Chinese and Vietnamese core societies and the upland peripheral frontier communities. In Tai-speaking communities, leaders of *müang* were referred to as *caw* (alternate transliterations include the Thai *chao* and the Shan *sao*), lords of varying degrees of power who received tribute and corvée labor from villages that sought the regional stability these military strongmen promised to provide.[46] Moreover, when a *müang* (or *po*) lost its leader, the other regions gathered together in a "competition," from which a new strongman who displayed leadership qualities would emerge.[47] While this position could be considered hereditary, the leading family had to maintain its stature as a powerful and effective leader, or it would face further challenges from its neighbors.

Leo Shin, who has studied the southwest border chieftaincy system in place during the later Ming period (1368–1644), after examining the autonomous nature of the smaller political units and the harsh manner in which larger chiefdoms preyed on their smaller neighbors, compares the network of relations among these regions to the feudal system of the Warring States period (Zhanguo Shidai) (475–221 BCE).[48] This competition between chiefdoms was recorded as early as the Tang dynasty (618–907), when the Nùng, Huang, Wei, and Zhou clans often invaded one another's territory. Even before the Song period, when Nùng leaders perceived that the opportunity for affirming their local preeminence had arrived, they acted in a manner consistent with the prevailing system of indicators of political power. The Chinese system of titles and appointments wielded authority beyond the immediate region in which the Nùng lived, but the clan required local symbols of power in order to protect itself at home.

Tôn Phúc's attempt to establish an independent kingdom on the frontier between the Song empire and the Đại Cồ Việt kingdom soon failed. Nonetheless, his efforts set the stage for the subsequent rebellions of his son Nùng Trí Cao and Trí Cao's wife A Nùng, which would sweep across the South China coast, to the horror of both Kaifeng and Thăng Long. Tôn Phúc's revolt marked the strongest expression to date of local political ambition that was clearly understood by the Han and Kinh Vietnamese in the region. One should note that Nùng Tôn Phúc's actions were not without historical precedent. On the one hand, past kingdoms had sprung up in South China during two major periods of dynastic disunion, the period of Northern and Southern Courts (222–589) and the Five Dynasties Period (907–60). On the other hand, perhaps more importantly, there was the example of the southwestern Tai-speaking Nanzhao kingdom.

The Nanzhao kingdom had managed to repel initial attacks by the Tang court, and it thrived in its position along the southern frontier of the Tang empire. The kingdom continued to maintain its tributary status as the Dali kingdom in the Nùng leader's own day. The successes of Nanzhao and Dali could certainly have encouraged Tôn Phúc to assert his claim to local independence with the possibility that his frontier kingdom would be allowed to survive. George Condominas argues, not without controversy, that the robust survival of the Nanzhao kingdom contributed directly to the spread of Tai political culture in the region, "to constitute a vast area of Thai principalities, extending from the southern confines of Nan-chao and covering the northern area of continental Southeast Asia in its wider sense from Hainan and Upper Tonkin to Assam."[49] Tributary issues should not overshadow consideration of this possible "Tai" path to power in exploring the reasons for this seemingly sudden outburst of violence along the Sino-Vietnamese frontier.

Conclusion

In studying the structure of frontier management along the Song period Sino-Vietnamese frontier, one must examine the differing goals that Chinese, Vietnamese, and local Tai-speaking leaders had in mind when considering their actions in this frontier region. For both the Chinese and Vietnamese courts, the frontier was a liminal area, removed from the locus of power within the court and the capital city or even the powerful home regions of the royal households and the clans behind the court's highest officials. Before the eleventh century, neither Chinese nor Vietnamese leaders turned regularly to this region for political support or economic enrichment. If anything, the frontier was a source of trouble, not of promise, an area that required surveillance and diligent control and offered very little in return. Weakness at court revealed itself first as turmoil in the border regions, so the popular saying noted, "chaos within translates into calamity without" (*neiluan waihuan*).

The Chinese court's willingness to leave Vietnamese authorities in charge of the border region was likely derived from the relative indifference of Chinese rulers to this frontier area. During the early Song, disturbances along China's northern frontier, generated by frayed relations with both the Liao and the Xi Xia nomadic kingdom, occupied most of the court's attention. When Nùng Tôn Phúc led his uprising, the Song emperor Renzong showed little interest in taking direct action to quell the unrest. Instead, he relied on the historical precedent of delegating a frontier representative, in this case, the ruler of Giao Chỉ, to perform such tasks. While threats to Song territory along the northern frontier involved militarily formidable foes and had a direct effect on Kaifeng's security, disturbances on the southern frontier were contained enough to be handled indirectly through the delegation of authority.

This decision was further conditioned by the hierarchical order at the heart of the tributary relationship the Song court had fostered with Vietnamese rulers. As a practice underlining the Song court's claim to being the region's central authority, Chinese rulers retained the privilege to grant special titles to subordinates for their services. The Song's granting of the title "king of the southern pacified region" to Phật Mã in 1039 signaled support for a defensive move against the Nùng clan rebels. The early Song court saw frontier stability as its prerogative but viewed the active policing of the southwest as the responsibility of its tributary neighbor, the Đại Cồ Việt kingdom.

Conflicts still erupted as appropriate spheres of authority and tributary protocol in the frontier region were determined. Jeffrey Barlow describes an episode from the fall of 1004, when an upland chieftain, probably Nùng, entered a frontier prefecture.[50] The local Song prefect invited him to an official audience. When the local chieftain refused to attend, the Song prefect offered a banquet in his honor at the Ruhong garrison. When the Vietnamese court learned of the preferential treatment Song authorities had offered to this local leader, it responded by attacking and looting the garrison citadel. Consequently, the Song court criticized local officials for mismanaging their duties and forbade all frontier authorities to offer such invitations in the future.

The balancing of roles and responsibilities between acting as a tributary king in the Chinese context and ruling with imperial authority in the Vietnamese context is echoed in a Vietnamese account of Lý Phật Mã's capture and execution of Nùng Tôn Phúc. Chinese court scholars once argued that, in the process of imposing this order, the Đại Cồ Việt court's severe treatment of the borderland communities led to further unrest and that the local situation only worsened.[51] More likely, it was Lý Phật Mã's initial unwillingness to eliminate the Nùng clan completely, hoping that the court could retain the clan's loyalty, that contributed to the crisis. Whatever motivated Phật Mã to intervene in the local uprising, this episode was followed by a series of rebellions that left an imprint on Sino-Vietnamese relations for years to come.

In 1041, two years after his father and uncle were executed by Đại Cồ Việt troops, Nùng Trí Cao and his mother led forces in a bid to regain Thăng Do prefecture. Nùng Tôn Phúc's effort could be understood as an effort by a local chieftain to mix local and imperial political symbols as a means of expressing his desire to increase his local power base. Moreover, the territory claimed by Tôn Phúc remained fairly limited. Despite the grandness of the titles he took, Tôn Phúc was primarily addressing his own followers as, in the words of O. W. Wolters, a "man of prowess." Had the Vietnamese ruler Lý Phật Mã allowed Tôn Phúc to retain the modest gains he had made in territory and power, while reviving the personal bonds between the Vietnamese ruler and his frontier vassal, further widespread upheaval may have been avoided.

Tôn Phúc's son Trí Cao, in contrast, laid claim to more territory and greater political stature. When the Song court left the response to Trí Cao's rebellion to its tributary vassal the Vietnamese court, the outcome was limited and too tentative. The different dimensions of the short-lived rebellion of Nùng Tôn Phúc suggest that the inability of both the Chinese and the Vietnamese leadership to face Nùng Trí Cao's revolt effectively in its early years began with their misunderstanding of his father's motives.

5

The Specter of Southern Power: Nùng Trí Cao's Insurrection, Court Reaction, and the Legacy of Nam Việt

In 1041, two years after his father and uncle were executed by Vietnamese troops, Nùng Trí Cao and his mother A Nùng led a small militia to seize control of Thăng Do prefecture.[1] Thus began a series of efforts by Trí Cao and his mother to carve out another semiautonomous polity in the Sino-Vietnamese frontier region. Trí Cao's series of revolts would far surpass efforts by previous generations of local leaders from the region, including that of his father. Nùng Trí Cao made three ambitious attempts to establish a borderland kingdom, in 1042, 1048, and 1052. Although his formidable challenge failed to produce a lasting political state, Trí Cao himself would become a symbol of resistance for subsequent generations of Tai-speaking leaders caught between Chinese and Vietnamese spheres of influence. The series of temples devoted to Trí Cao and his family still standing along the modern border between China and Vietnam attest to this local leader's position as a potent symbol of political possibility.

Within a network of collective and individual associations, the Nùng Trí Cao rebellions may be viewed as outbursts at the center of several sets of regional tensions. Trí Cao's rebellion meant different things to the contestants for authority in the region, the local inhabitants, and the Song and Vietnamese courts. Following the capture and execution of his father Tôn Phúc, Nùng Trí Cao's own rebellions emerged from the unstable state of political affairs along Song China's southern frontier. The Chinese court's response to the regional tensions reflected Kaifeng's increased interest in the natural resources of the Guangnan region. The Vietnamese court, in contrast, viewed Nùng Trí Cao's insurgency as an interruption in the orderly conduct of tribute relations. Drawing specifically on the Chinese model of tribute as signifier of political submission, the Vietnamese emperor saw Nùng Trí Cao and his followers as disloyal subjects of his domain and worthy of punishment for this reason.

As for the local concerns of the Nùng clan after the death of Nùng Tôn Phúc, disdain for the Vietnamese court may have compelled clan leaders to refuse to grant tribute, to form their own kingdoms, and to ally themselves with the Song state. As Nùng Trí Cao took each one of these actions, it would appear that he was highly dissatisfied with the Vietnamese ruler's behavior. Personal dislike for the Vietnamese ruler, however, represents only part of the motivation for establishing a separate kingdom between the Đại Cồ Việt and Song states. Nùng Trí Cao could also employ his followers' enduring memory of an ancient southern kingdom that once extended from South China to northern Vietnam, the Nam Việt kingdom. Taken together, these factors present a broader, more nuanced picture of political activity at the border between eleventh-century China and Vietnam. In this chapter, we examine the series of negotiations between border communities and representatives of the distant imperial courts during this crucial period of change in the history of the Sino-Vietnamese frontier.

Nùng Trí Cao's Early Life

The historical record has not left us with a clear picture of Trí Cao's earliest years. According to the *Official History of the Song Dynasty* (Songshi), Trí Cao's mother was a member of the clan in charge of Vũ Lặc prefecture and in control of the Right River region.[2] Following her first husband Nùng Tôn Phúc's capture and execution by Vietnamese authorities, A Nùng married a local wealthy merchant. Trí Cao seems not to have felt a strong bond with his stepfather. In fact, the *Official History* tells that Trí Cao, at thirteen years of age, murdered this man, allegedly crying out in his homicidal fury, "Where is it under Heaven that one may have two fathers?"[3] Importantly, *The Complete History of the Great Viet* (Đại Việt sử ký toan thư) and other Vietnamese sources contain no mention of this second husband and his murder, and when we take a closer look at this episode, we may discern other gaps in the historical record that prevent us from determining its authenticity. The actual timing of the murder is difficult to establish, given that short two-year span between Tôn Phúc's capture and the likely date of Trí Cao's and A Nùng's first attempted revolt. This tale could perhaps be a Chinese court historian's attempt to introduce Trí Cao as a violent but nonetheless morally aware individual, who did not accept that his mother's local authority could be publicly acknowledged as powerful enough to sanction her remarriage but instead chose to take matters into his own hands in restoring the proper Confucian moral order to his household. If this reading was intended, the Song court chronicler was reflecting his own thirteenth-century mores more than he was communicating social conditions in the frontier region during Trí Cao's day.

Following the alleged murder of his stepfather, Trí Cao and his mother took control of the Lôi Hỏa grotto settlement, located near the modern Guangxi village of Xia Lei. This area would serve as Trí Cao's base of operations of several of his major campaigns. At this time, A Nùng entered into her third marriage, to Nùng Hạ Khanh (dates unknown), the Nùng clan chieftain of the Temo *jimi* prefecture, which encompassed territory from modern-day Wenshan in eastern Yunnan to Jingxi in southern Guangxi.[4] This marriage expanded territorial control for both partners, while keeping control within the Nùng clan.

In the winter of 1041, Nùng Trí Cao, his mother, and their followers moved out from Lôi Hỏa to regain control of Thảng Do prefecture, Nùng Tôn Phúc's former court-appointed domain located to the northwest of Quảng Nguyên prefecture. At the age of seventeen, Nùng Trí Cao established his first kingdom with the title Kingdom of the Great Succession (Dali Guo), perhaps following in his father's footsteps.⁵ Jeffrey Barlow has suggested that Nùng Trí Cao may have been declaring fealty to the rulers of the neighboring Dali kingdom with this choice of homophonous titles for his dominion. As mentioned earlier, the Dali kingdom occupied a large section of what is now Yunnan in Southwest China before it finally fell to Kublai Khan and his Mongol invaders. The kingdom had been established by the ethnically Bai military commissioner Duan Siping as a federation of regional chiefdoms following the collapse of the formerly dominant Nanzhao kingdom. Although Trí Cao may have purposefully drawn this connection between his realm and the Dali kingdom, such an association may not have made sense to a local audience. In the modern dictionary of the Tai dialect spoken by the northern Vietnamese Nùng community, *li* 理 and *lik* 歷 are not homophones.⁶

The Vietnamese court responded to his announcement by attacking Thảng Do and taking control of the territory. Trí Cao was captured by Vietnamese troops and taken in chains to the capital Thăng Long. He was held at the court of the Vietnamese ruler Lý Phật Mã for a year before winning his release. There is no mention of A Nùng's capture, so one may presume that she managed to escape. Vietnamese court historians would later contend that Nùng Trí Cao was finally pardoned as a display of the devout Buddhist Lý Phật Mã's "benevolence" and that the ruler also managed to restore Quảng Nguyên prefecture to its former position as a dependency of Thăng Long.⁷ Trí Cao's "crime" was excused and he was allowed to return home.⁸ There is a sense in this account that the Vietnamese court had established a Chinese-style political order by granting the Nùng clan the right to administer Quảng Nguyên in the name of the Lý ruler.

The most important sign of authority Nùng Trí Cao received from the Lý court was the imperial seal, which was offered to him after his release from Thăng Long. The acceptance of this seal still resonates with all modern worshipers of Nùng Trí Cao; the popular Kỳ Sầm Temple on the outskirts of the city of Cao Bằng was established on the site of the official enfeoffment. During the ninth month of 1043, Lý Phật Mã sent his envoy Nguỵ Trưng to Quảng Nguyên to present the imperial seal to Nùng Trí Cao and confer on him the title "grand guardian" (*taibao*).⁹ The title had existed since the Zhou dynasty (1122–256 BCE) and designated a member of a distinguished group of court officials known variously as the "three preceptors" (*sanshi*) or the "three dukes" (*sangong*). This group also included the grand mentor (*taifu*) and the grand preceptor, or *taishi*. By the late imperial period, the title "grand guardian" indicated an official ranking of 1a, the pinnacle of the official bureaucracy.[10] The title was significant as an indicator of honorific position, implying that its recipients must "guard and protect one's lord and to lead by relying on virtue [*de*] and propriety [*yi*]." The title, as such, carried no inherent authority nor did it allude to any particular official responsibilities.[11]

Phật Mã likely conferred this title as an honorific position without specific official duties, considering the lack of regular communications between the central court and Nùng Trí Cao's home region. The Vietnamese leader was actually following a practice established locally during the beginning of his reign when Phật Mã rewarded loyal officials who put down rebellions by three of his brothers, who were contesting Phật Mã's ascension to the throne. To his three leading supporters, Phật Mã also granted the three titles "grand mentor," "grand preceptor," and "grand guardian."[12] Rather than cultivating institutional bonds with local leaders, the Lý ruler demanded personal loyalty from his subordinates and required them to visit the court at Thăng Long every year to swear oaths of allegiance. In this sense, the act of granting the title "grand guardian" and the gift of a court seal were likely linked to an expression of the closer personal bond the Vietnamese ruler wished to foster with Nùng Trí Cao.

The benefits of Nùng Trí Cao's new, warmer relationship with the Vietnamese court were by no means merely symbolic. Given control of Quảng Nguyên prefecture, Trí Cao gained local jurisdiction over Quảng Nguyên's "aboriginal settlements" (*dong*) of Lôi Hỏa, Bình An, and Tần Bà as well as the *jimi* prefecture of Tư Lạng, which bordered Quảng Nguyên to the north.[13] All this territory conferred on Nùng Trí Cao and his mother greatly expanded the manpower and resources at their disposal. In return for Trí Cao's freedom and these lands, the Lý court demanded a greater share of the territory's natural resources, particularly gold.[14] Gold and precious metals were among the Right and Left rivers region's most valuable resources.

Sources remain largely silent until seven years later when, in 1048, a militia under Nùng Trí Cao's command launched Trí Cao's second rebellion and took control of the mountainous Andezhou prefecture, today a part of the Jingxi district's Ande county in Guangxi. A victorious Trí Cao proclaimed himself ruler of the Kingdom of the Southern Heaven[15] and so launched the chieftain's second attempt to carve out a separate political space between the Vietnamese and Chinese spheres of authority.

More significantly, Trí Cao also adopted a new reign title, Auspicious Circumstances (Jingrui), to mark the establishment of this new kingdom. Such a decision was not unprecedented. Early on, the Sino-Vietnamese border communities had adopted the Han calendar of Heavenly Branches and Earthly Stems. However, these communities relied on their own separate calendars for measuring periods between agricultural phases of the year.[16] The Han practice measured political periods, while the local calendar measured the lives of the common people. The establishment of separate reign periods, of course, was an even greater political statement than merely claiming authority in a spatial sense. This claim resounded most loudly at the Chinese and Vietnamese courts, as Trí Cao was signaling this audience that great changes had been marked in his region.

One possible reason for Trí Cao's desire to continue his revolt is presented as dialogue attributed to the Nùng chieftain himself, found in the writings of Sima Guang. When Nùng Trí Cao, who had escaped with his mother, requested *neifu* status from the Song court, Chinese authorities rejected this request. Sima Guang contended that this occurred because the Chinese court feared losing the support of the Vietnamese court. Hearing of the court's decision, Nùng Trí Cao replied, "today I face the criminal acts of Giao Chỉ, and China once again will not annex my region. I have no way to endure this situation by myself, and so there is nothing to do but to rebel against it."[17] Here, Trí Cao appears to be completely aware of his difficult position in not being able to secure a patron for his tiny domain, leaving only the possibility of expanding his own territory in order to create greater security. The local chieftain's harsh condemnation of the Vietnamese court may better reflect the biases of the author of this account, Sima Guang. One should read this passage of dialogue with that possibility in mind.

During the ninth month of 1049, Nùng Trí Cao's rebel force attacked and pillaged the Yongzhou garrison. In 1050, the Vietnamese court launched an expedition against Trí Cao, laying siege to the rebel's stronghold. This time, Trí Cao's forces scattered into the surrounding mountains and forests. Vietnamese forces succeeded only in relocating the border leader and his closest followers farther north into Song territory. Xiao Gu (1002–1066), then serving as fiscal commissioner of the Guangnan West circuit, reported all these events back to Kaifeng, calling for greater readiness in the frontier region.[18]

At about the same time that Trí Cao launched his second rebellion, the Song court was reevaluating the system of frontier militia that had been in place since the dynasty's founding. With the aging of the court-appointed militia posted along the northwestern frontier near Shaanxi, and the retirement of many troops in its ranks, the court called for the enlistment of native militia to replace the deployed troops.[19] Existing armies in the frontier region were drawn into imperial defenses as "inner commanderies" (*neijun*) with a status similar to that of *neifu*. The court contended that it would save both provisions and wealth by making this change. The move toward dependence on local militia occurred elsewhere in the empire as well, including in the southwest. Quite possibly, Nùng Trí Cao had sought to gain the attention of Kaifeng with his earlier revolts in the hope that he would be given the status of a local militia leader. With court sanction, and little other outside involvement, Trí Cao could continue to expand and consolidate his personal political power without inviting retaliation.

The Song Court Response

The leadership at Kaifeng was in no mood to accept the existence of a militarily powerful local regime along the Sino-Vietnamese frontier, which, some leading officials asserted, the Song court had neglected for too long. Even in 1046, following Nùng Trí Cao's first revolt, the Song court's vice censor-in-chief, Zhang Fangping (1007–1091), had these comments:

When we consider [our empire's] past ambitions, in matters of territory the primary issue is *yin*. And *yin* refers to the proper duties of an official, care for the people, and care for the barbarians [*manyi*]. When we consider today's events, we must acknowledge the importance of matters between the interior and exterior of our empire. Therefore, we should not allocate authority to the border officials. If today's events cause us to worry, we should outwardly prepare to defend ourselves from enemies, and inwardly we should comfort the people. In the northwest there are two enemies [the Khitans and the Tanguts]. Because the court has been very worried about them, a policy for keeping these enemies outside our borders has been a central policy.[20]

Zhang then explained how official vigilance toward the Khitans and Tanguts had resulted in less attention toward China's southern border, leading, for example, to seven years of neglect for a widespread rebellion led by the Yao ethnic group. He wrote:

"The lands to the south of the seas" [Southeast Asian trading kingdoms] and Giao Chi are expanding their influence dramatically. Moreover, the routes from the Yong and Rong prefectures pass through the aboriginal region [*xidong*] inhabited by the Nùng clan. The matters of the South require a strategy for their management.... During the reign of the Tang Yizong [860–73], An Nam's protector-general Li Zhuo failed to pacify and control the region. The Southern Man barbarians pillaged the region and caused turmoil. General Li subsequently was forced to rely on his troops, and with these added expenditures he found it difficult to provide his tribute to the court. ... If similar events should occur today, misfortune will certainly manifest itself in chaos.[21]

Setting current events in a larger historical context, Zhang referred to the precedent of Tang failings in this region as justification for more active intervention in matters along the southern frontier. Relying entirely on local support for court-appointed leadership had not achieved the desired result in the past. For Zhang Fangping, turning to a local leader, particularly one with obvious political ambitions, to manage all aspects of the frontier was out of the question.

Representatives of Kaifeng were also instigators of instability along the frontier in this period. In early 1050, local officials in Yongzhou enticed Bộ Thiệu Tư, Bộ Thiệu Kham, and more than three thousand people from Tô Mậu Châu into entering and residing in the region under Song supervision. Lý Phật Mã appealed to the Chinese court regarding the allurement of his people. The Song emperor then halted their movement and had the people returned to Vietnam. He also issued an edict to the Lý court, ordering Lý Phật Mã to suspend local trade, in order to prevent plunder and intrusions on both sides of the frontier. Song Renzong seemed uncomfortable with the active manipulation of the frontier population attempted by the Yongzhou officials, and yet he did not wish to relinquish all control of the frontier to his tributary representatives.

Meanwhile, Nùng Trí Cao acted as if he had no inkling of this lingering indecision in the faraway Chinese court. As his personal power increased, Trí Cao very clearly manipulated both the institutions of tribute relations and the symbols of imperial power. In the third month of 1051, Nùng Trí Cao sent a tribute mission to Kaifeng to offer tame elephants and lumps of gold and silver to the Chinese court.[22] The Chinese initially refused these gifts. The Song emperor Renzong later concluded that because the Quảng Nguyên prefecture originally belonged to the northern Vietnamese kingdom of Giao Chỉ, if the two delegations approached the court together for a single audience, he would allow this offer to be submitted.[23] After that, Nùng Trí Cao again sent an offering of gold with a petition letter (requesting *neifu* status) to be passed to the emperor by the Yongzhou prefect Chen Gong (d. 1052). Chen did not grant this request, likely on grounds of procedural impropriety, but Trí Cao's attempt shows an awareness of the channels that had to be pursued if he intended to gain legitimacy. An independent position within the Chinese tributary system provided certain political stability and economic gain.

From pragmatic Song officials with personal experience on the frontier came other suggestions on how the court might benefit politically from the turmoil. Some viewed Nùng Trí Cao's rebellion as a rare opportunity for strengthening China's hand in the region. Fiscal Commissioner Xiao Gu again memorialized the throne in the second month of 1051, stating that the Quảng Nguyên Man barbarian Nùng Trí Cao had requested *neifu* status. This memorial may have been sent to Kaifeng shortly before Nùng Trí Cao brought tribute gifts of tame elephants, gold, and silver to Yongzhou in third month of 1052 to support his request.[24] First, Xiao Gu asked if it was not enough for the Vietnamese court to muster a punitive expedition against Nùng Trí Cao. He also added that Yongzhou's "military commander" (*zhihuishi*) had acted without authority by attempting to capture Nùng Trí Cao himself. As a result of this local attack, Trí Cao had turned to the central court at Kaifeng for assistance. As Xiao comments, because the Song court considered that Nùng Trí Cao's service was the right of the Đại Cồ Việt court, the emperor ignored the request.[25]

Xiao Gu pressed the court with this suggestion:

> Trí Cao will necessarily cause trouble for the southern region. I would rather grant him an official title in order to control him and then allow him to oppose Giao Chỉ.

Emperor Renzong responded to Xiao Gu, stating,

> If we had protected Giao Chỉ and had not antagonized Trí Cao, then he would not finally have begun his plundering. Therefore, you must question the reasons for this.

Xiao Gu then replied:

> The Southern Man barbarians seek self-interested opportunity before acting, and they invariably protect their own living quarters. These are not the qualities that are becoming of an official. I contend that, as of the present, our state's influence does not extend into the Man region. Regarding individuals such as Nùng Trí Cao, we must control him and that's all. As Trí Cao's military power increases, Giao Chỉ will not be able to continue to fend him off or restrain him. At that point, the Nùng will be able to fight back. After this, the Man people will fight one another, and we will be able to sit back and not have to become involved.[26]

Although the Chinese court did not adopt Xiao Gu's pragmatic approach to regional power brokering, his position takes into account the actual lack of Chinese influence on the southern frontier, while pointing to a practical, if somewhat opportunistic, remedy to this problem. Xiao dispatched Yongzhou's military commander Yuan Yun to reprimand local officials for mishandling the garrison's defense.[27] Yuan was then ordered to raise a militia and launch a counterattack on Trí Cao with the purpose of capturing the rebel leader. However, when Yuan had the opportunity to inquire locally as to the specific circumstances surrounding the violent outbreak, he became inclined instead to follow a grander strategy for this frontier region in which Trí Cao would be granted *neifu* status. Xiao Gu sent Yuan back to Kaifeng with local tribute for several years in succession in order to present a memorial in which Xiao argued for this change of policy. The emperor offered no response.[28]

Emperor Renzong's stubborn resistance to Trí Cao's request for *neifu* status revolved around the ruler's desire to see matters through the ancient relationship between China and An Nam.[29] Xiao Gu's suggestion took into consideration the pros and cons of Realpolitik, using Nùng Trí Cao as a threat to the Đại Cồ Việt kingdom, so that Guangxi and Guangdong could stand by themselves as a barrier between the two states.[30] The Song court could then have changed direction and manipulated developments between Nùng Trí Cao and the Vietnamese leaders. Because Renzong chose not to follow the dictates of the balance of power at the frontier, but instead desired to adhere to historical precedent, this policy was not followed.

Nùng Trí Cao's Third Rebellion

Scholars looking back over this period of transition point to a wide variety of causes for Trí Cao's third act of rebellion. Chinese sources argue that Trí Cao's lingering hatred of the Vietnamese court was the reason behind this particular act.[31] The Japanese scholar Araki Toshikazu is not as convincing in his argument that the Song court faulted Nùng Trí Cao for serving the Vietnamese rulers.[32] As noted earlier, the Chinese initially assumed that the Nùng clan owed its service to the Lý court.

They could not have been surprised when Lý Phật Mã granted Nùng Trí Cao the "grand guardian" title. The Song court maintained its distance from Trí Cao and ignored his gifts of tribute and requests for *neifu* status, because such requests circumvented the established boundaries of sovereign authority. However, the location of Trí Cao's planned kingdom was no longer strictly in territory directly controlled by Thăng Long but rather straddled both sides of the frontier. For that reason, the local chieftain was actually taking a defiant stand in the face of both Song and Đại Việt authority.

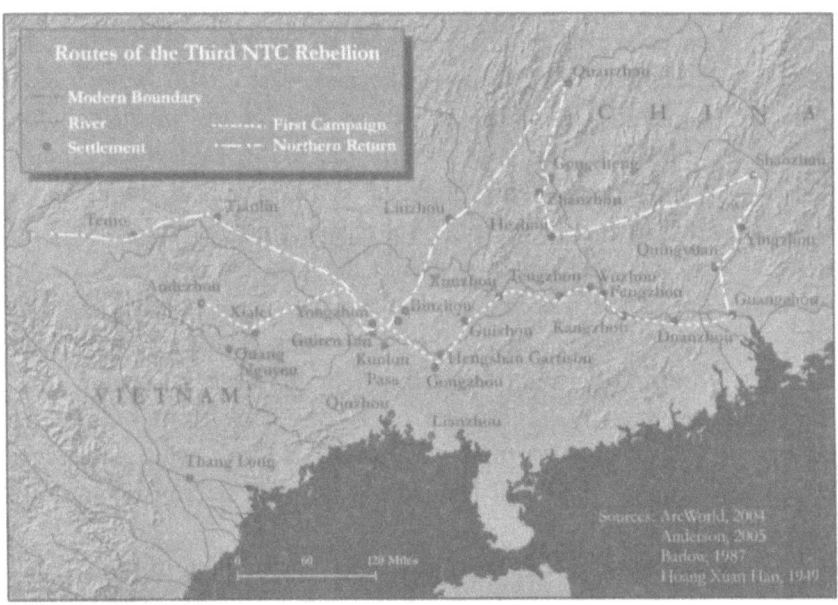

Map 4. Nùng Trí Cao's Third Rebellion (Elizabeth Nelson)

In his third attempt to gain regional recognition in 1052, Trí Cao revealed even grander plans to establish his own frontier kingdom. Initially, he had little trouble raising a militia force of "desperados" (*wangming*) from the various clans under his control.[33] Trí Cao was himself in full control of both the mountain passes and the fertile river valleys of his region, and he did not face any significant opposition to his claim to local hegemony. Chinese sources note that this force made several passes through the region, disguised in old clothes and supplied with simple rations so as to avoid undue attention. Reports soon came from the outlying grotto settlements that these militia groups were unable to feed themselves well enough with local provisions and that coordination of these groups suffered as individuals dropped out and returned home. Some sources allege that Trí Cao spread these rumors in order to disarm Song defenders who were observing movements in the countryside.[34] In any case, when Song authorities at Yongzhou learned of the troubles these rebel bands faced, Chinese military leaders decided that the rebels posed no significant threat and so took no special precautions to protect the garrison from possible attack.[35]

Trí Cao responded to his problems in retaining local militia by recruiting talent from outside the Guangnan West circuit region. Most remarkable was his ability to enlist the help of the *jinshi* scholars Huang Wei (d. 1052) and Huang Shifu (d. 1052), from Guangzhou.[36] The two Huangs were likely engaged in interregional trade, which brought them into contact with the Tai-speaking communities along the frontier. They were perhaps in search of the gold and mineral resources for which the region was known at that time.[37] Trí Cao also recruited other prominent leaders among the Nùng clan, including Nùng Kiến Hậu and Nùng Chí Trung. With the help of these influential local leaders, as well as the assistance of scholar elite from outside the region, whose participation must have given Trí Cao's cause heightened legitimacy among even local Han residents, the chieftain planned his next political move.

In the spring of 1052, Trí Cao ordered the burning of the villages under his control and led at least five thousand of his subjects in a revolt that would soon gain momentum and sweep across the South China coast to Guangzhou. Chinese sources report that Nùng Trí Cao's appeals for local support were backed up by brutal coercion. Addressing the crowd before the revolt in the fourth month of 1052, Nùng Trí Cao is described as having proclaimed: "As for all the belongings that you amassed during your lives, they were destroyed today by heaven's fire. You have nothing to live on, and you are considered poor indeed! You must grab Yongzhou and capture Guangzhou where I will establish myself as its ruler. If you don't do this, you will necessarily die."[38]

On closer inspection, the inclusion of Nùng Trí Cao's speech in the court's historical record looks to have been more of a literary device than a statement of historical fact.[39] Trí Cao is described as having committed acts of desperation, destroying his people's possessions so that they had nothing to lose by joining the rebels. Nùng Trí Cao's initial success is attributed to the cruelty of his methods, even if this had not actually been the case. By attributing these characteristics to the rebel leader, the Chinese scholars created a cunning, but barbaric, adversary for those who would defend China's frontier.

On the same day that Nùng Trí Cao reportedly made his "now or never" speech before his followers, he launched the first campaign of what would become a protracted but at first stunningly successful expedition across the entire South China coast. Trí Cao led his band of five thousand directly to the prefectural capital at Yongzhou. There, he met a spirited Song defense of the walled city. When the rebels first encircled the garrison town and began their siege, Chen Gong sent his military assistants to lead the defense of the city's main gates. The "controller-general" (*tongban*) Wang Qiangyou (d. 1052) took up his position at the Laiyuan Gate, the "provisional military director-in-chief" (*zhidujian*) Li Xiao (d. 1052) defended the Daan Gate, and the "commander" (*zhishi*) Wu Ji defended the Chaotian Gate.[40] Chen Gong also called for outside assistance from nearby Song authorities. Guangnan West circuit's "military director-in-chief" (*dujian*) Zhang Li (d. 1052) quickly brought reinforcements in from Binzhou (located in modern-day Binyang in central Guangxi).

The rebel force eventually claimed victory after a successful siege on the garrison. In the fighting, Trí Cao captured Chen Gong, the "garrison commander" (*duxunjian*) Gao Shian (d. 1052), Wang Qiangyou, and Zhang Li, among others. The Song defense force had been well organized and led by highly competent officers. Nevertheless, more than a thousand troops were said to have died in the fighting.[41] After securing the garrison, Trí Cao reportedly inspected the garrison's storehouse of military supplies and provisions, removing above all supplies of gold and armor with which to supply his troops. Recent Vietnamese scholarship contends that Trí Cao discovered enough grain in the garrison that he won over a great number of new recruits by distributing the grain among them.⁴² The Song historian Li Tao confirms that Trí Cao's army increased considerably after the taking of Yongzhou, where he collected five hundred piculs (approximately thirty-three and a third tons) of grain, likely rice, to feed a growing army of about twenty thousand men.⁴³

During his inspection of Yongzhou, Nùng Trí Cao is reported to have turned angrily to Chen Gong and said, "I had sought to follow official channels in establishing a connection with your imperial office, but you would not listen to my request. Why is that?" To Trí Cao's question, Chen Gong replied that he had received the memorial but had not reported it to the emperor.⁴⁴ Trí Cao then inquired as to whether or not Chen had memorialized the court to acknowledge that the local grain had not been harvested that year and then led Chen Gong outside.⁴⁵ Chen at this point appeared horribly shaken and reportedly shouted, "Long may you live!" (*Wansui*) to the collected rebel band.⁴⁶ Chen pleaded that he be spared so that he might follow Trí Cao in his insurrection. Trí Cao paid no attention to Chen's cries for leniency and instead had Chen and his colleagues executed on the spot.⁴⁷ According to the *Official History of the Song Dynasty*, Chen's comrade Zhang Li faced his execution without flinching, shouting curses at his tormenters as they took his life.

After securing control of Yongzhou, Nùng Trí Cao decided to express stronger political ambitions. He first set about establishing a military training ground at Zijin Peak, which was located in the southern reaches of Si En prefecture and to the northwest of the Yongzhou garrison.⁴⁸ Then he called for a new political realm free of all ties to the existing tributary arrangement that had once constrained his chiefdom's authority. Trí Cao not only proclaimed the founding of the Kingdom of the Great South with the reign period Inaugural Age (Qili) but also granted himself the title Benevolent and Kind Emperor.⁴⁹ His mother took the title "empress dowager." As his first act of imperial benevolence, Trí Cao issued a general amnesty to all inhabitants of the region surrounding Yongzhou, including its vanquished defenders.⁵⁰ All of Trí Cao's military advisers, including the *jinshi* scholar Huang Shifu and those rebel leaders under Huang, took official titles drawn from the Chinese bureaucratic model. Despite Trí Cao's faithful emulation of existing political practices, these changes could not possibly have been accepted peacefully by the region's dominant powers. A prince, or even a king, may exist within a system of tribute relations centered on the Chinese emperor, but a new emperor at the periphery of the Chinese empire, particularly one without the military might to support his claim, could never be left undisturbed.[51]

With his thousands of followers, Trí Cao struck out eastward by boat from his base camp near Xia Lei, traveling down the Yu River.[52] The rebels quickly laid siege to and finally crushed the Song forces that were protecting the Hengshan garrison (*Hengshanzhai*).[53] Hengshan garrison was located near modern-day Hengzhou, and it was the eleventh-century Guangnan West circuit's second-most important center of trade and communications. Because the rebels' first attack had so easily achieved its purpose, Nùng Trí Cao soon led his followers eastward on a sustained strike along the main trade route that followed the Yu River to Wuzhou (modern-day Wuzhou), where the Yu River is joined by the Gui River (Guijiang), both of which are tributaries of the Xi River (Xijiang). Nùng Trí Cao's army then turned southward along the lower reaches of the Xi River to its intersection with the Pearl River above Guangzhou. As a result, the nine prefectural capitals, and crucial trade nodes, of the South China region were soon captured: Hengshan, Guizhou (modern-day Guigang), Gongzhou (modern-day Pingnan), Xunzhou (modern-day Guiping), Tengzhou (modern-day Teng county), Wuzhou, Fengzhou (modern-day Fengchuan, in Guangdong), Kangzhou (modern-day Deqing, in Guangdong), and Duanzhou (modern-day Gaoyao, in Guangdong).[54]

The fighting was bloody along the entire route, and tales of individual conflicts have been preserved in various sources. Li Tao's account in *Draft for a Continuation of "The Comprehensive Mirror for Aid in Government"* (Xu *Zizhi tongjian* changbian), tells how the Fengzhou prefect Cao Jin commanded only a small militia and was unprepared for the approach of Trí Cao's rebel forces. Trí Cao initially indicated that he would allow Cao Jin to live after the prefect surrendered his garrison, provided that Cao join the rebels. Cao allegedly remarked, "Where is it that one in the service of the Son of Heaven would flee from bandits?"[55] After several days of torturing Cao Jin in an attempt to compel him to change sides, Trí Cao had the prefect put to death. The same source also describes how the Kangzhou prefect Zhao Shidan and his military director-in-chief Ma Gui were finally captured and executed by Trí Cao's men when the Song militia leaders ran out of arrows.[56] Such tales of bravery in this Southern Song source enhance the quality of martyrdom displayed by these officials as defenders of the orthodox center in the face of this "barbarian" assault from the periphery.

Nùng Trí Cao's mother A Nùng played a particularly active role in expanding her clan's power and control during this third rebellion. When Trí Cao's forces attacked local garrisons, the rebel leaders often relied on strategy she had devised.[57] The Chinese court depiction of A Nùng seems dictated by the fear and loathing male courtiers felt toward the powerful female figure they believed her to be. Her nature, they wrote, was "infused with poison."[58] A Nùng is described as a practitioner of an ancient, dark art of human sacrifice who had a fondness for the flesh of young children. It was even written that she was required to kill a child for every meal.[59] Such frightening and outlandish claims certainly express the confusion this non-Han, female figure of authority created for later Confucian scholars, who wished to present an understandable picture of the events surrounding the rebels' early military successes.

Nùng Trí Cao's and A Nùng's regional insurrection quickly spread eastward along the inland waterways of the South China coast. Official Song chroniclers noted wistfully that because Lingnan had been at peace for so long, the prefectural and county administrations were completely unprepared for widespread violence: "the troops were hurriedly assembled, but the leadership knew not what course to take."[60] The Song defenders and their commanders soon abandoned their positions and fled in panic. During the eastward expansion of Trí Cao's forces, numerous Song officials lost their lives, some three thousand troops died fighting, and approximately ten thousand others were captured.[61] The destruction caused by fire was said to have left nothing behind, and many local storehouses and granaries were burned to the ground.

In describing the events surrounding Nùng Trí Cao's final campaign, both Chinese and Vietnamese chroniclers evoked images of natural disaster. The Chinese account describes how, at one point in the years before Trí Cao's rebellion, a statue of the Buddha at Yongzhou rocked back and forth before another bandit attack, and a devastating fire soon broke out.⁶² Therefore, it wasn't surprising that the same statue began to shake on the eve of the rebels' assault. The Vietnamese account reports that on the fifth day of the first month of 1053, "there occurred an earthquake of the third degree of intensity."⁶³ This invocation of natural disaster in the midst of man-made chaos is an ancient historiographical device, well understood by both Chinese and Vietnamese audiences.

The rebel advance finally ended at the gates of the Guangzhou garrison, the primary center of political and economic power in the South China region. At this point, Nùng Trí Cao's army numbered as many as fifty thousand men.⁶⁴ As soon as Trí Cao and his forces arrived, Guangzhou's defender, the prefect Zhong Jian (d. 1052), ordered the city gates closed and refused passage to anyone from outside. Those who found themselves outside the gates at this time soon joined Trí Cao's following, enhancing the size and power of his military force. Prior to Nùng Trí Cao's attack on Guangzhou, the Song local official Wei Guan had ordered the city walls repaired and fortified and a new well sunk within the city limits to provide water for livestock.⁶⁵ Wei also installed a large crossbow on the rampart to improve the city's defenses.

When Trí Cao's troops arrived in Guangzhou, they raised scaling ladders against the city walls and launched a furious assault on the garrison. The rebels also cut off the free-flowing water supply to the city.⁶⁶ The Song defenders fought back furiously, employing the crossbow defenses, and the city remained stocked with both water and food. Faced with this staunch opposition, the attackers abruptly scattered, and Nùng Trí Cao lost his tactical strength. A short while after the rout of Nùng Trí Cao's troops, the prefect of Yingzhou (modern-day Yingde in north-central Guangdong), Su Jian (d. 1076), assembled his remaining militia at nearby Pangdu Village, intending to hold this strategic position along the rebels' main route to their home region.⁶⁷ At Panyu county, located in the northern suburbs of modern-day Guangzhou, Xiao Zhu (1013–1073), then serving as the "district magistrate" (*ling*), raised a troop of local militia to join a force of more than two thousand able-bodied men from the coastal area. Xiao threw these men into battle, and they fiercely resisted an attack by Nùng Trí Cao's seafaring detachment, setting fire to warships that were attempting to coordinate an attack on Guangzhou from the Pearl River. Having taken over for Xiao Gu as Guangnan West circuit's new fiscal commissioner, Wang Han (fl. 1043–63) also arrived with supplies and men from outside the region to enhance the defenders' preparations. Nùng Trí Cao realized that he was unable to pull back easily at this point, so he launched a siege on the Guangzhou garrison that lasted fifty-seven days until the seventh month of 1052, when he ended his assault on the city and left the region.

Fording the stream at Qingyuan to the northwest of Guangzhou, and passing through Lianzhou (modern-day Lianshan, in western Guangdong), Nùng Trí Cao continued his northern route as he returned to his home region. The rebel force ran into the militia led by Zhang Zhong and the Yingzhou prefect Su Jian and fought against them at Bai Tian hill, beside the Xiaohai River.[68] This time, the rebels prevailed, and Zhang died in the skirmish. Nùng Trí Cao then attacked Hezhou (modern-day Hezhou, in eastern Guangxi), although he was unsuccessful in his attempt to take control of the garrison. In a night assault on the Taiping "training ground" (*chang*) outside of Hezhou, the rebels killed the local Song militia leader Jiang Jie.[69]

In the ninth month of 1052, Nùng Trí Cao attacked Zhaozhou (modern-day Pingle, in Guangxi), and the Song commander Wang Zhenglun was killed in the fighting at the Guanmen "courier station" (*yi*).[70] Song sources record that scattered groups of inhabitants, totaling at most one hundred thousand, lived among the mountains of this prefecture. When the local people heard Trí Cao's troops approaching, they fled and hid in the surrounding countryside. Trí Cao learned of this effort to escape his force's advance, and he responded by ordering fires set throughout the area. Many of these people were killed in the blaze.[71] Trí Cao's army then moved to the southeast during the tenth month of 1052 to attack Binzhou again.[72] Later in the same month, Nùng Trí Cao attacked and recaptured Yongzhou, where he planned to establish himself as king.[73] Trí Cao's first defensive move was to dispatch a group of his men to Kunlun Pass (Kunlun Guan), to the north of the city, to guard against a Song advance from that direction. Another group worked day and night felling trees with which to build new boats, likely to prepare for an attack from the Yong River, a tributary of the Xi River, which flowed along the southern edge of the city.[74] That winter, Trí Cao himself reportedly spread the word that he would attempt again to advance on

Guangzhou. In the twelfth month of 1052, his forces once again defeated another Song force under the leadership of the Guizhou (modern-day Guilin) prefect Chen Shu at Guizhou's Jincheng courier station.[75]

Meanwhile, when word of Nùng Trí Cao's rebellion first reached Kaifeng, the court ordered Chen Shu and other local officials already posted to the Guangxi West circuit to attack and crush the insurgents. Finally, with all the destruction that resulted in the first months of fighting, the court ordered a group of high-ranking military leaders and officials, including Yang Tian (1007–1062) and Cao Xiu (dates unknown), to lead new forces into the mountain region and confront the rebels. The court also called on Yu Jing (1000–1064) and the newly appointed "military commissioner" (*anfushi*) Sun Mian (996–1066) for both Guangnan circuits. In the first encounter with Nùng Trí Cao's forces, Yang Tian and Cao Xiu both panicked and fled the area with their men.[76]

According to the compilers of the *Official History of the Song Dynasty*, Nùng Trí Cao grew more reckless after scoring this victory and started stirring up the southern region again. During the fighting, he sent a letter from his military camp to Kaifeng, seeking the position of military commissioner for Yongzhou and Guizhou prefectures. Trí Cao's actions severely irritated the court at Kaifeng. Upon hearing of Nùng Trí Cao's intentions, the assistant palace secretary Liang Shi (1000–1069) remarked, "What is this? There is no court located within the two Guangnan circuits!"[77] Trí Cao's active recruitment of official staff, along with, as asserted by Araki Toshikazu, his strong classical training, bespeak a political leader who, even in light of local myths that he defied imperial authority, regarded the Chinese model as the preferred medium for the expression of political power in the region.

The Song emperor Renzong and his advisers considered this situation to be disastrous, and so they turned over responsibility for the counterattack to a well-regarded campaigner along the northern frontier, the military leader Di Qing (1008–1061), who had already voiced opposition to the earlier court policy of inaction. Renzong named Di Qing "pacification commissioner" (*xuanfushi*) and put him in charge of all troops and their commanders then involved in the campaign against Nùng Trí Cao. Troops from the Jiangnan East and West circuits (modern-day Jiangxi) and Fujian East and West circuits, among others, were called up to form a large expeditionary force under Di Qing's command.[78] As written in the *Official History of the Song Dynasty*, Chen Shu became concerned that Di Qing would quickly achieve the military success that had eluded Chen for so long and therefore abandoned his effort. Nùng Trí Cao's forces quickly defeated Chen's men.[79]

Meanwhile, disruption in the regular procession of tribute missions had sufficient impact on the local economy that local officials chose to support Vietnamese intervention on purely practical grounds. Song officials also feared that an uninvited military force led by the Lý court might enter the region to take advantage of the chaos that was spreading in the wake of Nùng Trí Cao's string of skirmishes. One of the Song officials sent principally to suppress the rebels, the newly appointed Guizhou prefect Yu Jing, adopted a strident but likely heartfelt tone when he reported to the Chinese throne in the twelfth month of 1052:

> Giao Chi [the Vietnamese] ought to bring tribute this year, but due to Nùng Trí Cao's activities, the route [between Giao Chi and China] has been cut off. I have long entreated the court to assemble troops to launch a punitive expedition against these bandits, but even after this period of time the court has yet to make the announcement. Observe that this request is utterly sincere. Because I am not yet able to attack and exterminate this gang of bandits, please allow me to disassociate myself from this situation so as to avoid duplicity. Trí Cao has been classified by Giao Chi as a rebel, and appropriately the Lý ruler should be allowed to send out troops. Do not obstruct his good intentions. If you do not let the Lý ruler act today, he will certainly become stronger and subsequently lend support to Trí Cao's revolt. For this reason, it is most beneficial to permit him to act.[80]

Renzong followed Yu's request and commanded that twenty thousand strings of cash be offered to cover military expenses along with thirty thousand strings of cash as a reward for those Vietnamese border officials who assisted in returning peace to the region. As will be mentioned shortly, other Song officials charged with the suppression of Nùng Trí Cao's activities were strongly opposed to any involvement of the Vietnamese military, and eventually the emperor would offer a hefty reward to persuade the Vietnamese leadership in Thăng Long to stay out of the counterattack efforts. The success of these court officials in defeating the call for direct cooperation from the Lý court would have repercussions in the period that followed the rebellions.

The Vietnamese offer of assistance to the Song is presented quite differently in Vietnamese and in Chinese sources. The Vietnamese account notes that the Vietnamese ruler Lý Phật Mã offered to send troops to assist with the punitive expedition, adding that "the Song ruler appropriately allowed for this."[81] Lý Phật Mã sent twenty thousand troops along the sea route into China to assist the Song imperial forces. The Chinese court diplomatically showed its appreciation for the Vietnamese leader's offer, but Kaifeng ultimately refused to accept the help of Vietnamese troops. In Vietnamese sources, the Song court's refusal appears to have been the result of Di Qing's efforts at persuasion. When Di Qing took charge, he subsequently memorialized the court, saying "I have no use for false 'outsider' troops in this matter of 'insider' rebel activity. As for Nùng Trí Cao, the forces of Guangnan East and West circuits combined were not enough to control him. Moreover, among those false troops from the outer frontier are some that have caused this turmoil to break out. How will they stop it?" The account concludes: "In that same year, the Song issued the order to prevent our military assistance. Then Nùng Trí Cao requested troops from us, and the Vietnamese court permitted his request."[82]

Chinese accounts contain a more dispassionate description of the manner in which high-level officials presented reasons for opposing Vietnamese assistance in the punitive attack on Nùng Trí Cao's forces. Di Qing demonstrated his opposition to this policy by memorializing,

> [Lý Phật Mã] has claimed that he commands an infantry of fifty thousand men, with one thousand riders for assistance, but in fact this is not the case. Moreover, using these counterfeit troops from outside [China] to wipe out a domestic rebellion is of no benefit to us. When Trí Cao and his forces once trampled the two Guangnan circuits from west to east, we did not have the force to oppose this. We then made use of the Man barbarians as soldiers, but the Man desired control while forgetting righteousness. For this reason, they began their rebellion, so how will we stop it? I wish then to

stop Giao Chi from using its troops, and also to call to arms any troops who can bring peace to the region and can stop obstructing the passage of envoys from Giao Chi.

This account notes that Renzong finally put Di Qing's plan into effect.[83]

In the third month of 1053, the Song emperor dispatched the special envoy Chen Qingming to present Lý Phật Mã with rare objects and coins, with the request that Phật Mã not send troops to assist with the expedition. The fortunes of the Song court changed only when additional leadership came to bear on the problem. Liu Ji (1008–1088), the prefect of Binzhou (Linxian, in modern-day Shanxi), feared that Guangnan had already been lost. Nevertheless, Liu quickly traveled to the Hunan city of Changsha for a meeting with Di Qing, who had recently arrived in the area with his forces. Liu allegedly made his case for an effective attack plan to the general, saying, "if the bandits are able to fall back to their lair and defend it, their poisonous influence will spread through the region. You ought to instruct your troops to wait before beginning their attack. If you are certain of victory at the time you choose to go into battle, you will indeed succeed in capturing these rebels."[84]

During the first months of 1053, Di Qing, the elderly Sun Mian, and Yu Jing all assembled their armies at Binzhou for the first stage of their attack on Nùng Trí Cao's forces. The Song troops included a combined force of more than thirty-one thousand local militia.[85] Following the dictates of military law, Di Qing had Chen Shu executed for abandoning his post, and thirty-three other officers, including the local (Tai-speaking?) military commander (*zhihuishi*) Yuan Yong were punished for disobeying imperial orders. Di Qing wished to take quick, decisive action to shake the remaining troops back into shape and to restore discipline on the eve of the big campaign.

After putting his troops in order, Di Qing ordered a coordinated attack on the rebels. The commander himself took the advance line of troops, while Sun Mian commanded the second line, and Yu Jing led the rear guard. Sources note that Di Qing wore a bronze mask into battle.[86] The ethnographer Wolfram Eberhard surmises that the Song military leader wished to appear to the local people to be a deity.[87] Such an appearance might compel some of the rebel's followers to abandon their cause. In terms of military strategy, Di Qing had planned a night attack on Trí Cao's forces at the Guiren Inn (Guiren Pu) (located in Santang village, outside modern-day Nanning) near Kunlun Pass. When Nùng Trí Cao received word that imperial troops had succeeded in cutting off the narrow pass, he was caught completely unaware. He ultimately managed to rally enough of his army to fend off the attackers. Trí Cao's troops, dressed in their crimson uniforms, grabbed their long shields and struck back furiously, advancing on the Song troops, as the court chroniclers describe, "like a fire" (*wang zhi ru huo*). Di Qing's line was briefly forced into retreat, and his longtime comrade-in-arms and highly decorated soldier Sun Jie was killed in the counterattack as he led the Song's frontal assault.[88] Liu Ji had taken command of the right flank, and it is noted in his biography that he came to Di Qing to propose a new battle strategy after a day of fighting.[89] Di Qing then signaled to his various mounted troops to fall back and positioned the left and right flanks of his troops to pass through the retreating horsemen and engage Nùng Trí Cao's forces. According to Liu Ji's battle plan, the left flank moved right and the right flank moved left. Then, suddenly, the two flanks reversed course, with the left flank moving left and the right moving right again. Nùng Trí Cao's troops did not know how to react to this advance and were soundly defeated.

By that evening, Nùng Trí Cao had again taken Yongzhou, ordered his troops to set fire to the walls and ramparts, and fled the city.[90] He allegedly withdrew a short distance to Tianjing Peak, where he maintained a reserve force of men, horses, and supplies.[91] At this point, the rebel commander chose to escape to the west, crossing at the Hejiang River into the nearest independent kingdom founded by another highland society, the Dali kingdom.

The Nùng forces had suffered a massive defeat, leaving, according to Chinese accounts, 5,341 dead on the battlefield. Di Qing's troops immediately set to the task of repairing the city's temple sites and restoring the property of more than ten thousand residents who had been made homeless in the fighting.[92] The Song forces seized nine "false" imperial seals created for Nùng Trí Cao's use. They also captured fifty-seven officials of Trí Cao's court, including Huang Shimi. These prisoners were executed, and their heads were placed upon the city wall for public exhibition.⁹³ The Song troops also seized the numerous horses, cattle, and other valuables that the rebels had accumulated in their campaigns.

By the time Chinese forces led by Di Qing had begun to drive back the rebel army, Nùng Trí Cao looked south of the border for support. Vietnamese sources record that in the tenth month of 1053, Trí Cao sent his envoy Lương Châu to the Vietnamese court to "beg" (*qi*) for troop support. The Vietnamese emperor then commanded that the tribal military commander Võ Nhị lead a force to assist the rebels.⁹⁴ This account does not quite match the Chinese version noted above, in which the Song emperor essentially bribes the Vietnamese ruler to prevent him from becoming involved. It is also noteworthy that the forces described as being sent are from another borderlands ethnic group, and not from the Vietnamese imperial guard. In this manner, the Vietnamese court adopted a position similar to the one taken by the Song at the rebellion's outbreak, when the Renzong emperor called on his frontier guards, the Vietnamese leadership, to take care of the problem.

When Nùng Trí Cao finally fled Kunlun Pass, he and his mother took different routes. A Nùng retreated to the northwest corner of Temo *jimi* prefecture, where her third husband was Nùng clan chieftain. There, she assembled some three thousand men, the remnants of the rebel army, to practice for warfare on horseback and prepare for a return to Yongzhou.⁹⁵ However, the Song army had planned an advance on this rebel stronghold. Early in 1054, Yu Jing assembled an expeditionary force, including his retainers Huang Fen, Huang Xiangui, the Yongzhou native and *jinshi* scholar Shi Jian, and the *jinshi* scholar Wu Wuju.⁹⁶ Shi Jian had earlier assured Yu Jing that A Nùng and her forces did not have the unanimous support of the Tai-speaking chiefdoms in the area.⁹⁷ Therefore, the Song leaders were able to assemble a native militia group to undertake a surprise attack on Temo.

Yu Jing's men managed to capture A Nùng, Trí Cao's younger brother Nùng Trí Quang, and Trí Cao's two sons Nùng Kế Tông and Nùng Kế Phong and brought them back to the Song capital. Sources do not indicate specifically how Song authorities treated their prisoners. The *Official History of the Song Dynasty* contends that the court initially had not considered executing them but rather wished to hold these family members hostage in order to attract Trí Cao back into Song territory.

This account records that the prisoners were provided for while Song troops continued to search for Nùng Trí Cao in the westernmost reaches of Guangnan.[98] As soon as the court believed that Nùng Trí Cao was dead, the entire family was put to death in a public execution.

A memorial soon arrived in Kaifeng from Xichuan, a *jimi* prefecture now located in the Ninglang "Yi-minority autonomous district" (*Yizu zizhixian*) in northwestern Yunnan. The memorialist contended that Nùng Trí Cao was indeed still alive and that he had planned an attack on Lizhou (near Hanyuan county, in south-central Sichuan) and Yazhou (Yaan, in south-central Sichuan). Yazhou played a vital part in the Song court's military defense of the western frontier, safeguarding the "tea and horse" trade routes that originated in Yazhou and ended in Lhasa, passing to the north of the Dali kingdom.[99] Moreover, Yazhou was home to many non-Han communities, with more than fifty *jimi* prefectures established in the region since the Tang dynasty.[100] Fearing perhaps that Trí Cao would attempt to disrupt the lucrative trade or seek allies among local chieftains, the Song court ordered that proper military precautions be taken to thwart an attack on these prefectures. Moreover, the "vice censor-in-chief" (*yushi zhongcheng*) Sun Pu (996–1064) requested that an imperial order be issued to the prefect at Yizhou (modern-day Chengdu, in Sichuan) to make the necessary defense preparations and ease tensions among the native inhabitants of the Shu region (present-day Sichuan).[101] The anticipated and feared counterattack never came. Instead, the account in the *Official History of the Song Dynasty* ends with the statement that news of Trí Cao's death had proved inconclusive, and "whether he lives or has perished, there is no one who knows."[102] By some local accounts, the rebel was offered escort into the northern Thai region, where his descendants continue to thrive today.

Conclusion

The Song court responded to its victory with a general amnesty for the region's inhabitants, as the Song dynasty chroniclers wrote, to "relieve the ulcers" of local distress and suffering.[103] Other local supporters of the court's efforts were granted special recognition. For his collaboration and provision of important military intelligence, Yongzhou native Shi Jian was given the honorific title "assistant minister in the court of judicial review" (*dali cheng*) and the official position of Yongzhou's "military commissioner" (*jinglue anfushi*).[104] Other members of the court officialdom had their own reactions.

Sima Guang soon composed his account of the Nùng rebellion, reserving his strongest criticisms for Song officialdom. Peter Bol has quoted Sima Guang as writing that "the first concern of policy is the effective administration of government."[105] Sima Guang's approach to problems involving national defense required reforms at the bureaucratic and administrative levels. He favored adjustments to the imperial order rather than outright rejection of existing institutions, as would be more the case with his apprentice and future rival Wang Anshi.[106] In this context, Sima Guang showed a strong interest in Nùng Trí Cao's rebellion. He also held the Đại Cồ Việt court responsible for turning Trí Cao into a rebel.

Sima Guang's version of events is as follows:

> Trí Cao was crafty and difficult to control, and Giao Chi hated him. The Vietnamese ruler sent troops to capture his father and to take him back to Giao Chi as a hostage. Trí Cao was powerless to do anything, and in that year his loss of gold and possessions was very great.

This account does not recognize material gifts to the Vietnamese court as tributary obligations. Instead, from the vantage point of the Song central court, demands for such gifts verge on acts of thievery. As Sima Guang continues:

> A long while passed, and his father died. Trí Cao was angry at the Giao Chi authorities. Moreover, he was afraid that their actions would finally lead to his ruin. So he rebelled against Giao Chi, crossed the river [between China and the Đại Việt kingdom], and took up residence in Andezhou prefecture. He then sent an envoy to the Yongzhou garrison city to request that the Chinese court make him a regional chief by decree. The Chinese court often

granted this title to local leaders within the *jimi* system. Because the court had heard that Trí Cao had rebelled against Giao Chỉ before arriving, they were afraid that the frontier would be disturbed, and so they did not allow this. Trí Cao became angry about this, and he thereafter often entered [our land] as a bandit.[107]

In his account of the rebellion, Sima Guang alternately heaps praise and blame on the Song defenders who attempted to slow the rebels' advance toward Guangzhou. At one point, he remarks, "Jiang Jie from the West Circuit Command made light of the situation. He put his forces into operation as a crazy person would. When the army reached Taiping plateau, the troops were from the very start unprepared for fighting."[108] Because Sima Guang's focus was on the Chinese bureaucracy in action and the lessons that could be drawn from its successes and failures, issues involving the Song court's relations with its neighbors were of secondary importance. Sima Guang maintained primarily that both the Vietnamese and the Nùng were brash, ritually heterodox neighbors who merely served to test the ability of Chinese bureaucrats.

Nùng Trí Cao's choice to rebel against both Vietnamese and Chinese authorities may not, as Sima Guang might have assumed, come from his unfamiliarity as an "outsider" with the institutions of these courts. Instead, Trí Cao's ambitions may have emerged from an intimate understanding of the system of local administration in his frontier region and the knowledge that he would be forever excluded from positions of power unless he challenged the system itself. Araki Toshikazu makes the very interesting claim that Nùng Trí Cao's greatest motivation for carrying out his rebellion after his incarceration at Thăng Long was his failure to gain court recognition as a successful "civil service examination" (*keju*) candidate.[109] Araki contends that Trí Cao had the opportunity (and the family resources) to take the "prefectural exams" (*jieshi*) at the Yongzhou prefectural seat several times during the 1041–48 period.[110] Trí Cao's name was not forwarded to the "metropolitan-level exams" (*shengshi*), owing to his family history, Nùng Trí Cao's association with the Vietnamese court, and his own reputation for rebellious behavior. These circumstances would explain Trí Cao's ability to attract the services of the Chinese *jinshi* scholars Huang Wei and Huang Shifu, from Guangzhou. Moreover, Nùng Trí Cao's reliance on the symbols and institutions of Chinese imperial rule demonstrate his acquired knowledge of this political tradition, knowledge that would be expected of any examination aspirant.

The evidence supporting Araki's claims points to an important new cultural influence that entered the border region with the changing Song policy. Successive Song rulers extended access to the civil service examination system farther and farther into the empire's hinterland. "Fiscal commissioners" (caoci) appointed to the Guangnan circuit were given the additional responsibility of administering these exams.[111] By the Southern Song period (1127–1279), all exams given outside of Nanhai (Guangzhou) were administered from the prefecture seat at Jingjiangfu (located within modern-day Guilin). Moreover, the court made special allowances for non-Han examination aspirants. Famous travel writer and former Guilin vice-prefect Zhou Qufei notes that "the quota for candidates to be forwarded" (jie-e) from the tiny aboriginal "grotto settlement" (xidong) districts to the metropolitan exams offered spots for two exam takers.[112]

It is difficult to verify whether similar conditions existed in Trí Cao's day, but the trend toward incorporating outlying districts in the empirewide exam system started as early as the reign of Taizong, the second Song emperor, who ruled from 976 to 997. Moreover, the same source describes the trade in books and writing materials at the open-air market established by the Hengshan garrison, a locale accessible to traders from the indigenous frontier communities as well as to merchants coming up from the Đại Việt kingdom. There are accounts of Chinese paper and brushes being sold to Vietnamese region customers in the coastal market at Qinzhou "in quantities about which enough cannot be said."[113] There is even a report that the ink produced from the great pines of Guangxi's Rongzhou region was a local specialty, prized by buyers in the Vietnamese region.[114] If such an active trade was evident during the Southern Song period, the reader could expect that these materials were accessible during the earlier Song period as well. With reference to the exams, all of these materials had to be present if candidates were to prepare effectively for the tests.

An important final issue to explore is whether or not Nùng Trí Cao intended to found a separate kingdom that would stand between the Song and Vietnamese empires, or if he wished simply to carve out a semiautonomous space within the existing political order that would allow him more local authority and perhaps enrichment through regional trade. Regarding this particular point, there is the possibility that Nùng Trí Cao sought to breathe new life into the ancient legacy of the independent Nam Việt, or Nanyue, kingdom (207–111 BCE). At the height of his political power, Zhao Tuo (Triệu Đà), the kingdom's founder, governed from Guangzhou over a vast southern region including modern-day Guangdong, Guangxi, Hainan Island, and northern Vietnam to the Red River delta. Huang Xianfan, the leading Chinese scholar of Nùng Trí Cao, notes that following Trí Cao's capture of Wuzhou during his third rebellion, he announced: "Now I will found Nan Yue."[115] Huang argues that in establishing a frontier kingdom, Nùng Trí Cao's wish was not to found a state to rival that of the Song but instead to establish a dependency that could thwart Vietnamese expansionist intentions in the region.[116] While Huang has evidence for this claim, the allegation that Trí Cao chose to side with the Song by attacking the Song remains controversial.

Another interpretation expressed in recent Vietnamese scholarship is that Trí Cao may have been resurrecting the ancient kingdom of Nam Cương. The kingdom's former capital at Nam Bình is on the outskirts of Cao Bằng city in the Hòa An district, where, incidentally, a modern temple dedicated to Nùng Tri Cao is still located. Other modern scholars do not consider Trí Cao's allusions to the Nanyue legacy and other kingdoms late in his revolt to be sincere expressions of his original intentions. As Jeffrey Barlow writes, "Nong Zhigao, who attempted to establish a Zhuang kingdom based at Guangzhou and entitled *Yue*, was not one of the powerful sinicized or collaborative elites but a 'wild' leader from the hinterlands who had tried and failed to be recognized by the [Song] regime. Only after that failure did he declare a Zhuang kingdom, aspiring to seize Guangzhou, in some senses an archaic goal."[117] Barlow argues that Han penetration of the southern frontier after the decline of the Tang dynastic order was one of the primary reasons for local chieftains' shift away from the establishment of independent polities and toward collaboration with neighboring regimes.

Whatever the case may be, the series of rebellions led by Nùng Trí Cao forced the Song and Đại Cồ Việt courts to pay even greater attention to effective regulation of the Sino-Vietnamese frontier. The leadership in Kaifeng still feared that disturbances elsewhere along the frontier could well erupt in communities sympathetic to the rebels' aims. In 1053, an edict from the Song court ordered that "frontier troops" (*shubing*) who had served in the region for at least two years be decommissioned and sent home and that the local "military administrator" (*qianxia*) instead employ native militia that would serve one-year tours of duty. At the time of Nùng Trí Cao's rebellion, frontier troops in the region numbered more than twenty-four thousand men. These troops eventually obeyed the order to return home, leaving defense of the borderlands in the hands of the native militia.[118]

Moreover, even in the court-approved description of Nùng Trí Cao's exploits, there is some recognition that desperate economic conditions played a role in causing local communities to side with the rebels. At the very end of the Song court account, the authors included a local saying: "What the peasants grow, the grain merchants harvest."[119] Today, tales of Nùng Trí Cao's daring acts and Di Qing's stunning victory are both part of local folklore among communities along the Sino-Vietnamese border. And the theme of social justice denied, implied by the saying above, has remained part of the narrative as well.

Nùng Trí Cao's rebellion had a lasting effect on Sino-Vietnamese relations, in terms of both tribute and trade. The Chinese court's response to the regional tensions reflected Kaifeng's increased interest in the resources of the Guangnan region. The Vietnamese court, in contrast, also recognized the importance of this region, due to the volume of trade that passed through the settlements the Nùng rebels had targeted, as well as the weakness of the local Chinese militia charged with its defense. From this period, the Chinese pacification campaign launched against Nùng Trí Cao's followers in the 1050s and the subsequent submission of strategic Tai-speaking frontier communities to direct control of the Song court contributed directly to the outbreak of the Sino-Vietnamese borderlands war of 1075–77.

6

Tempting "Treacherous Factions": The Manipulation of Frontier Alliances on the Eve of the 1075 Sino-Vietnamese Borderlands War

No one in either Thăng Long or Kaifeng was likely to have imagined that the suppression of Nùng Trí Cao would lead to war. Nonetheless, the official containment of the frontier chieftain eventually had the effect of escalating rather than decreasing tensions along the Sino-Vietnamese frontier region. In fact, the pacification campaign launched against Nùng Trí Cao's followers in the 1050s and the subsequent submission of strategic Tai-speaking frontier communities to the direct control of Song authorities contributed directly to the outbreak of the Sino-Vietnamese borderlands war of 1075–77.

As important as it was, the factor of shifting alliances between the two courts and these frontier communities was not all-determinative in the conflict that brought about the breakdown in relations between the Chinese and Vietnamese courts. Among the other crucial influences were the Chinese court's efforts to increase frontier economic activity under the Song-sponsored reforms of the new policies initiated by the grand councilor Wang Anshi during the period 1068 to 1085 as well as the consolidation of peripheral fiefdoms undertaken by the Lý court during an accelerated period of state building. Nevertheless, despite other factors that aggravated regional tensions, in the aftermath of open hostilities, the two courts conducted talks to negotiate a fixed border between the Đại Việt kingdom and the Song empire.[1] These talks and the establishment of a fixed border marked a diplomatic watershed in Middle Period Sino-Vietnamese relations. In these negotiations, one must consider the role the frontier Tai-speaking communities played in shaping this firm dividing line between Chinese and Vietnamese domains. Control of these communities and their resources was an important consideration in the positions taken by both the Song and Lý negotiators. Moreover, the line of demarcation established upon the conclusion of these talks remained largely in place up to the present day.

Inferring the true nature of frontier relations in this period proves to be a difficult task when a cursory reading of existing historical sources reveals only a battle between two imperial powers staged among dispossessed Tai-speaking communities. The available Chinese sources do not readily disclose local concerns, because most of the language used even by Song frontier officials in their memorials to the court couched matters in court-centered contexts. Likewise, extant imperial Vietnamese sources view this period from the perspective of the Lý ruler and his closest advisers at court. Efforts to gain a clearer understanding of regional interaction along the frontier in the premodern period owe a great deal to Vietnamese scholars working in the Democratic Republic of Vietnam after 1954. This group of scholars was the first to question the paradigm of a Chinese political and cultural monolith employed by French colonial writers in their assessments of Vietnamese history. Patricia Pelley notes that, "by emphasizing the ethnic heterogeneity of China, by underscoring the tenacity of regional politics in China, and by calling attention to South China's historic links to Southeast Asia, revolutionary scholars managed to reduce the apparently monolithic and overwhelmingly Han dimensions of China."[2] Where these historians saw a diversity of interests among the subjects of Chinese rulers, they often read solidarity and unity among the subjects of Vietnamese kings. The unified, invariant picture created by these revolutionary scholars, of an eleventh-century Vietnamese society filled with Kinh and non-Kinh in a "united front" against Chinese aggression from the north, does not fit neatly with the picture presented in this chapter.

Much of the above-mentioned scholarship has also relied on the assumption that the Lý court prevailed in its efforts to woo the Tai-speaking communities of the region over to the Vietnamese. While this conclusion could be inferred from existing sources, there is a strong nationalist bias to these findings. Patriotic Vietnamese scholars in the twentieth century have long been interested in overcoming the picture of Vietnamese regional and ethnic disunity promoted in earlier French colonial scholarship. Shortly after the seizure and colonization of Vietnam in the late nineteenth century, much French colonial academic effort was devoted to the reconstruction of Vietnamese premodern society as a key to explaining the relative ease with which Vietnam fell to French domination.

Pelley notes that, "to overcome this characterization, revolutionary writers were supposed to recite haranguing clichés about the essential unity and homogeneity of [Vietnam] and its indomitable spirit in the fight against foreign aggression."[3] Regarding the eleventh century, an influential voice that inspired this group of revolutionary scholars is the historian Hoàng Xuân Hãn (1908–1996), who contends in his seminal 1949 work *Lý Thường Kiệt* (Lý Thường Kiệt) that the Lý court had a special ability in "giving heart to" (*phủ dụ*) the upland peoples, promoting the Lý court's prestige among "the mountain dwellers" farther north, and helping to maintain peace along the Đại Việt kingdom's inland frontier.[4] Later, he argues, when Thăng Long sought to attract supporters among Tai-speaking communities on the eve of the general Lý Thường Kiệt's (1019–1105) invasion of the Song frontier, the Vietnamese court soon benefited from the local knowledge and logistical support provided by these communities.[5]

In his book, Professor Hãn describes the Nùng clan as the local representatives of the Lý court and characterizes the lands they occupied as sovereign Vietnamese territory. At one point, he writes, although the frontier leader and Nùng Trí Cao's kinsman Nùng Tông Đán (b. 1013) and his relatives had approached the Song court and offered Song authorities the northern frontier grotto settlements of Lôi Hỏa and Kế Thành, both of which would later be incorporated into the Song's Pacified Prefecture (Shun'an Zhou), "the family of Tông Đán still maintained control of his old territory, which therefore was territory that still belonged to Vietnam."[6] Hoàng Xuân Hãn's opinions continued to influence future generations of Vietnamese scholars, who saw an undeniable unity of purpose between the Vietnamese court and the upland frontier peoples in the face of Chinese aggression in the mid-eleventh century.

Other Vietnamese historians have noted Nùng Tông Đán's participation in Lý Thường Kiệt's preemptive attack on Song territory as a clear sign that the Lý court had wisely cultivated strong relations with its Tai-speaking neighbors. Conservative scholar and former prime minister Trần Trọng Kim (1883–1953) notes in his influential historical survey *Việt Nam sử lược* (A record of Vietnamese history) that Tông Đán held a high leadership position in the Lý military force, perhaps even on a par with Lý Thường Kiệt.[7] The expatriote scholar and anti-Communist activist Nguyễn Ngọc Huy (b. 1924) notes in his work on the Lê Code that "one result of [the Lý court's] benevolent policy toward minority leaders was their effective support for the dynasty in the successful campaigns against the Sung."[8] Paris-based scholar Lê Thành Khôi contends that the Lý policy of fostering alliances with the upland communities eventually "bore its fruits," and he notes Tông Đán's leadership role in Lý Thường Kiệt's military force as a prime example of this success.[9] Professor Phan Huy Lê of Hanoi National University, in turn quoting Hoàng Xuân Hãn, writes, "Generally speaking, all of the Lý court's wise policies [regarding local chieftains] were successful, and they held an important significance during preparations for the victorious battle with the Song during the years 1075–77."[10] In another recent study produced by the Bureau for National Defense in the Vietnamese Institute of Military History, Lê Đình Sỹ writes, "The Lý were concerned to protect 'the silk and brocade' [i.e., our beautiful] fatherland's territorial integrity, as well as the independence and the autonomy of our people."[11] Ethnologists working on the history of Tai-speaking groups in Vietnam have voiced similar opinions. Hà Văn Thư and Lã Văn Lô wrote in 1984 that "when the Song invaded our country, all of the local militia [composed of upland people] joined together in the cause at strategically important sites, carrying out surprise attacks on the military gatherings and supply lines of the enemy."[12] A more recent ethnographic work reiterates this same event in the historical introduction.[13]

I would argue that many of these Vietnamese scholars were influenced by the historiographical imperative mentioned above in asserting that the Lý leadership benefited more from upland support than did the Song leadership when the two courts engaged in open conflict in 1075. On the contrary, I maintain that the Chinese authorities successfully cultivated relations with these upland communities, particularly with the declared followers of Nùng Trí Cao and his clan, and that this change in frontier policy alarmed the lowland Vietnamese court and its upland supporters to such a degree that the military strategy of "the best defense is a good offense," promoted by the Lý military aide Lý Thường Kiệt, was eventually adopted.

Growing Chinese Interest in the South

Through the 1060s, the Song and Lý courts viewed their frontier communities as a ready pool of able personnel who could contribute to what Jeffrey Barlow has termed the "military labor market."[14] Chinese regimes had in the past used militia assembled from Tai-speaking frontier communities in armed conflicts with Vietnamese forces based in the Red River delta region. During the Five Dynasties period, the Southern Han founder Liu Yin (r. 907–11) recruited troops from the southern Guangxi region, among them archers, to assist in the war then being waged against the kingdom of Chu (907–51).[15] These troops were well known for their ferocity. In 930, the Southern Han ruler Liu Gong (r. 911–42) recruited more local militia to help with the invasion of northern Vietnam, then under the command of the Vietnamese strongman Khúc Thừa Mỹ (r. 917–30). Fifty years later, in 980, when the Song court launched its punitive attack on Lê Hoàn, the Chinese army gathered another contingent of southern militia from the frontier region to supplement its northern forces.[16] Given its reputation for bravery in battle, this Tai-speaking militia was considered a valuable military asset and a worthy ally in frontier conflicts. By 1065, some 44,500 militia soldiers from these communities had been enlisted by local Song authorities.[17] These numbers could suggest that the Chinese court was eager to tap this source of military manpower, and, importantly, the increase in recruitment could also reflect a rapid shift in political loyalties in the region.

Frontier inhabitants from modern-day Cao Bằng province also served the interests of the Vietnamese court as military leaders. During the same 980 conflict between the Lê and Song armies, a fisherman, Quan Triêu, marshaled a local militia and called on the powers of a local tutelary spirit to fight off the invading Chinese army.[18] Following Lê Hoàn's victory against the Chinese forces and their upland allies, the Vietnamese ruler rewarded Triêu with the titles "Red Lotus Duke" (Hồng Liên Công Vương) and "Imperial Guardian of the Kingdom" (Phụ Mã Hộ Quốc Công). As the nineteenth-century author of a local history wrote, "Quan Triêu as the Red Lotus Duke had joined forces with the mysterious powers to come to the aid of the kingdom's frontier militia."[19] A local inhabitant and the indigenous forces he commanded had presented a supernatural first line of defense against threats from the north. Therefore, by the late eleventh century, both Chinese and Vietnamese courts had taken the opportunity to call on their frontier subjects in military exercises against each other.

The successful expedition of the Song general Di Qing against the Nùng rebels and the Lý court's refusal to intervene on either side brought a tentative peace to the frontier region. For nearly twenty years after Nùng Trí Cao's defeat, frontier disturbances were minimal and Chinese and Vietnamese military resources swiftly contained any disorder. In this period, Han homesteaders and discharged soldiers also moved to the area, settling in existing Chinese communities and on the outskirts of *jimi* regions. At the same time, new local leaders took control of the decimated but still remaining frontier communities. The regional peace would not last. With the changing ethnic balance along the frontier, new political challenges emerged, which could no longer be lessened by the existing order of frontier administration. This environment, of a growing Song imperial presence on the edges of a frontier that the Lý leadership also desired to control, pushed the two courts closer to a violent confrontation. When several influential Nùng leaders sided with the Vietnamese court in the ensuing conflict, Kaifeng realized that it had to establish an entirely new arrangement for frontier relations.

Manipulating the Frontier

Nùng Trí Cao's revolt of the 1050s had revealed weaknesses in the Song's administration of its southern region. Furthermore, frontier unrest threatened to begin anew with a new generation of Nùng leadership. In the tenth month of 1060, the Guangnan West circuit fiscal commissioner Wang Han memorialized the throne, stating that Nùng Trí Cao's fellow clansman, Nùng Tông Đán, had already crossed back into Song territory in 1057.[20] Tông Đán had since assembled a following and was now threatening to plunder the region. Following rumors that Nùng Trí Cao was actually still alive, Wang visited Tông Đán's camp at Lôi Hỏa and spoke with Trí Cao's son Nùng Nhật Tân (fl. 1050–78). According to the *Official History of the Song Dynasty* (Songshi), Wang made the following statement to the frontier leader's son: "If you seek *neifu* status with the Song court, you will be seen as an enemy by the Vietnamese. If you remain outside [China proper] as a loyal frontier militia leader, you can expect to be rewarded with tempting profit. Therefore, there is no need for scheming. Now, return home to report this news to your father and then to choose the path that offers the greatest benefit."[21]

Wang Han feared that the Nùng clan's resurgence could spell the end to peace on the frontier. Therefore, he requested the enactment of a new policy. The Song court responded by ignoring Wang's specific recommendation and instead requesting that the Nùng communities, along with other ethnic groups, be given *neifu* status in the Song empire. In this manner, troubles between the Song and its frontier regions temporarily subsided. Nùng Trí Cao's followers achieved the elevated *neifu* status Trí Cao and his father had initially been seeking, although at the cost of many lives. However, Nùng Trí Cao later fought for no less than his own kingdom stretching across southern China. Such an independent polity within China's borders would not emerge until the Warlord Period (1916–28).

Moreover, the Song court acknowledged the Nùng clan's continued regional influence by accepting Tông Đán's renewed local leadership. Xiao Gu, then the court-appointed military commissioner, advised the court to return Tông Đán's followers to official service by peaceful means, including a treaty alliance and new honorary titles. By the summer of 1061, even the emperor was lamenting the fact that Tông Đán, the "Nùng Bandit," and his family had strayed so far from the observance of their frontier duties that they might never really return to the imperial fold.[22] Yet when, in 1062, Tông Đán requested that the territories under his authority be incorporated into the Chinese empire, Emperor Renzong accommodated this request.

The Chinese ruler then extended a new set of titles and nominal positions to leading members of the frontier communities, at a level of authority below the titles granted to the Vietnamese court and its officials. The *Draft of Documents Pertaining to Song Official Matters* (Songhuiyao jiben), by Song Xu, records that the "loyal warrior" (*wuzong jiangjun*) Tông Đán, whom the Song court regarded as the prefect of Lôi Hỏa, recently renamed "Pacified Prefecture," was granted the title "personal guardian general of the right" (*you qianniu weijiangjun*).[23] Nùng Trí Cao's younger brother Nùng Trí Hội (fl. 1062–85) received the title "personal guardian general of the left" (*zuo qianniu weijiangjun*). Other members of the Nùng clan who were former followers of Trí Cao also received official recognition. Nùng Binh, Nùng Lượng, and Nùng Hạ Khanh, local leaders from the Temo *jimi* prefecture, swore their loyalty to the Song court.[24] As mentioned in the previous chapter, Nùng Hạ Khanh was almost certainly the third husband of Nùng Trí Cao's mother, A Nùng, which may or may not have been known to Xiao Gu and the other Song officials administering the area. Even Trí Cao's former rebel commanders Lư Báo, Lê Mạo, and Hoàng Trọng Khanh were granted official titles that denoted service at the local level to the Song court.[25] In all of these titles, there is an element of reorienting local authority so that it is much more dependent on the centralized authority of the Song court. These titles were granted with the condition that they could be withdrawn at any point if their holders did not live up to the official obligations the titles implied.

In the wake of all these administrative appointments, the *jimi* prefectures lost their autonomous status in the eyes of the Song leadership. The change was not limited to new titles alone. Local militia along the southern frontier were reorganized and trained to comply with new court standards for frontier defense. In 1065, the local "military commission" (*anfusi*) of Guangnan West circuit, under the direction of the new Guizhou prefect Lu Shen (1012–1070), took charge of the organization of communities along the southern frontier.[26] The forty-five grotto settlements in the Left and Right rivers region were all appointed to the rank of "grotto militia leader" (*dongjiang*). The commissioner then surveyed the region's population of able-bodied men, from which he selected groups to be led by "guard commanders" (*xiaochang*) from the area's prominent households. Each guard commander then received a specific "signal banner" (*qihao*) that would distinguish his group. Groups of thirty men were organized into self-regulating units of local governance known as "tithings" (*jia*).[27] Tithings received different leaders when they were organized in groups of five led by a "troop commandant" (*dutou*), groups of ten led by an "aboriginal commander" (*zhijunshi*), and groups of fifty led by a "commander-in-chief" (*duzhijunshi*).

As noted above, some 44,500 local men along the southern frontier may have been registered under this new system. At least on paper, these efforts to organize frontier militia went far beyond any previous attempts under the existing *jimi* frontier system of management. The tightening of frontier defenses on the Song side did not sit well with the Vietnamese court, which saw its own flexible and personally oriented systems of local control being gradually undermined.

Moreover, greater numbers of Song subjects from the north were moving into the region during this period. Scholars have noted a sharp increase in population along China's southwestern frontier by the end of the eleventh century. During the period 976–84, the total population of the prefectures of Yongzhou, Binzhou, Xiangzhou (modern-day Xiangzhou county, in central Guangxi), Rongzhou (modern-day Rongan county, Guangxi), Hengzhou, Liuzhou (modern-day Liuzhou city), and Yizhou was estimated to be in the area of 17,760 households, and by the period 1078–85, the population in the same area had increased to 56,596 households.[28] Moreover, figures for the entire Guangnan West circuit for 1080 place the region's population at 287,723 households, a 133 percent increase from an earlier Tang census in 742.[29] One should note that these figures include both indigenous communities and the more recent Han settlements. Improved methods of recording household registration may indeed explain some of the increase. However, the trend toward increased Han settlement remains clear through these changes;

an increase accounted for by both the community of soldiers who had followed Di Qing in his campaign against Nùng Trí Cao's forces and the merchants who provided support for the Song military.

The Republican period gazetteer *A Record of Fengshan County* (Fengshan xianzhi) makes this point: "Before the Tang, this county was settled by the Miao barbarian people. There were no traces of Han settlers. In 1053, The 'Great Martial Leader' Di [Qing] put down the rebellion of the Quang Nguyên barbarian Nùng Trí Cao, and the troops following the general's expedition remained in the region to open up and settle the wasteland. Their settlements extended throughout this county."[30]

Li Wenxiong, in his early-twentieth-century gazetteer *A Record of Longjin County* (Longjin xianzhi) (modern-day Longzhou county, Guangxi), extends this population shift right down to the frontier in his observations:

> Longjin County before the Tang was a part of Giao Chỉ [or Vietnamese] territory. Its inhabitants were subjects of Giao Chỉ. In 1052, Zhao Ding, following the success of the Di [Wuxiang] Qing in his campaign against the barbarians, was appointed to the hereditary position of local administrator.[31] A division of General Di's soldiers from the Shandong region entered the area to settle down. Because of this event, many settlers from north of the Yangzi River moved into the area to live. After the barbarian wastelands had started to be controlled [by the Song court], settlers from Fujian [*min*], Jiangxi [*gan*], Hunan [*xiang*], and the Guangdong [*yue*] region daily flocked to the region. Some came to take positions as local officials, and they married into the local community. Some came as merchants, marrying into the region as well. Most of these Han homesteaders settled in the larger towns or the marketplaces. However, there were certainly those gathered in the rural villages to conduct their business.[32]

Throughout the Song empire, word spread that new opportunities could be found in this southernmost outpost of imperial control, and many were more than willing to try their luck in its settlement.

A cultural shift had also begun to take place in the region, with an increased emphasis on North Chinese or Central Plains practices.

The earliest signs of change are described in *A Record of the Empire's Borders and Dimensions during the Taiping Period* (Taiping huanyuji), by Yue Shi (930–1007). As Wang Xiangzhi (d. after 1221) noted in *A Record of This Region's Merits* (Yudi jisheng), this trend accelerated during the period after the fall of North China to Jurchen armies: "following the Song's 'Southern Push' (Nandu), i.e., fall to the Jin, when many northerners moved south to escape their homelands, clothing styles, ceremonials caps, rituals and music then became the same as those practices in North China."[33] These social practices were actually brought into the region by Di Qing's troops and the accompanying cadre of local officials. If the Guangnan region had not already had strong ties with court culture during the early Song period, these ties were laid in place and strengthened with each wave of northern settlers that poured into the frontier.

Meanwhile, the Vietnamese court pursued a policy of expansion, with military expeditions to the south against neighboring Champa in conjunction with pacification campaigns to assert direct court control over indigenous communities located along the northern frontier. Lý Phật Mã died late in 1054, and the Khai Hoàng prince Lý Nhật Tôn ascended the throne to preside over a Vietnamese kingdom that had become increasingly "united and self-assured."[34] Lý Phật Mã had already started a court-organized movement toward frontier settlement and control, and this trend continued unabated throughout the period of unrest involving Nùng Trí Cao.

Soon, there was more evidence of Viet expansion in the frontier region. In 1059, the Lý court made an additional effort to take direct control of its frontier and the local manpower. The court divided the northern frontier in the Left and Right rivers region into the new administrative units Ngự Long, Vũ Thắng, Long Dực, Thần Điện, Bồng Thánh, Bảo Thắng (Bảo Thắng county, in modern-day Lào Cai province), Hùng Lược, and Vạn Tiệp.[35] To each of these units the court assigned an official serving Thăng Long's interests. In the most expressive gesture on regional dominance, Lý Nhật Tôn ordered that militia units be established among the local communities and that conscripts all have the characters "Army of the Son of Heaven" (Thiên Tử Quân) tattooed on their foreheads.[36] This practice had existed since early times and had last been followed by Lê Hoàn in assembling his own militia forces. Emphasis on the control of regional manpower reflects a distinctly Southeast Asian system of statecraft.[37] Most importantly, it indicates that the Lý desired to tap its frontier resources in a novel manner in order to fuel efforts at regional expansion. Resources at this point in time meant largely human resources.

During the early 1060s, the Sino-Vietnamese frontier experienced numerous local disturbances among the indigenous communities, in response perhaps to the influx of settlers from the north. Moreover, there were clashes between troops serving both the Chinese and Vietnamese courts. In the spring of 1060, Thàn Thiệu Thái, the elderly chieftain of the frontier prefecture Lạng Châu (present-day Lạng Sơn) and an imperial in-law through a marriage alliance, crossed into Song territory to raid frontier settlements for cattle and new militia recruits.[38] In the attack, Thiệu Thái also captured the local Song military leader Yang Baocai. In the autumn of 1060, Song troops crossed the frontier. However, the Chinese were unsuccessful in their attempt to bring Yang back.[39]

Kaifeng soon dispatched the newly appointed military commissioner Yu Jing (1000–1064) to the Guangnan region to quell unrest stirred up by Giáp Đồng natives led by Thiệu Thái. Fighting there had already claimed the lives of five "military inspectors" (*xunjian*).[40] Once he reached the south, Yu Jing also sent a court representative secretly to Champa to enlist Cham support for a possible allied attack on Vietnamese communities in Guangnan.[41] This increased activity along the frontier naturally drew the attention of the Vietnamese court, which reportedly had also caught wind of the Cham plot. As the Song court took a greater interest in the frontier region, a new policy emerged of wooing local leaders directly rather than relying on the assistance of the tributary representative in the Vietnamese court. Such a shift in behavior undercut the local authority once granted Thăng Long through official tributary relations with the Chinese. As the Song court began to seek local leaders to implement its regional interests, even in opposition to Vietnamese interests, the Đại Cồ Việt court sought ways to make its presence felt along the frontier.

However, the Lý court likely saw merit in defusing what had become a tense relationship with the Song. A delegation from Thăng

Long led by Bi Gia Dụ traveled to Yongzhou one year later to negotiate terms for peace with Yu Qing himself.[42] Lý Nhật Tôn instructed his court to "send an envoy into China to convey thanks [for quelling the earlier disturbances] but continue to collect more intelligence on Cham troops, Yu Qing's forces, and other troops stationed in the Guangnan West circuit."[43] The Chinese delegation again requested the return of Yang Baocai, but the request was denied.[44] Given the recent unrest, the Chinese emperor Renzong hesitated to raise tensions further along the southern frontier, and he ordered the delegated leaders of his local military commissions to refrain from assembling troops in the region. The Song ruler then allowed a tribute mission from Thăng Long to travel to Kaifeng for an imperial audience. On February 8, 1063, the two Vietnamese envoys offered tribute to the Song emperor that included nine tame elephants, a gift that Vietnamese leaders then considered their most precious offering.[45] Sino-Vietnamese relations appeared at this stage to have reached a new equilibrium.

Within months, the relationship between the two courts had changed once again. On March 30, 1063, the emperor Renzong passed away, and the heir apparent Zhao Shu (Yingzong [r. 1063–67]) came to power. Vietnamese envoys soon arrived in Kaifeng to congratulate the new emperor on his ascension. On April 7, 1063, Yingzong made an important imperial gesture by sending gifts, such as calligraphic compositions in the hand of the late ruler Renzong, to the Vietnamese court. Such a gift was likely an acknowledgment that the Vietnamese ruler and his advisers were learned enough to appreciate the literary refinement of these works and fell within the wider circle of Central Plains culture. Yingzong also granted the ruler Lý Nhật Tôn the post of "concurrent manager of governmental affairs in the secretariat-chancellery" (*tongzhong shumen xiaping zhangshi*).[46] The Song emperor's purpose in granting this office was likely to reinforce from the outset of his reign the image of the Vietnamese court as an extension of the Chinese central court and to preserve Lý Nhật Tôn's position as both a frontier official and a participant in the formulation of central court policy. Despite this nod to historical precedent, the Song court's gesture did not completely ameliorate tensions on the frontier.

On the same day that the Vietnamese envoy Lý Kế Tiên prepared to depart Kaifeng, news arrived from the south that a frontier militia under the leadership of errant clan leader Thàn Thiệu Thái had engaged in yet another attack on settlements within Guangnan West circuit.[47] A Guangnan official sent an urgent plea to Kaifeng for an immediate punitive attack on the southern intruders. Chinese sources record that the Song court had come to the conclusion that Thàn Thiệu Thái was "reckless and mad," perhaps as a conscious effort to divorce his actions from those of the Vietnamese court. In the meantime, an envoy from Thăng Long had already been dispatched to Kaifeng to ask forgiveness for the attack. Yingzong, therefore, did not raise an army to deal with this problem. Local Song officials may have wanted a stronger response from Kaifeng, but the Song ruler maintained that his vassals were still capable of self-regulation.

More than a year passed before any further troubles arose. On November 18, 1064, the Guizhou prefect Lu Shen memorialized the throne during a court visit by Vietnamese envoys. Lu reported that a military delegation from Thăng Long had allegedly come across the frontier in search of Nùng Tông Đán's son Nùng Nhật Tân and his followers and that this same delegation showed an interest in taking control of a section of Song territory, including the Wenmen Grotto *jimi* district (located near Hurun village, in modern-day Jingxi county).[48] Although the court took no specific action as a result of this memorial, Lu appeared determined to expand the Song's military presence in the south so as to thwart such exploratory expeditions by his Vietnamese neighbors.

After delivering his memorial, Lu Shen set out along the frontier to Yongzhou. As mentioned earlier in this chapter, he commissioned forty-five local aboriginal leaders from the Left and Right rivers region as military officers in his growing militia. When he had assembled the above-mentioned 44,500 seasoned troops, he ordered his force to repair and fortify military installations in the region. He also requested local Song administrators to cast special seals for his militia leaders. Lu petitioned the Song court with a request that the Left and Right rivers region be exempted from the payment of all back taxes.[49] He took all these measures in order to gain the loyalty of those communities that, one generation previously, had joined Nùng Trí Cao in his rebellion against the throne. The effort to provide military training for the leaders of this frontier militia was a variation on existing court policy, but Lu's methods built on Kaifeng's growing interest in more direct incorporation of these frontier areas.

After witnessing these events along the frontier, Vietnamese officials became quite concerned. Leaders in Thăng Long immediately dispatched a tribute-bearing envoy to Kaifeng to "send their greetings" as well as to remind the Chinese court of the precedent of relying on Vietnamese authorities to settle frontier matters. Meanwhile, Lu had again memorialized the throne, requesting that the court offer special training and indoctrination to one local militia leader each year. Following this training regime, this militia leader would be made a member of the official bureaucracy after three years.[50]

At about this same time, it appears that the frontier leader Nùng Tông Đán decided to switch political allegiances. It may have been that the local chieftain saw his traditional base of power eroding rapidly under the new system of frontier management set in place by Lu Shen. The evidence is rather scanty. According to the *Official History of the Song Dynasty*, sometime after late 1065, Tông Đán made overtures to Lý Nhật Tôn and the Quảng Nguyên chieftain Lưu Ký.[51] Fearing a potentially hostile coalition so close to home, Lu Shen sent an envoy to announce this news to the Song court. Emperor Yingzong, a mentally weak and distracted ruler by this point, apparently took no other action than to reassign Tông Đán his honorific titles. This lack of attention from the center was to have a harmful effect on the vitality of the Song presence along the frontier. As highlighted in the Vietnamese sources, Tông Đán then became a willing and able ally of the Lý court and would perform a key military role in the 1075–77 conflict.

This alliance between Tông Đán and the Quảng Nguyên chieftain Lưu Ký had its roots in Nùng Trí Cao's third rebellion. In *Notes from Mengxi* (Mengxi bitan), Shen Kua argues that Lư Báo, Lê Mạo, Hoàng Trọng Khanh, and Liệu Thông were among Trí Cao's chief supporters for his initial assault on the Hengshan garrison prior to the attack on Yongzhou.[52] When the rebellion was finally suppressed, Lư Báo called together Trí Cao's disbanded rebel army and eventually returned to Quảng Nguyên, where the entire group had pledged its loyalty to Lưu Ký. As mentioned earlier in this chapter, the Song court rewarded members of this group with official titles, despite their direct participation in Nùng Trí Cao's insurrection and their ties to Lưu Kỷ. Song support for these local leaders had mixed results. By 1069, Lư Báo and another of Trí Cao's kinsmen, Nùng Trí Hội, had announced their support for the Song court, while Nùng Tông Đán and Lưu Kỷ cast their lot with the Vietnamese court. The greatest change in the balance of relations in this period came with the rise of the young emperor Shenzong, who ushered in a new approach to frontier management in Kaifeng.

On January 8, 1067, Yingzong passed away, and his son Zhao Xu (Shenzong [r. 1067–85]) ascended to the throne. Shenzong emulated the practice of his father by rewarding all well-wishers generously during the first days of his reign. The new emperor appeared to pay special attention to the Vietnamese delegation. When Thăng Long dispatched a mission to greet the new emperor, Shenzong presented the envoys with a lavish array of gifts: a set of official robes for the Lý household, a golden belt, two hundred *liang* of silver ingots, three hundred bolts of silk, two horses, and a saddle inlaid with gold and silver plating.[53] On February 9, 1067, Shenzong decreed that Lý Nhật Tôn should be granted the title "king of the southern pacified region." The young emperor's initial aim appears to have been to reestablish the tributary relationship between the two courts according to terms set at the beginning of the dynasty. At the same time, Chinese frontier officials in the emperor's service were training for military action along the southern edge of the empire.

By late 1067, there was more movement on the Song side of the frontier region. The new Guizhou prefect Zhang Tian (fl. 1068–77) reported to Kaifeng that

> through interviews I have heard that the Quảng Nguyên Châu official Lưu Kỷ maintains ties with Lư Báo, despite the fact that Lưu Kỷ is an official in the service of Lý Nhật Tôn. Lư Báo is a member of Nùng Trí Cao's treacherous faction, still located in Quảng Nguyên Châu. Lưu Kỷ is currently planning to cause mischief of some sort, and Lư Báo now intends to seek personal glory by crossing over into Chinese territory. I want to halt Lư Báo and crush his followers.

The Song court's "bureau of military affairs" (*qumiyuan*) replied to this report with the following:

> Lư Báo is certainly a member of Nùng Trí Cao's treacherous faction. However, any action against Lưu Kỷ cannot be allowed. If commoners choose to cross the frontier [into Song territory], they will be targeted and executed. However, it is not necessary to send military officials to pursue their leaders and the Vietnamese army. The court does not treat prisoners according to the ritual protocol expected of outer barbarians [*waiyi*]. If this Lưu Kỷ chooses to transfer the administration of his prefecture back to China, such action ought to be accepted. Therefore, it is not necessary to attract these people, but instead officials should record the fact that Lưu Kỷ is approaching, and that Quảng Nguyên has no other leader. It is not necessary to launch a defense of our territory until Lưu Kỷ has advanced into Han-controlled territory. If he doesn't, then let the situation settle and the problem will fade.[54]

The Song court chose to follow this policy, suddenly abandoning the balance of power along the frontier that it had always advocated in its tribute relations with the Vietnamese leadership.

By 1069, Lư Báo had instead offered his allegiance to the Song court, while Lưu Kỷ remained in the Quảng Nguyên region, nominally under the control of Thăng Long.[55] In the late summer, the Vietnamese court sent a tribute mission north to maintain good relations with the court at Kaifeng. Shortly thereafter, perhaps to counter Tông Đán's defection, the young Chinese emperor confirmed the Nùng clan's frontier status by conferring on Nùng Trí Hội, now seen by the Chinese as the sole leader of Quảng Nguyên's adjoining settlements of Guwu and Shun'an (Lôi Hỏa), a variation on Tông Đán's former title, "great general and personal guardian general of the right" (*dajiangjun wei youqianniu*).[56] The Chinese leadership hoped to maintain a solid ally in the region, even through this period of rapid change.

In late 1071, local Song officials again apprised the court of shifting allegiances among local leaders. The Guangnan military commissioner reported to Kaifeng that "the Vietnamese official Lưu Kỷ has been sighted at the head of more than two hundred men in the vicinity of Shun'an prefecture. We have not yet determined how many Vietnamese have joined his entourage."[57] Lưu Kỷ's action had been deemed particularly interesting, given his earlier overtures and the recent alliance he had forged with Quảng Nguyên's other influential leader, Nùng Trí Hội. The Song court responded to the military commissioner's memorial: "Recently I have received repeated reports that Quảng Nguyên's barbarian bandits [*manzei*] have been gathering [for unlawful reasons], and there seems to be no end in sight for these occurrences. These disturbances have now unsettled the general populace in the grotto settlements. I'm concerned that the bandits cannot help but to act in a crafty manner."[58] The Song court was well aware of the effect that locally influential leaders still had in a region where Kaifeng now wished to have some say. The only effective strategy appeared to be to manipulate chieftains with significant followings and hope that these individuals would not later switch sides.

Political changes on the Vietnamese side of the frontier caused further changes to the extant network of relations. By the 1060s, Lý rulers had become more comfortable viewing themselves as a dynastic power, with the imperial authority and apparatus of power needed to maintain long-term command over their expanding territory. The second ruler of the dynasty, Lý Phật Mã, had set an important precedent for his followers with his ambitious efforts in territorial expansion and the court's establishment of regional dominance over the leaders of local communities, and his son sought to improve upon his father's reign.

The maintenance of free passage through the frontier region was an important aspect of regional dominance. On November 26, 1068, Lý Nhật Tôn made this declaration at court:

> The military commanders of Guangnan and Jiangnan prefectures always make their presence known along the main route by which we carry memorials to the Song court. Persons traveling this route face difficult obstacles. The high official Nguy Trọng Hòa reports that people taking this route face disruption in many counties and prefectures, including all kinds of fees that they must pay. I have ordered the commander of the Sea-based Second Circuit Prefectural Army to act according to ancient rules of protocol when receiving

persons along this major thoroughfare. However, in the event that this route is disrupted or cut off, we must not show fear but instead launch a vigorous defense of the Việt kingdom.[59]

In that year, Lý Nhật Tôn established new offices for his own government that strengthened the institutional control of his family. Lý dynastic power would remain strong through the end of his reign.

With Lý Nhật Tôn's death on February 2, 1072, a crisis in the imperial household nearly broke down the imperial authority built up by earlier generations. The crown prince Lý Can Đức (Lý Nhân Tông [r. 1072–1127]), son of a commoner consort, Ỷ Lan (1044–1117), was only six years old when he took the throne. The young Vietnamese ruler and his regents, including the "defender in chief" (*thái úy*) Lý Thướng Kiệt, were soon busy consolidating his authority in the face of court opposition from Lý Nhật Tôn's principal wives. Toward this end, the young ruler turned to the frontier for political backing. The court of Can Đức soon announced a general amnesty for all "outlaws" (*tù*) in the "protected prefectures" (*đô hộ phủ*), referring to the frontier region.[60] The anonymous thirteenth-century court chronicle *A Survey of the History of Việt* (Việt sử lược) records that, in gratitude, the local chieftain of Lạng Châu, Dương Cảnh Thông, presented a white deer to the court as tribute followed by numerous officials paying their respects.[61] Can Đức's court ordered that Cảnh Thông be granted the title "grand guardian" (*thái bảo*), after the precedent set by Lý Phật Mã of cementing ties with frontier officials with the use of this ancient Chinese honorific title. By late summer of 1072, Can Đức appears to have felt that his mandate to rule was clear, and he embarked on numerous imperial activities, all of which culminated in the construction of five additions to the imperial palace complex.

Wang Anshi's Economic Activism and the New Vision of Frontier Management

By early 1073, some of the most important changes in the Sino-Vietnamese relationship during the Song period were just beyond the horizon. These changes were influenced by two main factors: first, the increasing self-confidence of the Lý court in the projection of its autonomous regional authority and, second, elements of Song court–sponsored programs of economic activism and military enhancement, urged by the reform-minded official Wang Anshi, that touched on the frontier region. Wang's vision of a single, centrally directed state enterprise for the management of the empire's resources eventually came into conflict with the Vietnamese court's notion that it should manage the frontier as its rulers saw fit. When the Song leadership was no longer content to administer frontier matters from a distance through its vassal representative, conflicts along the frontier quickly escalated into open, armed hostilities.

Wang Anshi had a vision for an economically and militarily revived Song imperial order that could once again make manifest the grand principles of "original intent" proclaimed by the sage-rulers of antiquity.[62] Because, as Peter Bol observes, Wang Anshi maintained that "all things are in principle part of the greater whole," it became necessary for the state to reconcile and ultimately unite the individual interests of various social groups under the court's leadership. As Bol notes, where conservatives such as Sima Guang saw a distortion of underlying principle in the trend toward greater commercialization of Song society, for example, Wang Anshi saw an opportunity to use this trend to combine the energies of public and private interests in a more efficient and constructive manner. Extending the state's reach to the frontier region was an extension of Wang's vision of holistic order to the Song empire and a rationalization of that empire's potential.

In the interim between Nùng Trí Cao's rebellion and these events, the Song court had been forced to reevaluate its traditional frontier policy and chose to administer the area more directly. Recent scholarship has identified the personal political ambitions of the Shenzong emperor as the motivational force behind most changes in frontier management during this period. As Paul Smith writes, "fanned as they were by imperial passion, irredentism and frontier adventure emerged during [Shenzong's] reign as a potent form of political capital that swept a new constellation of men — including general, eunuchs, and hawkish bureaucrats — into power."[63] Vietnamese scholarship for this period has traditionally fixed the blame for territorial expansion in the Sino-

Vietnamese frontier region on Wang Anshi and his immediate supporters. However, the emperor himself had called for a more aggressive frontier policy wherever the Song bordered on lands formerly under Han control. Throughout the 1060s, military officials were dispatched from Kaifeng to the prefectures of southeastern Guangxi to take up positions as local administrators. Imperial troops were transferred to the region, and the number of warhorses increased considerably.[64] During this same period, Shenzong's court closed down the border markets along the Song frontier with the Tangut-led Xi Xia kingdom, and the emperor himself commended a Song general who had led an unprovoked attack on a Xi Xia border town.[65] The emperor's own desire to recover "lost" territory opened the possibility of experimentation with Wang Anshi's policy for strengthened frontier administration.

One aspect of Wang Anshi's 1060s program of "economic activism" affected this general region — the court's extended reach into the frontier area for new sources of revenue and strategically valuable items. As Paul Smith notes in a discussion of the "tea and horse agency" (*duda tiju chama si*) in Sichuan, "by grafting native recruitment onto the strategy of bureaucratic entrepreneurship, reform policymakers decentralized operational and personnel authority to the men who had most to gain from state economic activism and thus acquired for the state unprecedented access to Szechwan's surplus product."[66] Although the Guangnan West circuit region had less to offer the court economically, horses and precious minerals either passed through or were found in close proximity to this area. One of Wang's earliest reform measures in mid-1069 was to grant fiscal intendants in six of the Song's southern circuits the right to disregard local quotas on tribute items and instead to fill government orders by buying and selling these items according to prices on the open market.[67] Under Wang Anshi's New Policies reforms, Song officials paid greater attention to seeking out loyal supporters of the empire who could assist with the systematic extraction of these resources.

Wang Anshi's policies did not proceed uncontested at court, and this news spread beyond the frontier. Chinese officials also heard that Lý Thường Kiệt had argued publicly in Thăng Long that Wang Anshi, in his plans to expand the training of militias into the frontier region, had already demonstrated the Song court's desire to take control of the frontier and ignore the precedent of tributary responsibilities. Wang had recently sent a memorial to the emperor Shenzong, calling for action by Song imperial troops.[68] For these reasons, Chinese officials announced that the Vietnamese court was once again in danger of losing legitimacy. Cross-frontier tensions had reached a breaking point, and any single event could spark a violent reaction.

In 1075, the Quảng Nguyên chieftain Lưu Ký unexpectedly launched an attack on Yongzhou. Nùng Trí Hội, then administering Guihua prefecture (or Wuyang grotto settlement), was able to ward off the attackers.[69] As a result of this attack, or perhaps to preempt future disturbance, emperor Shenzong issued an edict that the members of the native "Five Clans" (Wu Xingfan) of northern Guangnan should present tribute to the court every five years.[70] In 1073, a group from these communities had made a large tributary offering to the Chinese court, and thereafter missions had continued on an erratic schedule. The Song emperor likely desired to standardize relations with these communities without alienating them, given the defection of other groups across the frontier in this period. The *Official History of the Song Dynasty* estimates that the Five Clans amounted to a sizable population, because they were able to muster a delegation of 890 for their 1073 tribute mission.[71] The Chinese emperor would need a large number of local allies if he were to mount a successful attack in the region.

Given the changing conditions and shifting alliances along the frontier, by 1075, relations between Song and Đại Việt authorities had soured considerably. The Chinese court's interest in further militarizing the frontier region north of the Nùng clan's home region was a local indication of the deteriorating relationship. In the spring of 1075, Shenzong sent two officials, Hanlin Academy member and director in the "ministry of justice" (*xingbu langzhong*) Shen Qi (1017–1088) and former prefect of Qianzhou (today located in southern Jiangxi) Liu Yi (1017–1086), to take up the administration of Guizhou, at the site of modern-day Guilin.[72] Shen and Liu were instructed by the court to train the local militia in techniques of riverine warfare. Moreover, the Song court ordered the local people to cease all trade with subjects of the Đại Việt court, further isolating communities that lay on the northern and southern edges of the frontier.

The Vietnamese court was well aware of these activities, and it prepared a response. As is well known to Vietnamese readers, Lý Thướng Kiệt had anticipated an attack from the north, and he chose what later Vietnamese historians would call an "attack in self-defense." He divided his army into two groups. The objective of the first unit, under the control of his new frontier ally Tông Đán and with a strong contingent of upland inhabitants, was to invade Guangxi in order to attract Song troops stationed at Yongzhou south into the frontier region.[73] At the same time, the principal army, under the command of Lý Thướng Kiệt himself, would deploy along the South China coast to occupy those places that would then be left defenseless.

In the autumn of 1075, Tông Đán took control of the Guwan, Taiping, Yongping, and Qianlong garrisons.[74] These four garrisons, along with the Hengshan garrison, had been established under the direction of Di Qing in the aftermath of Nùng Trí Cao's last rebellion, and they protected the strategically important aboriginal settlements along the eastern portion of the Sino-Vietnamese frontier. While Tông Đán's forces

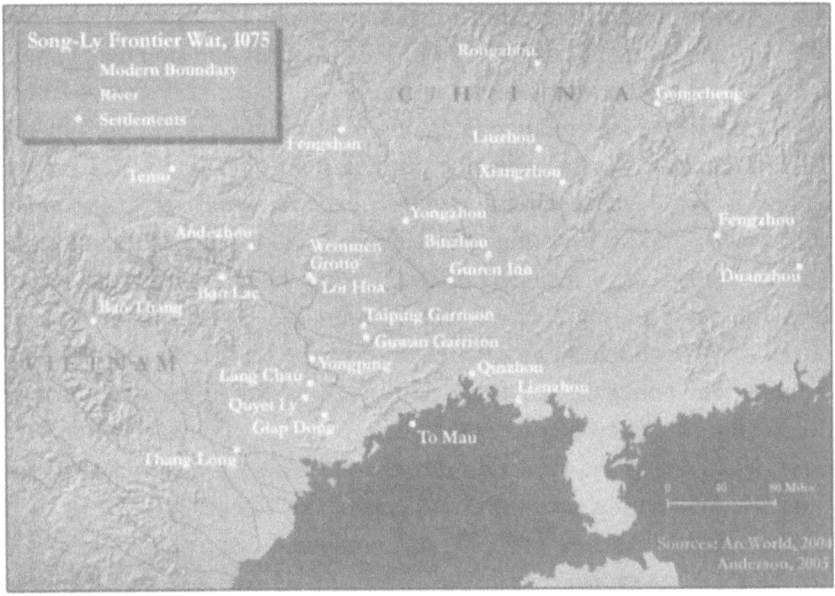

Map 5. The 1075 Song-Lý Frontier War (Elizabeth Nelson)

were advancing, the fleet of Lý Thường Kiệt seized the two prefectures of Qinzhou and Lianzhou and then moved farther into Song territory.⁷⁵ To alleviate fear and to keep local Song subjects off his rearguard, Thường Kiệt proclaimed that he came only to apprehend a rebel (Lưu Kỷ perhaps?) who had taken refuge in China and whom the Chinese prefect had refused to repatriate. Thường Kiệt also was presented as a liberator of the Chinese people, who had been impoverished and oppressed by Wang Anshi's reforms.⁷⁶

Lý Thường Kiệt arrived with Tông Đán at Yongzhou in the early spring of 1076 and devastated a local Song militia force under the leadership of Zhang Shoujie, the "governor-general" (*dudu*) of Guangnan West circuit. Zhang himself was beheaded in the fighting at the Kunlun Pass.⁷⁷ After forty-two days of intense resistance, and at the end of their resources, the defenders of Yongzhou succumbed under a furious attack. Thousands died in the fighting. The city fortress was completely razed, and its commander, Su Jian, killed his entire family and committed suicide by refusing to leave the blazing building.⁷⁸ A large unit of the Song army soon approached, and the Lý forces withdrew, along with an enormous amount of spoils and thousands of prisoners.⁷⁹

Shortly before launching the Song attack, Lý Thường Kiệt had also led a successful campaign in 1069 against the southern Cham kingdom. Therefore, the Song court called on Cham and Khmer forces to join the Chinese in retaliating against Vietnamese aggression.⁸⁰ In late 1076, combined forces under the command of Guo Kui (1022–1088), acting as the "Annan circuit punitive expedition officer" (*Annandao zhaotaoshi*), and his assisting officer Zhao Di launched a counterattack.⁸¹ The combined army included more than one hundred thousand men.⁸² One hundred mounted cavalrymen under the command of Tao Bi (1015–1078) entered the frontier by way of the Left River region.⁸³ The frontier was penetrated at three points. The Song force quickly took possession of Quảng Nguyên prefecture, crushing resistance among the Đại Việt loyalists and capturing the region's leader, the aforementioned Lưu Kỷ, and setting fire to the settlement's dwellings.⁸⁴

By the beginning of 1077, the combined Song land forces had crushed Lý resistance from Cơ Lang and Quyết Lý, and Chinese forces were rapidly approaching Thăng Long. The Song armies met on the northern bank of the Như Nguyệt (or Cầu) River, also known in Chinese sources as the Fuliang River, in modern Bắc Ninh province.[85] Lý Thường Kiệt regarded the defense of this river to be absolutely crucial to the Vietnamese cause, not only because it provided the last possible opportunity to protect the delta region in which the capital was located, but also because this region contained the home village of the dynasty's founder as well as the tombs of former rulers alongside the Thiên Đức River.[86] Lý Thường Kiệt had ordered his men to build a wide earthen rampart on the river's southern bank, protected by several lines constructed from piles of bamboo. Most of his fleet crossed at the mouth of the Bạch Đằng River in order to prevent the Chinese fleet from joining its supporting infantry units.[87]

Nevertheless, the Song front line was able to cross the river, and its cavalry riders soon were no more than several miles from Thăng Long. In an effort to encourage the counterattack, Lý Thường Kiệt ordered one of his officers to hide in the temple of the god of the river, Trương Hát, and to recite the following stanza, known to Vietnamese schoolchildren worldwide:

> Over the peaks and rivers of the South reigns our emperor.
> Such is the destiny fixed forever on the Celestial Book.
> How dare the Barbarians invade our land?
> Their foolish audacity will witness their bloody rout![88]

As legend has it, Thường Kiệt's troops were so inspired by this stirring verse that they held their ground and beat back the first wave of Song attackers. The Chinese tried again to cross the river and were again pushed back, sustaining one thousand casualties.[89] Meanwhile, Vietnamese defenders held back the invading naval fleet at the coast and so prevented it from providing the support necessary to continue the attack. The Song foray into Vietnamese territory came to a standstill.

The two opposing forces faced each other on the banks of the river. Song forces bombarded Lý positions and supporting junks. When Lý Thường Kiệt tried to take the offensive, he suffered a significant defeat at the Kháo Túc River, and two Lý princes perished.[90] However, logistical problems, the tropical climate, and disease had decimated the Song army, which had lost more than half of its effectiveness. On the other side of the conflict, the Vietnamese court feared that a prolonged war would not produce any positive result. At this point, Lý Thưởng Kiệt made peace overtures. The Song agreed to withdraw its troops but retained control of five disputed regions of Quảng Nguyên (then renamed Shun'an Zhou) — Tư Lang Châu, Môn Châu, Tô Mậu Châu, and Quang Lang — which comprised a major part of the modern Vietnamese provinces of Cao Bằng and Lạng Sơn. Guo Kui, the leader of the Chinese assault, had left Shun'an Zhou under the administration of his cavalry commander Tao Bi.[91] Chinese sources note that the Vietnamese had seized a section of Song territory along the frontier as well. The war lasted fifteen months. When the dust settled, the Đại Việt armies had managed once again to hold off a well-equipped Song military force.

Border Negotiations and Demarcation

In the aftermath of open hostilities, the two courts conducted talks to negotiate a fixed border between the Đại Việt kingdom and the Song empire. These talks and the establishment of a fixed border marked a diplomatic watershed in Middle Period Sino-Vietnamese relations. The Chinese leadership had by this point recognized the futility of any effort to wrest control of the southern frontier region away from the Vietnamese. The only reliable way of maintaining influence in the region was to entice the Vietnamese leadership with elevated titles and grander imperial pronouncements while refusing to break ties with maritime tributary kingdoms that had become trade competitors of the Vietnamese.

After a long period of strained silence between the two courts, Thăng Long agreed in 1082 to give back to Kaifeng the captured prefectures of Lianzhou, Qinzhou, and Yongzhou along with their inhabitants and prisoners of war. In return, Chinese authorities relinquished four prefectures and one county seized from the Vietnamese court, including Nùng Trí Cao's birthplace and the Nùng clan home base Quảng Nguyên.[92] To some observers, this trade strongly favored Vietnamese long-term interests. In the aftermath, a poem circulated throughout the Song empire, one line of which read "Because we had a craving for Giao Chỉ elephants, we gave up Quảng Nguyên gold" (Pin Jiaozhi xiang, que shi Guangyuan jin).[93] The Song court's desire to reestablish its tributary relationship with the Lý outweighed the potential material gains to be found in retaining this mineral-rich territory.

This resolution of the border dispute did not come without a few vengeful acts by both courts. In the late spring of 1079, Song authorities in Guangnan captured and beheaded Nùng Trí Xuân and took his wife and children as hostages.[94] In 1083, under the pretense of pursuing Nùng Trí Hội, Vietnamese troops attacked his home prefecture of Guihua. The *Official History of the Song Dynasty* reports that when Trí Hội approached the military commissioner Xiong Ben (1026–1091) to plead for fresh troops to fight off the Vietnamese, Xiong instead had the chieftain brought into custody for questioning. Lý Can Đức then assembled the troops to "thank" Xiong Ben and to request the return of "the eight động," that is, the six counties of Bảo Lạc and the two aboriginal settlements of Susang.

The two courts soon recognized that the time had come to resolve their differences regarding sovereignty over the border regions of Quảng Nguyên and Guihua. In 1084, the Vietnamese court sent the "director of military personnel" (*binh bộ thị lang*) Lê Văn Thịnh (fl. 1075–96) to negotiate the border issue with the Chinese. Xiong Ben sent the Left River region's military inspector, who was also a Wang Anshi supporter, Cheng Zhuo to argue the Song's case. In the vicinity of the Left River, surveying delegations from both courts inspected the area separately and then convened at the Song-held Yongping garrison in southernmost Guangnan.[95]

Negotiations proceeded from July 6 to August 8, 1084. The Vietnamese delegation spoke of designating the Quảng Nguyên and Guihua prefectures as two sides of a "fixed border" (*qiangjie*) region between the two states. The *History of the Great Viet* (Đại Việt sử ký) contains these comments about the Vietnamese negotiator: "Lê Van Thịnh should be regarded as a good official. He was someone who got along with others. He did not seek to vex [his Chinese counterparts] or cause trouble, and so he was able to change the attitude of the Song emperor. As for the six counties that Đại Việt troops had invaded, the resources of this territory had not yet been utilized by anyone. The leader of the Vietnamese delegation chose a negotiation strategy that avoided the ill will that might have emerged from China's defeat at the hands of Vietnamese troops."[96]

Lê Van Thình also proved to be a tough negotiator, and the Chinese officials present found it very difficult to challenge his points.[97] When the Song emperor heard of the Vietnamese court's proposal, he ordered his officials to look into Lê Van Thình's reasons for wanting to retain control of Quảng Nguyên. He then offered Lê Van Thình the lavish gift of an ornamental belt, a robe, and five hundred bolts of thick silk. By the end of the negotiations, however, Lê Van Thình had retained control for the Vietnamese court of the area beyond the Eight Passes (Bát Ải), that is, Bảo Lạc and Susang. With the successful conclusion of the negotiations, the official Song history compilers noted, "the South's turmoil was thus quelled."[98]

The Song court quickly placed the overtures for negotiations in the context of tributary protocol. Concerning the prefectures and counties seized by Song troops, the Chinese emperor issued the following edict:

> You, my nobleman, as the administrator of the southern kingdom of Giao Chi [Nanjiao], have for generations maintained hegemony over this region. However, you have now lapsed in virtue by disobeying my orders and by robbing the frontier towns. You have cast aside the notions of paying heed to your ancestors and to assumptions of loyalty and obedience. And you have added annoyance for this court by launching your attack. Your troops have advanced deep into Song territory, and they are on the verge of heading home only after becoming exhausted. The signs of their crimes are many, and there is no need to list more of your transgressions. Now you are sending envoys to reestablish tribute relations. I have examined your messages and opinions. Clearly, you have repented. I am in charge of a myriad of kingdoms, and I do not distinguish between those kingdoms close at hand and those far away. However, I see that the people of Yongzhou and Qinzhou, displaced by fire and theft, long ago lost their native lands. I will wait until I have sent these people back to their border region before I give Quảng Nguyên and the other lands back to Giao Châu.[99]

The *Official History of the Song Dynasty* has this comment regarding the territory considered during the negotiations:

> Shunzhou [or Quảng Nguyên] is located in the extreme southern region, and this region was used to defend [the Song empire's] frontier. Due to the dense fog and pestilent conditions, many of the region's inhabitants died of illness. Tao Bi actually died while posted here. The court knew that this area was of no use, so the Chinese negotiator returned a total of four prefectures and one county. However, Quảng Nguyên was formerly attached to the Yongzhou administration region as a loose-reins aboriginal district. It originally did not belong to Giao Chỉ.[100]

Although all Song rulers through the period described above had allowed Vietnamese leaders to regulate frontier affairs in this region, the thirteenth-century Yuan period compilers of the *Official History of the Song Dynasty* had already altered this perception to claim a precedent for direct control of this territory by Chinese authorities.

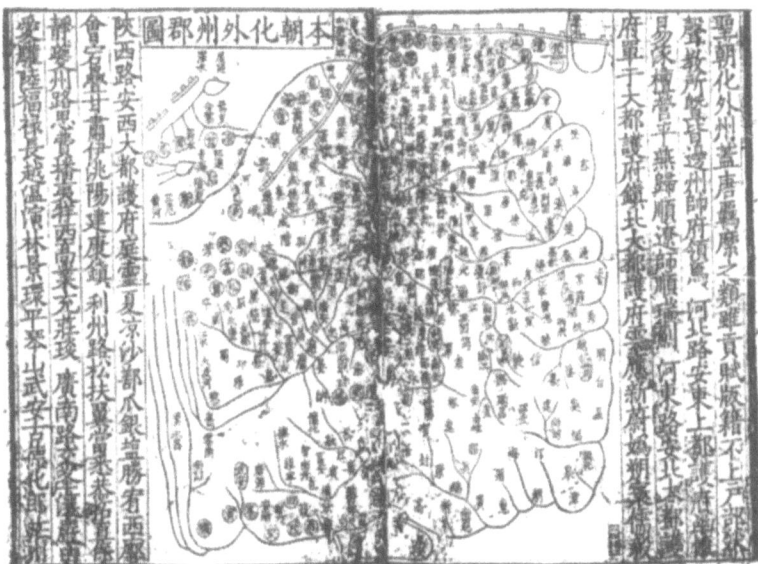

Figure 6.1. An Illustration of Prefectures and Commandaries Beyond the Influence of Our Dynasty (Shanghai Guji Pub., 1989)

By the end of the Northern Song in 1126, rulers in Kaifeng understood that the Đại Việt region occupied a place one step further removed from the influence of the Chinese central court. According to *An Illustration of Prefectures and Commanderies beyond the Influence of Our Dynasty* (Benchao huawai zhoujun tu), the region labeled "An Nam" is clearly outside the Song empire, and the prefectures captured during the borderlands war but later returned to the Đại Việt kingdom had achieved the status of the well-known Sixteen Prefectures that had once been lost to the Liao.[101] According to the legend on the Ming edition of this map, the "lost" southern prefectures include Ái, Bình, Cầm, Cảnh, Điền, Diễn, Giao, Hoan, Hoàn, Lâm, Lục, Nghiêm, Nhương, Ôn, Phong, Phúc Lộc, Sơn, Trướng, Việt, and Vũ An. However, the home region of Nùng Trí Cao, Quảng Nguyên, was placed back within Song territory.[102]

Conclusion

Historians certainly have not been in total agreement when describing the state of affairs along the frontier in the aftermath of Nùng Trí Cao's rebellion. The clearest discernible school of scholarship may be found among modern Vietnamese historians, who argue that the frontier communities rallied in support of the Lý leadership's nation-building efforts. Much of this scholarship begins with the assumption that the Sino-Vietnamese frontier region had remained vaguely defined with the advent of the Đại Việt kingdom and its recognition by China.[103] Such a statement depends heavily on very modern notions of political boundaries and the rights and responsibilities of nation-states, which maintain these boundaries. Nevertheless, a premodern frontier can lack a clearly delineated physical demarcation and still be divided into unambiguously understood spheres of administration. In the case of the Sino-Vietnamese frontier before Nùng Trí Cao's revolt, the Song court, through the precepts of tributary protocol, expected the Vietnamese court to manage affairs in this region in the Chinese court's name. When disturbances arose, the Chinese leadership turned to Vietnamese authorities for rectification.

However, the Nùng Trí Cao rebellion and its aftermath changed everything. The Chinese court's response to regional tensions also reflected Kaifeng's increased interest in the resources of the Guangnan region. The Song court, facing frontier opposition in both the northern and southern regions of the young empire, implemented new policies that emphasized stricter definition and regulation of its internal territory.[104] Even changes in the content of *jinshi* examination questions reflected this shift toward a more aggressive borderlands policy.[105] For its own part, the Vietnamese court viewed Nùng Trí Cao's insurgence as an interruption in the orderly conduct of tribute relations. The Vietnamese court also viewed the rebellion as an obstacle standing in the way of the court's expansion into the northern frontier. Suppressing the rebellion, however, led to a curtailing of this expansionist policy.

In his summary of changes to frontier policy in the late Northern Song, Okada Koji has argued that between 1068 and Song Huizong's Chongning reign period (1102–6), the Song court attempted to pursue a more assertive frontier policy through border negotiations with the Lý court, abandoning the *jimi* prefecture system and opening up *jimi* territories for economic development, but, he asserts, the new policy ultimately failed.[106] Okada attributes the failure to two factors. First, abandoning the existing *jimi* system necessarily involved the establishment of a formal administrative arrangement that included posting officials to these outlying areas. Funding such new positions put a greater strain on court resources at a time when Kaifeng could not afford the extra financial burden.[107] Second, for purposes of taxation, the Song court treated Han settlers and non-Han frontier inhabitants outside *jimi* administrative regions in a similar manner. These non-Han communities were soon expected to shoulder the greater tax burden that resulted from the construction of new fortification and road systems along the frontier. For this reason, the Tai-speaking residents of the frontier protested violently when large groups of Han settlers began to flood into the region.[108] By the beginning of the twelfth century, the court suspended this policy and reinstituted *jimi* administration.

To the south of these *jimi* areas, the Vietnamese leadership also changed its frontier policy and adopted a less territorially aggressive approach. Thăng Long's northern expansion was reversed after the

1075 conflict, which altered the Vietnamese court's direct control over local communities as well. The *Official History of the Song Dynasty* notes that soon after the frontier war, in 1082, Lý Nhân Tông agreed to return the three captured Song prefectures Lianzhou, Qinzhou, and Yongzhou, along with one thousand prisoners of war; he also sent a group of 221 people to the Song court. Men over the age of fifteen all bore the aforementioned tattoo reading "Army of the Son of Heaven," and men over twenty bore the mark "conscripts of the Southern Court" (*tou Nanchao*). Women bore the tattoo "official guests" (*guanke*) on their left hands.[109] While the Vietnamese court had earlier marked this population as servants in the Lý cause of expansion, turning them over to Chinese authorities as a gesture of goodwill was also a sign that these frontier communities were no longer of such great importance by the 1080s. The successful conclusion of border negotiations marked more than a provisional resolution of differences between the three parties along the frontier. Chinese imperial might no longer served as a strong deterrent in the face of the Vietnamese court's expansion of regional power, and the Song could hardly control the refashioning of the Lý in the image of the Chinese imperial model. The Chinese remained the stronger of the two parties, and Vietnamese leaders carefully maintained their tributary ties with the Song court out of the conviction that this system was, in the final analysis, the best option available. As soon as clear boundaries were drawn, major military tensions quickly subsided. Trade issues, and not border conflict, defined Sino-Vietnamese exchanges by the late eleventh century. The bonds of the tribute system remained strong, but both sides regarded the material benefits of close ties to be more important than the quest to iron out political differences. Lý leaders, for their part, turned inward for the expansion and elaboration of their own empire, and Chinese leaders had more than enough to occupy their attention along the northern frontier.

In the aftermath of the 1075 borderlands war, the territorial concessions granted at the bargaining table remained unchanged, while trade in the area continued to develop. During the reign of Song Zhezong, from 1086 to 1100, the emperor refused to consider a Vietnamese request for the Wu-e and Wuyang aboriginal settlements from the frontier region. During the reign of Song Huizong, from 1101 to 1125,

Tempting "Treacherous Factions" 151

Vietnamese tributary officials came to the capital asking to be allowed to trade for book materials. Although there was some court opposition, the emperor ordered that their request be respected and that they be allowed to purchase all books except for banned books, divination texts, Daoist texts, calendar guides, numerological texts, military treatises, officer manuals, current administrative manuals, books on frontier installations, and geographical texts.[110] By 1118, the Chinese emperor had announced that because the people of Vietnam had not caused any disturbances since 1085, he would permit a specified relaxation on prohibitions against borderlands trade.[111] So began a new period in Sino-Vietnamese relations.

7

Monumental Pride: Sino-Vietnamese Cross-Border Commemorations of Nùng Trí Cao

Nowhere else is Nùng Trí Cao more revered than in his own home region within the Tai-speaking communities along the modern border between China's Guangxi Autonomous Region and Vietnam's Cao Bằng province. Many families with the Nùng surname still reside in the border region, and most consider themselves to be direct descendants of Nùng Trí Cao, his father Nùng Tồn Phúc, and his mother A Nùng. Moreover, there exist many public displays of regional pride in the Nùng leaders' accomplishments in the form of temples and locally sponsored monuments. However, the tale of Trí Cao's public commemoration among Zhuang communities of southern Guangxi has differed dramatically from the history of such activities conducted across the border in northernmost Vietnam.

Sites of veneration for Nùng Trí Cao are not evenly distributed across the Sino-Vietnamese border region. Northern Vietnam, on the one hand, supports numerous sites that celebrate the deeds of Nùng Trí Cao. In the province of Cao Bằng, annual festivals have long been observed to honor Trí Cao and his parents. Moreover, at least three temples still exist in Vietnam for the specific worship of these figures. On the other hand, there is little physical evidence from any premodern period to mark the existence of temples sites dedicated to

Trí Cao in South China. In fact, most relevant Chinese sources describe only stelae and temples that honor the names of the Song generals who crushed Trí Cao's bid for independence.[1] So the question is, why does Vietnam have a number of temples devoted to Nùng Trí Cao, in addition to an active worship community, while southern China has few such sites or communities?

In this book, I explore the effect of Nùng Trí Cao's rebellion on Sino-Vietnamese relations in the mid-eleventh century. In the course of my study, I was prompted to give more thought to another question, namely, where does the figure of ancient "local hero turned local deity" fit in today's cross-border community affiliations in the Guangxi–Cao Bằng region? When this once remote and largely ignored region gained importance as a "local place" within the larger scheme of twentieth-century nationalism (occurring earliest in China), Nùng Trí Cao, the historical personage, was inserted into two, often mutually exclusive narratives (Chinese and Vietnamese) of proto-nationalism and anti-imperialism. As such, Trí Cao was grandfathered in by both sides with all the rights and obligations of a modern citizen of the two nation-states. Only recently have these nationalist narratives been challenged by renewed cross-border contact between professed descendants of Nùng Trí Cao and groups wishing to revive pride in Trí Cao's local, not nationwide, achievements.

This last chapter undertakes a brief exploration of the historical implications for this cross-border difference in public commemorations of Nùng Trí Cao from the Imperial period through the modern age. These commemorations have been closely linked to differing Chinese and Vietnamese policies of frontier and, later, border management as well as differing local responses from communities living on the Vietnamese and Chinese sides of the border. Of course, the topic of this chapter extends well beyond the book's historical focus on the Nùng Trí Cao Rebellion and its effects felt in the 1075–77 Song–Đại Việt border conflict, and so I do not draw a direct correlation between Nùng Trí Cao's act of rebellion and the political attitudes of his modern descendants. Instead, I examine how an event such as the deification and worship of a regionally revered ancestral hero has shaped local identity among communities that reach across a modern political divide. The modern cult of Nùng Trí Cao appears to be a particularly apt focus for such an examination.

One factor that has played an important role in shaping local identity in the Sino-Vietnamese border region is regionalism, in the sense that Diana Lary uses "political regionalism" in her study of Guangxi local politics in the early twentieth century. A precarious balance of local loyalties and loyalties professed to distant central authorities certainly existed the closer one traveled to the heart of the Sino-Vietnamese frontier region. Moreover, as Lary notes, "Regionalism responds to situations; the external situation decides which form is called for, not the regionalism itself. From a system of layered loyalties is selected the one which fits the situation best."[2] Through the many centuries, during which the Chinese and Vietnamese courts were not strong enough to control their common frontier directly, "regional" loyalties and identities could be defined on a clan-to-clan or village-to-village basis. However, when court authorities from Thăng Long or Beijing garnered enough economic and military power, local loyalties were expected to include the lowland political centers manned by local Han and Kinh officials as well as the upland home regions. Finally, when the nation-states were at the height of their strength, regional loyalties were to be subordinated to national unity.

To complicate this unambiguous theoretical vision of local events, we must consider that frontier communities globally have often remained on the outside of centrally dictated national trends, benefiting less from changes effected at the center and therefore less enthusiastic about enacting them. The two sides of the Sino-Vietnamese frontier often had more in common with each other than with the distant metropolises from which their leaders ruled. Moreover, although Sino-Vietnamese court relations were structured by the protocol of the Chinese tribute system, the two courts conducted relations with communities on their mutual frontier very differently. Therefore, we turn first to a comparison of these historical differences and how they affected the emergence of a cult of Nùng Trí Cao in the region.

The Tale North of the Border

As mentioned in chapter 1, the Chinese frontier policy served the "centering" function of the traditional tributary system. Nùng Trí Cao's resistance to this order in the mid-eleventh century tipped the balance of power by turning state attention back to the periphery. Therefore, once the Chinese military had forcibly subdued Nùng Trí Cao and threatened his followers, the court made a great effort to restore peace by replacing symbols of local resistance with more acceptable, redefined commemorations of loyal acts by capable servants of the court. In 1053, almost as soon as the dust had settled from Di Qing's efforts to suppress Nùng Trí Cao's revolt, the Song general had a large stela erected on the left side of the face of Zhennan Peak, which is located near modern-day Guilin. The "suppressing the Man barbarian" (*pingman*) stela eulogized the Song general's pacification of Nùng Trí Cao and listed the "barbarian bandit" (*manzei*) Trí Cao's "crimes" and the martyred Chinese officials who died in the attempt to capture him.[3] The stela also left no doubt as to the court-centered rather than locally defined perspective that the Song court expected local residents of the frontier region to adopt regarding the recent disturbances. This official version of events would not change during the Imperial period.

The cult of Nùng Trí Cao could have begun in the period between the eleventh and the thirteenth century, which witnessed a surge of activity related to popular religion in the region. If so, the Nùng Trí Cao cult would have remained closely tied to regional and lineage identification at a time when many local cults throughout southern China (and northern Vietnam) were increasingly "interregional" through growing social mobility and additional long-distance trade contacts.[4] However, regarding physical signs of worship activity, there is little evidence from any premodern period of temples sites dedicated to Trí Cao in South China.

In general, premodern Chinese references to material sites associated with the commemoration of Nùng Trí Cao focus on the deeds of his attackers. In a Southern Song period unofficial history, the author Wang Cheng (fl. early twelfth century) refers to a temple erected by the local residents of Fengzhou to commemorate the deeds of the locally appointed official Cao Jin, who died in the early stages of Trí Cao's third rebellion.[5] The early-nineteenth-century Qing *Guangxi Gazetteer* (Guangxi tongzhi) notes that at the Kunlun Pass located to the northwest of Yongzhou, there is a gazebo and a plaque commemorating Di Qing's defeat of Nùng's forces.[6] The gazetteer also notes that local people raised a temple at the site, on which the Great Left-Hand Guardian General (Dazuo Weijiangjun), likely Di Qing's supporter Wang Sui, successfully quelled a Man revolt, which is probably a reference to Nùng Trí Cao's rebellion.[7] In another early Qing account by the well-known Han scholar and anti-Manchu activist Gu Yanwu (1613–1682), there is a reference to a Yang Guang Temple (Yangguang Tang) erected on the site at which the military aide to Di Qing (mistakenly recorded as Qiu Qing), Yang Wenguang, finally caught up with Nùng Trí Cao and his rebel army. Gu notes that local people erected the temple on this site to commemorate the event. Later in the same entry, he mentions that the Nùng clan was at that time the most powerful family in the region, followed by the Sha clan.[8] Both of these incidents imply that the local population felt gratitude for these outside military interventions and so raised the monuments to express its thanks.

There is additional evidence that the community commemoration of Nùng Trí Cao was once more common. In 1956, in modern-day Tiandeng county, local authorities produced a rubbing of a stela raised in 1706 to commemorate the construction of the Zhongxiu Dujunshen Temple (Zhongxiu Dujunshen Miao), which was located at that time in Dujun Village (Dujuncun). The stela describes how the His Highness Nùng the Great Spirit (Nong Dalingshen Dianxia) made a name for himself as the lord of the region, first by valiantly commanding his troops and then by becoming a strong *ling*-spirit to protect the Guangxi region.[9] The patrons of this temple were many, and they came predominantly from the Huang, Lin, and Zhao clans. Of these three surname-groups, the Zhao clan provided the greatest numbers of donors. Given that most Nùng clan members were forced to take the Zhao surname after the defeat of Nùng Trí Cao and his followers, it is not surprising to find so many Zhao among this temple's eighteenth-century patrons.

The lack of textual references to sites of worship for Nùng Trí Cao in the South China region could, of course, be due to a lack of interest among local literati to make note of such sites. However, the explicit mention of these other, officially sanctioned commemorations does express the court's desire to shape impressions of Nùng Trí Cao and his revolt among local communities. In Chinese official circles, the Nùng clan did not fare well until the late twentieth century. This lack of specific references in Chinese sources stands in stark contrast to the accumulation of specific illustrations found in imperial period Vietnamese sources.

After the Qing empire fell, the new Nationalist administration had numerous political challenges to face, and ethnic divisions were initially downplayed or ameliorated by conciliatory measures. Earlier Manchu policies had ignored the varied regional and ethnic character of China's border region and aggravated inter-ethnic tensions to the point that local leaders either rebelled or joined in calls for greater autonomy. Moreover, as Pamela Crossley notes, Qing imperial characterizations of certain subject constituencies and the court's unwillingness to subdivide these ethnic groups further into less easily disguisable parts informed the creation of "minority nationalists" in the early Republican period.[10] The post-1911 Chinese nation was nominally a "Republic of Five Nationalities," encompassing the Han, Hui, Manchu, Mongolian, and Tibetan peoples. During Chiang Kai-shek's (Jiang Jieshi [1887–1975]) Nanjing Decade (1927–37), the government pursued a de facto assimilationist policy in the attempt to consolidate the nation under Han leadership.[11]

Focusing on the overwhelming Han majority was an integral aspect of early Chinese nationalism. As Dru Gladney notes, "By drawing together the collective imagination of one Han people, the Nationalists thought they could prevent the total dismemberment of the Chinese state."[12] In fact, local leaders of other groups such as the Hui and other Chinese Muslims gradually felt less liberated from the bonds of Manchu servitude and therefore less beholden to the central government. Instead, after 1916, these leaders often sought to pursue power as independent warlords within the fragmenting Chinese state. The Communists benefited from this ethnic unrest in their own mobilization efforts during the civil war and pursued a more organized and comprehensive effort to win the political cooperation of China's ethnic groups, now "national minorities," in the post-1949 era.

Local activities among Zhuang frontier communities did not attract much attention from Chinese authorities in the early Republican period, given the greater economic prosperity and political influence of the coastal metropolitan areas. Diana Lary notes that French colonial authorities remarked on Guangxi's extreme levels of poverty and lawlessness when comparing this region with the French protectorate of Tonkin to the south.[13] The region's situation had dramatically deteriorated in the aftermath of the Taiping Rebellion (1851–64), leaving the region desperately poor and peppered with bandit groups. Even by the beginning of the twentieth century, the existing infrastructure of the Guangxi region was shattered. By the time of the Communist takeover and the founding of the People's Republic of China fifty years later, improvements to Guangxi's roads and railway routes had occurred almost exclusively in Han-dominated areas in eastern Guangxi. By 1949, more than 2,173 miles of roads had been built in the region, but scores of villages in western Guangxi still remained out of reach.[14] Communication systems such as the postal service were understaffed and underfunded for such a large region, and the inadequacy of these systems contributed to the area's overall fragmentation.

In this period, "regionalism" in western Guangxi, where Nùng Trí Cao's descendants could be found, was limited to local grassroots loyalties. There was very little social cohesion among the communities of this region, which the central government would later label as Zhuang. Villages were organized largely by lineages or by *zhixi* (branches), and these regional loyalties were much stronger than any more general sense of ethnic unity through the province. Today, *zhixi* are not officially acknowledged in Guangxi, but they are still recognized in Yunnan, where they are divided into three main clans — the Nong, the Sha, and the Tu.[15] The Nong and the Sha, as noted earlier, have a long history of association in Nùng Trí Cao's home region. In general, Guangxi was not as aggressive in its interaction with state authorities during the Republican period.[16] The central government therefore paid much less attention to this region than to the regions of Mongolia and Tibet, for example. Local loyalties were largely left undisturbed through the early 1950s.

After the founding of the People's Republic of China in 1949, Chinese Communist party leaders, while drawing up plans for the socialist reconstruction of China, worked out a strategy for bringing the non-Han populations of the country into the socialist fold. As Stevan Harrell notes, "Communist doctrine resisted both the empire model, in which ethnic groups were legally unequal, and the nation-state model, in which equality was based on the real or promised erasure of ethnic distinctions."[17] Party leaders then sought a third way by which to identify the numerous non-Han peoples present throughout the territory controlled by Beijing and to locate a sufficiently independent place in the new political order for these groups that would ensure their loyalty to the State.

Throughout the 1950s, such efforts were made throughout China with numerous ethnic groups. Eventually, although more than four hundred petitions were filed for special recognition, fifty-five separate ethnic-minority groups were identified and acknowledged.[18] The government also continued the trend toward establishing distinct autonomous regions for the largest of these groups, although "autonomy" explicitly excluded the option of political secession. Moreover, the new national minorities policy also demanded that all new ethnicities be encouraged to develop economically and culturally in line with the nation's "universal progress" toward Socialism.[19] Such encouragement necessarily involved government intervention, coercive or not, at certain periods and in certain political climates.

Katherine Kaup, in her study of the Zhuang in modern China, describes several stages of identification and local reorganization and indoctrination that the Chinese Communist Party employed. Kaup terms the first stage "Central Administrative Consolidation," which lasted from the founding of the People's Republic of China in 1949 until the beginning of the Cultural Revolution in 1966. This first stage involved recognizing a Greater Zhuang ethnicity, choosing and organizing an indigenous corps of Zhuang party cadres to assist with the implementation of party policy in local areas, and motivating the local populace to see their own stake in working with the Han majority toward the success of a socialist China.²⁰ Kaup designates September 1952 as the point at which the central government decided to recognize the ethnic uniqueness of the Zhuang and grant them special political status, in effect, creating them as a distinct national minority in China. The Guangxi Zhuang Autonomous Region was established during this stage.

In Guangxi, this was also the time when serious scholarly effort was devoted to producing a local history of the Zhuang people that would complement the Marxist framework of historiography then being applied to Chinese historical research in general. The government drew attention to public events, such as the springtime courtship and song festival Sanyuesan, which served as a party-approved expression of ethnic unity among members of this newly unified ethnic group. By the 1980s, this festival had become pan-ethnic in nature and served more to showcase ethnic diversity for tourists rather than to reinforce ethnic solidarity among the Zhuang.²¹

The major political upheavals of post-1949 China had some effect on the country's non-Han populations, but the impact varied by region. In Xinjiang, efforts in 1962 to form collective communes met with intense resistance from the region's Uighur communities, causing as many as eighty thousand Uighurs and others to flee across the border into the neighboring Soviet Union.²² While the Cultural Revolution (1966–76) slowed further political change throughout China, the outright persecution of the Zhuang, for example, was not as pronounced as the political violence directed against other non-Han ethnic groups in China. The greatest effect this period had on the region was the influx of "sent down" (*xia fang*) youth and intellectuals who came to live in once predominantly Tai-speaking, or at least non-Han, areas of the border region. Kate Kaup argues that this change contributed to a new sense of "Zhuang consciousness" among the villages' original inhabitants.²³ For many local residents, this was their first encounter with large numbers of Han. In the process of meeting and interacting with these outsiders, Zhuang villagers eventually came to appreciate a greater variety of differences between Zhuang and Han cultures.

This acknowledgement of ethnic difference spread further after Deng Xiaoping and his supporters took power. In an effort to distance themselves from the political environment and seemingly impoverished Han culture that had spawned the Cultural Revolution, many urban Chinese were attracted to the untainted "traditional culture" that rural Chinese, among them the non-Han, supposedly enjoyed.[24] In southwestern China, a regionwide interest in a unique Zhuang culture took root in the initial post-1978 period of reforms, with a flurry of new publications on Zhuang history, folklore, and culture and a renewed effort to promote the widespread use of the Zhuang written language. While many of the new publications were in fact works produced in the early 1960s, subsequently shelved in the dark days of the Cultural Revolution, and then produced belatedly, the appearance of so many works had the effect of drawing the public's attention to the special nature of Zhuang culture.

In what Louisa Schein describes as "Chinese internal orientalism," the ethnicities of rural peasants and non-Han peoples were publicly extolled without being judged as equal to dominant Han culture. Schein writes, "Collectively stamped as backward, the deftly amalgamated classes of minorities, women, and peasants, by virtue of their consociations in dominant representations, remained consigned to a secondary position in the Chinese social order — no matter how stridently their quaint practices were lauded in public discourse."[25] In the post-Mao and now post-Deng era, special recognition has not led directly to equal status within the Han-led social order formed to contain the corporate "Chinese nationality" (*Zhonghua minzu*).

In the post-1978 period, new obstacles emerged that prevented the eager acceptance of Zhuang culture across the border region. Zhuang scholars who desired to promote Zhuang writing and Zhuang culture lived primarily in Guangxi's urban areas and even in Beijing. Residents of the rural areas along the border were more concerned with poverty alleviation and job training with a national application.[26] Meanwhile, some promoters of Zhuang culture also felt the need to speak out against persistent Han-Zhuang economic disparities in the workplace in Guangxi.[27]

The image of Nùng Trí Cao continued to follow the shifts taken by the central government's minority policy. From the Republican period through the early years of the People's Republic of China, all official mention of Nùng Trí Cao included references to his barbarity.[28] By the late 1970s, Nùng Trí Cao had been rehabilitated as a "hero of the people," perhaps in response to the central government's liberalization of policies toward all national minorities. Among the numerous scholarly works on the Zhuang and Zhuang history to emerge in the early 1980s was Huang Xianfan's *Nong Zhigao* (Nong Zhigao). Huang treats the figure of Trí Cao as the centerpiece of a rich local history, but he carefully preserves the image of the rebel leader's "Chineseness." In the aftermath of the 1979 Sino-Vietnamese border conflict, Huang interpreted Trí Cao's rebellion as a struggle against the corrupt "feudalism" of a Song court that refused to provide Chinese border communities with adequate protection against marauding bands from the Đại Việt kingdom.[29] By the late 1980s, a series of folklore collections also were published, many of which contained tales of Nùng Trí Cao's heroism. All of these changes contributed to the mood among inhabitants of Trí Cao's home region that a public commemoration of his life should be established.

Figure 7.1. Commemorative stele to Nùng Trí Cao at Xia Lei, Guangxi, China, 1997 (James Anderson)

Only in the last decade has the issue of a public memorial to Nùng Trí Cao in China been addressed. On January 8, 1997, a local group of Trí Cao's descendants and their supporters from the township of Jingxi and the tiny village of Xia Lei took the initiative to revive interest in this rebel's life and deeds. A modern stela was erected on the supposed site of Trí Cao's birth and his first kingdom's military training grounds. On December 7, 1996, the vice-director of the Center for Zhuang Studies in Nanning, Pan Qixu, was invited to Xia Lei to authenticate the discovery of the cave that was believed to have been Nùng Trí Cao's dwelling and storehouse. A large group of provincial officials and leading academics from Guangxi reportedly attended the commemoration ceremony.

Funds for this stela were raised privately, and organizers of the event told me that high-level political figures avoided involvement in the project, voicing concerns over its "separatist" implications. However, the goal of bringing Nùng Trí Cao back into the public eye was largely successful, as suggested by the long list of small donors to the stela installation. A quick study of the list of large donors reveals that thirty-two out of the thirty-four people included have the surname Nong. This might suggest that older *zhixi* associations shaped local identification with this site. Nùng Trí Cao could also appeal to two audiences if the image of Nùng Trí Cao as the recently created ethnically Zhuang hero serving the Chinese nation is separated from that of Nùng Trí Cao as the native son of the Xia Lei region and great ancestor of the Nong clan, with whom local residents identified through clan association rather than ethnic affiliation.

The Tale South of the Border

As discussed in chapter 6, the heightened level of Chinese imperial privilege granted to Nùng leaders who had once answered locally to the Vietnamese court aggravated border tensions and contributed to the outbreak of hostilities between the Song and Đại Việt courts within the decade. Nevertheless, the shift in political orientation remained in effect after bilateral negotiations in 1078 fixed a firm line of demarcation between the Chinese and Vietnamese domains. From this point onward, the Tai-speaking communities north of this border, including the Nùng clan, became sinicized by accepting a greater degree of integration into the imperial tribute system, and the Tai residing on the Vietnamese side primarily continued to maintain patron-client-type ties with the Vietnamese central court.

Because Vietnamese imperial power was always strongest in the lowland wet rice–cultivating villages, upland Tai-speaking communities in the mountainous areas of the Việt Bắc region, such as the Nung, were allowed to select local leadership. These communities interacted nearly exclusively with the Vietnamese Các Lái, the Kinh merchants who had received government licenses for trade in the uplands in return for collecting annual tribute from these villages and delivering it to the Vietnamese court.[30] Although these upland groups were not forced to conform to lowland Kinh cultural practices, some individuals did adopt lowland dress, speech, and practices as a means of social advancement. Such changes would necessarily involve leaving the region for a lowland settlement, and so these individual acts of assimilation did not affect the upland region as a whole. For those families who were able to live in peace and relative prosperity under the terms of lowland-upland relations set by the Vietnamese court, cultural conformity with lowland society was not necessary for survival, in contrast to the situation on the other side of the border.

Marxist-trained Vietnamese scholars in the 1950s painted a picture of ethnic solidarity among upland and lowland groups in the Việt Bắc region through the modern period, upset only by the occasional self-centered rebel leader. Marriage alliances between the Vietnamese court and upland chieftains gave way to the *thổ ty* (Ch., *tusi*) system, wherein court-appointed officials, either upland or lowland leaders, administered the frontier regions. A similar system by the same name had been employed for frontier management by Chinese courts since the early Ming dynasty (1368–1644). The *thổ ty* officials passed their inherited titles on to their clans' next generation, and so the powerful clans of the eleventh century — the Bế, the Hà, the Hoàng, the Ma, the Nguyễn, the Nông, and the Vy — remained the powerful families, or Seven Local Clan Chieftains (Thất Tộc Thổ Ty), through the early modern period.³¹ Vietnamese scholars have also noted that these *thổ ty* officials gained absolute authority over the area they administered and that their influence remained even after their own lifetimes. The earliest *thổ ty* were later revered by local inhabitants as the creators and sustainers of the first communities, and their spirits (also known as *quang*) were worshiped locally.³² This practice is most certainly the source of the deification of Nùng Trí Cao and his family members. No stronger *thổ ty* leader had lived in this region than Trí Cao, and all subsequent Nùng leaders must have measured their own achievements against his example.

Although a large standing army along the Vietnamese frontier does not appear to have been a priority until late imperial times, by the early years of the Nguyễn court, there apparently was court-sanctioned military expansion in the region. In 1810, there were 1,778 troops for the four frontier prefectures of Thạch Lâm, Thượng Lang, Hạ Lang, and Nùng Trí Cao's home region of Quảng Nguyên, with 456 troops stationed in Quảng Nguyên alone.³³ Moreover, active local intervention by court authorities met with stiff and often violent opposition.³⁴

The most dramatic example of this tension was the 1833 insurrection led by the local chieftain of Cao Bằng's Bảo Lạc district, Nguyễn Văn Nha (also known as Nùng Văn Vân), which spread throughout Tuyên Quang, Cao Bằng, Lạng Sơn, and Thái Nguyên provinces and resulted in the deaths of the high court official Nguyễn Đình Trạc and the Cao Bằng provincial military governor Phạm Văn Lưu.³⁵ Nguyễn Văn Nha reportedly launched his revolt when he learned of the Lê Văn Khôi Rebellion (1833–35), which occupied the Nguyễn court's attention to the south.³⁶ After three years of fighting, Nguyễn Văn Nha was unable to take advantage of his early victories. When local Qing officials denied him refuge in 1835 during a retreat to the north, Văn Nha and his followers fled instead to Tuyên Quang, where they were defeated by Nguyễn troops; the battle ended with the death of Văn Nha in a forest fire set by his attackers.

For the most part, descendants of Nùng Trí Cao still residing in the Cao Bằng region lived in harmony with the distant courts throughout the imperial period. These communities probably paid tribute to the Vietnamese and Chinese authorities simultaneously or in some alternating pattern. The Vietnamese imperial presence did not become a permanent feature of the region until the nineteenth century, and this change came as a result of factional fighting and banditry that likely had originated on the Chinese side of the border. In such cases, interfering in the local rites and ceremonies of Nùng and Tay frontier communities could not have weighed too heavily on the minds of Vietnamese court representatives.

Although there is slight concrete evidence to indicate when the first temple devoted to Nùng Trí Cao was established in the Cao Bằng region, there are several intriguing clues. In a late-nineteenth-century rhapsody written by a local scholar, Trần Huy Phác, a short entry suggests that the founding of the shrine to Nùng Trí Cao, the Great King of Kỳ Sầm Temple, on the western outskirts of metropolitan Cao Bằng, was connected to the suppression of local rebel leader Bế Khắc Thiệu by Lê dynastic forces in 1431; this event occurred shortly after Lê Lợi and his supporters had driven out the Ming and founded the Đại Việt kingdom.[37] The text notes that Lê Lợi was interested in consolidating

Figure 7.2. Kỳ Sầm Temple, Cao Bằng city, 1997 (James Anderson)

support from the border communities by acknowledging the variety of powerful genie from this region, a strategy the Lý dynastic founders employed effectively in their day.

There is ample evidence that the worship of Nùng Trí Cao was widespread by the late Imperial period and had become popular on both sides of the Sino-Vietnamese frontier. Another local scholar, Nguyễn Đức Nha, reported in 1897 that during the previous year, local authorities had arranged with leaders of the Nùng clan to renovate the Kỳ Sầm Temple. Nha noted that an annual festival was held on the tenth day of the first lunar month. During this festival, "Han Chinese" from the Qing empire, both male and female, so flooded the area around the temple that Cao Bằng resembled nothing more than another region of China.[38] Nha wrote that traders from outside the region also arrived to do business during the festival. Moreover, the temple in Quảng Nguyên prefecture hosted a market festival in the third lunar month during the Thanh Minh (Tomb Sweeping) Festival, which offered another opportunity for men and women to socialize and trade.[39] Clearly, by the late nineteenth century, festivals devoted to the spirit of Nùng Trí Cao were regionally important occasions on many grounds. It is equally apparent that the distinguishing features of these Vietnamese festivals — that is, their appeal beyond clan or ethnic affiliations to the general populace — had already developed in this period.[40]

As for conditions along Vietnam's northern border, in the late nineteenth century, French colonial authorities developed an interest in cultivating the loyalties of northern Vietnamese upland communities in their search for local allies to support the regional domination of Nguyễn court–appointed officials. Colonial French authorities, particularly military advisers stationed in the Tonkin Protectorate, saw the Nùng as potential converts to the colonial order, having supposedly suffered historically under Chinese and Vietnamese domination. As noted in a 1908 military dispatch by a Commandant LeBlond, "subjugated and held ransom during many long centuries, sometimes by the one, sometimes by the other, the [Nùng] race has become flexible and is frequently able to ascertain the stronger [neighbor], to which it would turn instinctively. French domination appears soft to him and benevolent, compared with that of Annamites or the Chinese."[41] Nevertheless, LeBlond was quick to note that "[the Nùng] would reject [French rule] without hesitation, if we were not the strongest [power regionally]." As Mark McLeod notes, the failure of the Defend the Sovereign (Cần Vương) Royalist Movement at the end of the nineteenth century provided evidence that northern upland people, such as those communities now labeled Nùng, had little vested interest in supporting the lowland Kinh Vietnamese struggle against the French.[42] The French colonial administration could argue that without a direct benefit or change in the status quo likely to come from such cooperation, upland groups wished only to stay out of the conflict.

Liu Yongfu's (Lưu Vinh Phúc [1837–1917]) Black Flag Army (Heiqijun) was one significant force through which Tai-speaking frontier groups played an important role in supporting the Chinese and Vietnamese courts in their combined efforts to check the French colonial advance. Liu himself was Hakka (Kejiaren), born in a village near coastal Qinzhou. However, many of his early associates and later followers, including former Taiping rebels and assorted bandits, were Tai. Among Liu's collaborators in the 1850s was the Tai-speaking militia leader Wu Lingyun (d. 1862), who, according to one Chinese historian, launched a "Zhuang peasant uprising" in an attempt to found the autonomous frontier kingdom of Yanling (ca. 1861–62), near Xinning, outside modern-day Nanning.[43] Other local allies included the anti-Manchu Heaven and Earth Society (Tiandi Hui) triad leaders Zheng San and Wu Yazhong, who also reportedly led mostly Tais in their militia bands.[44] When Liu fled south into Vietnam in 1857 to escape a Qing expedition, he finally settled his militia forces among upland villages in Bảo Thắng county near modern-day Lào Cai, then a strategic trading port on the uppermost reaches of the Red River. Liu dispatched a trusted supporter, Nông Tú Diệp, to lead two battalions of men to another rebel stronghold near the Chinese border at the river port of Hà Dương (near modern-day Hà Giang), on the banks of the Clear River (Sông Lo), a tributary of the Red River.[45] Liu's faith in Tú Diệp's leadership ability demonstrates the close working relationship he shared with members of the Tai-speaking communities along the frontier.

Soon after arriving in Bảo Thắng, the Black Flags abandoned banditry and submitted to Chinese authority. They began performing their own mopping-up missions against other bandits along the frontier for the benefit of both the Qing and Nguyễn courts. Liu also quelled a Miao rebellion in the upper Red River valley in order to gain Vietnamese court support for his presence in the region and succeeded in driving out Huang Chongying's Yellow Flag Army, who had allied themselves with the Miao and other non-Tai upland groups.[46] Liu's Black Flags are best known, however, for their success in skirmishes with the French military and French-led local militias during the period of French expansion. French efforts in 1868 to navigate the Mekong River into Yunnan first brought the Europeans into contact with many militias, including the Black Flags, who had established themselves in northern Vietnam after the retreat of the Taipings. The 1873 death of the French officer Francis Garnier in Hanoi during a skirmish with the Black Flags initially cooled French interest in establishing a protectorate in northern Vietnam. However, the subsequent three-way negotiations between French, Vietnamese, and Chinese authorities established a French diplomatic and economic presence in the Red River region. When French forces eventually gained supporters among the Black Flags' chief rival, the Yellow Flags, and the upland groups that supported the Yellow Flags, the Europeans had a formidable local force with which to attack the Nguyễn military and its Black Flag allies. The Black Flags' victory against Henri Rivière's forces in 1881, and the death of Rivière himself, proved effective in the short term, but the battle's greatest significance would be as a prelude to the devastating Sino-French War (1881–84), after which China was forced to renounce its tributary relationship with Vietnam and the Nguyễn court lost control of its northern territory. Following the French victory in this conflict, colonial authorities eventually found some important supporters among remnants of Black Flag forces still residing in Tai areas of the Upper Tonkin. Descendants of these individual supporters would remain allies for the French through the First Indochinese War (1946–54).[47]

The French soon scored an important local victory when Auguste Pavie cultivated a personal relationship with the powerful leader of Sip Song Chau Tai (in northwestern Vietnam), Deo Van Tri (1849–1908) (also known as Kam Oum in Laotian), and prevailed on Tri to sign a protectorate treaty on April 7, 1889.[48] As a result of this agreement, the

White Tai of Sip Song Chau Tai became longtime allies of the French, while, as Jean Michaud notes, neighboring Tai-speaking communities continued to avoid French subjugation.[49] The French continued to follow the ancient policy of joining in local alliances with specific chieftains while tending not to interfere in local decision-making in the region.

Opium production in the highland region became an important component of French-controlled areas.[50] The French colonial administration in Laos worked directly with upland Hmong poppy producers because the lowland river valleys were unsuitable for poppy production. The Hmong living along the Sino-Vietnamese frontier were scattered and did not respond to French efforts at political organization. In this region, French colonial administrators in northern and northwestern Vietnam sought allies among influential Tai leaders, who controlled trade in the region that passed through the lowland markets.[51] Alfred McCoy notes that "to make the Tai leaders more effective opium brokers, the French suspended their forty-year policy of culturally Vietnamizing the Tai by administering the country with Vietnamese bureaucrats."[52]

Eventually, local Vietnamese political leaders interested in enticing these groups to join the anti-French resistance received guidance from the Program of Action, the general nationalities policy of the Indochinese Communist Party (ICP), which was introduced at the time the party was founded in 1930. Although the policy remained rather vague, it suggested that upland people and other ethnic minorities would be given the right to full autonomy once the French colonial order had been overthrown.[53] McLeod cites Stein Tønnesson in his comment that the ICP's minorities policy resembled that of the Soviet Union in that autonomy was granted on paper, with the assumption that life in the socialist state would make such a course of action unnecessary.[54] However, the ICP's central leadership paid little attention to its own minorities policy before 1941, when active support of these upland communities became a strategic necessity.[55]

At this point, the ICP and later the Việt Minh worked hard at persuading upland peoples, among them, Nùng villagers, to join in guerrilla activities or at least to give tacit support. In doing so, Vietnamese activities and organizers sought to fit older forms of regionalist loyalties among upland communities into the cause of modern nation building. As Nùng ethnic guides at the famous revolutionary landmark, the Pác Bó Cave, will tell anyone who listens, Hồ Chí Minh (and the Việt Minh in general) would have had a much more difficult time remaining active without enthusiastic Nùng support.[56] In 1997, outside the Nùng Trí Cao temple in the Quảng Nguyên commune, historically considered Nùng Trí Cao's home prefecture, I interviewed an elderly gentleman, Mr. Liêu Ngọc, who told me that the village had been engaged in anti-Japanese, anti-French fighting from 1937 to 1945 and that he himself had been sent to Beijing for political training from 1950 to 1954.[57] Moreover, he reported that the Nùng Trí Cao temple in the commune had been partially destroyed in some incident linked to anti-French activities. It is not entirely clear which side of the conflict the commune residents took; however, the message I received nearly half a century later is that the French were not nearly as attentive to local customs as were the Việt Minh.

The battle for the loyalty of upland communities continued during the First Indochinese War. The French had some success in attracting upland support from White Tai along the Lao border, leading to the establishment of a Tai border kingdom under the control of collaborator Deo Van Long.[58] However, such efforts close to the Sino-Vietnamese border generally backfired or failed to attract followers in numbers as large as those who joined the Việt Minh's efforts. By 1953, the Việt Minh had managed to take the upper hand in the Việt Bắc region, as so many more upland communities, both willingly and under duress, came to support the anti-French cause. Still, most Nùng villages were self-ruled, and with most of the actual fighting taking place farther south and to the west of the villages in which I found evidence of the modern-day worship of Nùng Trí Cao, issues of political loyalty and local identity likely were not often raised until after the founding of the Democratic Republic of Vietnam. Although life in Tai-speaking communities along the Sino-Vietnamese border was disrupted during the period of government-directed land reform, forced relocation of some villagers to lowland areas, and the flight of others (former French supporters?) to the south after 1954, the basic nature of village life in Nùng communities remained intact.

The Nùng villages of the Việt Bắc region emerged from the Second Indochinese War (1955–75) with very little damage, without the devastating levels of violence and disorder inflicted on the upland communities of the Central Highlands region. It should also be noted that the northern region received no preferential treatment once the fighting ended. McLeod argues that central authorities showed little interest in supporting regional autonomy for upland groups after 1975. Fortunately for the border communities, although the DRV had since 1954 supervised state-sponsored migration to all upland areas under its control, the north did not feel the impact of a massive influx of Kinh Vietnamese, as occurred through government-sponsored resettlement programs in the central and southern regions of Vietnam.[59] Perhaps for this reason alone, the ethnic balance around the areas supporting the Nùng Trí Cao temples remained fairly constant, and all groups in the region felt comfortable paying homage to a local hero, who could have been construed as only a Nùng hero.

Another recent event has reinforced regional support for Nùng Trí Cao. The 1979 Sino-Vietnamese conflict had a ruinous impact on Cao Bằng and Lạng Sơn, where these communities are located. Since Nùng Trí Cao was seen first and foremost as one who rebelled against the Chinese imperial order, support for his cult in Vietnam could be read as an anti-Chinese act of defiance. Moreover, this cause could have attracted some Zhuang support from across the border, from individuals who felt lingering resentment toward local Han authorities.

The modern-day veneration of Nùng Trí Cao in the northern Vietnamese province of Cao Bằng is closely tied to the shared regional identity of people from this region. Andrew Turton has described the activities associated with commemorations of other deities in regional Tai societies as "locality cults," noting that such cults today "are often (practiced) within hierarchical encapsulation, which allows for a degree of variation and autonomy for local and ethnically distinct practices."[60] Although I have not discerned any hierarchical structure to the schedule of events associated with the commemoration of Nùng Trí Cao's feats, the rebel remains a hero and a powerful "man of prowess" in diverse Nùng and Tay communities. The worship of Nùng Trí Cao includes practices that highlight the particular strengths of Trí Cao, his willingness to face up to the aggression of both Chinese and Vietnamese authorities, and his ambition to unify and heighten the status of his region's people.

The connection between the spirit world and political power has deep roots in this region. The renowned Han historian Sima Qian was allegedly quoting local chieftains when he wrote that "the Yue peoples by custom believe in spirits and in all our temples one can see spirits, who exercise effective powers. In the past, the Eastern Ou [Dong Ou] kings revered the spirits, and they lived to be as old as 160 years. Later generations dismissed or neglected the spirits, and this was the cause for the disintegration of their political realm."[61]

Even with this political legacy, the modern cult of Nùng Trí Cao certainly does not mask a brewing separatist movement among the Nùng and Tay people of northern Vietnam. However, the local focus of veneration regarding this figure, given his controversial position in history, clearly enhances the identity of the region's Nùng and Tay people against the background of a larger and pervasive state-controlled identity of "Vietnamese-ness" that would encompass and restrict these local identities.

Five temples dedicated to the cult of Nùng Trí Cao remained active well into the twentieth century, and three of these temples survived French colonial administration, guerrilla warfare, and police action and remain in use even today. The extant temples include the Kỳ Sầm Temple (known also by the name Linh Ân), on the outskirts of Cao Bằng, and a temple at the Quảng Nguyên commune, long considered the home prefecture of Nùng Trí Cao. A temple located in Sóc Hà village in Hà Quảng county was very active until it was destroyed in the severe fighting that broke out in the valley during the 1979 Sino-Vietnamese conflict.[62] Hà Quảng county alone once supported three other temples, at Xuân Hoà, Trương Hà, and Đào Ngạn.[63] Moreover, there also once existed the Bản Phân Temple at Đức Long (Thạch An) and the Đồng Mu Temple at Bảo Lạc (Cao Bằng). Furthermore, the Nã Lư Temple on the bank of the Bằng River, dedicated to the Lê royal house in 1682 following the defeat of the Mạc, is said to have been the site of the citadel of Nùng Trí Cao's father, Nùng Tồn Phúc. During my visit to the region in February 1997, I discovered that Nùng Trí Cao's mother A Nùng was being worshiped in a small makeshift temple in the western suburbs of Cao Bằng city.

Figure 7.3. Stele from destroyed temple at Sóc Hà Commune, Hà Quảng County, Cao Bằng, Vietnam, 1997 (James Anderson)

Figure 7.4. Temple at Quảng Hoà Commune, historically considered the home prefecture of Nùng Trí Cao, 1997 (James Anderson)

Figure 7.5. Site of Nùng Tồn Phúc's citadel with more recent Mạc garrison and Nã Lư Temple structures, 1997 (James Anderson)

Figure 7.6. Suburban Cao Bằng city temple devoted to A Nùng, 1997 (James Anderson)

Annual festivals, spaced throughout the year, are performed in their honor in the Vietnamese border provinces. In the city of Cao Bằng, on every tenth day of the first month (according to the lunar calendar), local residents and well-wishers from afar gather to present offerings of fruit and incense. At the demolished temple in the Sóc Hà commune, a large festival was held annually during the third month, shortly after the Thanh Minh Festival.[64] At the Quảng Nguyên Temple, specific ceremonies in Nùng Trí Cao's name were once performed every three months, and the festival held on the first and second days of the third lunar month was regarded as the most important.

The largest temple, Kỳ Sầm, located very close to the urban center of Cao Bằng, is reportedly packed with well-wishers of all ethnic backgrounds for every festival holiday.[65] The regional popularity of the Kỳ Sầm Temple is evident in the nineteenth-century source I examined. It is also true that the families with the hereditary duty of maintaining these temple sites identified themselves as Nùng. For example, the keepers of the Kỳ Sầm Temple have always borne the surname Nùng (or Nông).[66] While Nùng and Kinh Vietnamese linguists developed a romanized script for the Nùng language, the temple keepers and worshipers of the Nùng Trí Cao cult appear to prefer Chinese, and some modern Vietnamese, for the texts maintained within the temples themselves. This preference for Chinese texts is also true of the Zhuang site in Xia Lei, where the organizers could have used the phonetic Zhuang script had it been considered more appropriate for such a memorial.

Despite this clear picture of local worship, the Kỳ Sầm Temple has recently been "renovated" by local authorities so as to convey a more nationalist image of Nùng Trí Cao as a protective deity. During my most recent visit to the region in March 2001, I found a completely refurbished and quite attractive Kỳ Sầm Temple. A smooth, resurfaced driveway now leads to the temple from the main road. Not only has the temple's roof been repaired and the entire exterior restored to a nearly immaculate appearance, but a tall wall has been built around the entire temple grounds. A padlocked gate is now the only point of entry, and the temple keeper, who had to be summoned from her work in the fields to let us in, held the key. Inside the temple, I discovered that while the colophons on the exterior and interior pillars have been retouched with the original text, the longer Chinese-character inscription on the front altar and the Vietnamese *quốc ngữ* inscriptions on the walls to the right and left of the front altar have been completely removed. The old texts had boldly proclaimed that "King Nùng" had "raised high the banner proclaiming independence" and that "the spirits of divine troops, aged but strong and durable, like gold are preserved here ... and remain loyal to the command of the King's kinsmen." Appropriated "folk art" floral patterns and pictures of horses, a symbol associated very generally with folkloric heroes from this region, have taken the place of this provocative text.

Figure 7.7. Kỳ Sầm Temple, 2001 (James Anderson)

Outside the temple, there is now a sign, erected by the Cao Bằng municipal bureau of culture, that describes the historical deeds of Nùng Trí Cao and the reasons for the temple's existence. At the end of the driveway, another large sign describes the temple as a historical landmark. These changes indicate without a doubt that Cao Bằng authorities have decided to include this temple among their "cultural heritage" sites, with the hope that such a designation will put Nùng Trí Cao on the itineraries of incoming tourists and thus generate revenue.[67] By removing the locally oriented, and potentially worrisome, texts from the temple and replacing them with generic symbols of "ethnicity," the cultural bureau has preserved the physical site while undermining the sense of unique local identity it once engendered.

Conclusion

The recent Guangxi memorial and the continuing success of the various temples devoted to the Nùng clan in Vietnam are signs that the region has largely recovered from the dark days of the 1980s, when the border was prone to sporadic violence and frosty diplomatic relations kept a lid on official cross-border activities. The border communities involved in efforts to heighten the public profile of Nùng Tri Cao are now regionally privileged groups. Early in the twentieth century, these groups gained privileged positions as landowners and so have been able to exercise control over their upland shifting-cultivator neighbors, such as the Yao and Hmong (Miao) peoples. These groups had to pay for their privileged positions by accepting the vision of society promoted by the region's dominant powers.

Local commemorations of Nùng Trí Cao remain a sensitive issue in the eyes of central authorities, north and south. It may well be that some official concern is justified given the fluid nature of communities in the Sino-Vietnamese border region. In her study, Diana Lary wrote that "borders are seldom lines of absolute demarcation; the existence of a border does not preclude the existence of a commonality of social and political attitudes on both sides."[68] Lary continues with an observation that has direct bearing on the region examined here: "Border zones tend to be isolated and poverty-stricken, their inhabitants are thrown together against the more prosperous inhabitants of the central areas in both provinces." Lary describes relations between the modern Chinese provinces of Guangdong and Guangxi; however, her point applies equally well to the relationship between Beijing and Hanoi. The Vietnamese province of Cao Bằng and the Chinese province of Guangxi continue to be plagued by greater levels of poverty compared to other regions of their respective national economies. Moreover, rapid economic development, and not merely poverty alleviation, in these regions will not be a government priority for either China or Vietnam at any point in the near future. According to a 1995 Asian Development Bank report, Vietnam's Northern Growth Zone for rapid development extends only from the seaport of Haiphong north along the coast to Ha Long Bay and inland through the Red River delta region to Hanoi. A slower-growth Development Zone extends farther to the northwest, to Lao Cai, but still skirts the northernmost reaches of Cao Bằng province, the region in which the Nùng Trí Cao temples are located.[69] In Guangxi, the Nanning Economic and Technological Development Area joins the provincial capital with the Beihai, Fangcheng, and Qinzhou port cities to the east and the border town of Pingxiang to the south. Comparatively little attention has been paid to the economic development of southwestern Guangxi, where Xia Lei is located.

Map 6. Temple Sites in the Modern Sino-Vietnamese Border Region (Elizabeth Nelson)

Nevertheless, the Chinese central government has included the southwestern border region in its overall plan for greater involvement in Southeast Asia in order to provide wider strategic and economic support in Beijing's quest for further integration into the global marketplace. Tourism is an important part of this expansion. The official Xinhua News Agency recently reported that the Guangxi regional government had spent ¥67 million of a projected total of ¥130 million (approximately US$15.7 million) on the construction of a 634-mile "tourism belt" along the Sino-Vietnamese border, which will highlight the region's unique physical and historical features as well as the "diverse customs of ethnic inhabitants."[70] The Chinese government's incentive to pursue this project appears in large part to be financial gain. According to an earlier report, nearly three million people crossed the Sino-Vietnamese border into China in 2001, and these visitors brought ¥1 billion (about US$120.5 million) in tourism revenue to the Guangxi region.[71] Whether the increased revenue will remain in the border region or be diverted for use by the central government remains an important unanswered question.

This tourism belt is one of many projects that collectively reveal greater economic cooperation between southwestern China and the nations of mainland Southeast Asia. For example, since 2001, the Vietnamese government has established twenty-seven border economic zones along its shared boundary with Cambodia, China, and Laos, and these efforts have been quite successful. The Sino-Vietnamese border zone at the Quảng Ninh provincial capital Móng Cái alone showed a 100 percent increase in the volume of trade, totaling $553 million in 2002.[72] These changes have led to a variety of local reactions. The author of a recent study of South China explains that "globalization has also witnessed a proliferation of local and regional articulations of cultural forms, in the reality of local responses and resistances to globalizing forces."[73] Recent national projects that encouraged greater cross-border integration have also produced local movements that aim to reaffirm local identity in terms of common culture or shared history. In such efforts, the image of Nùng Trí Cao and the revised history of his deeds have begun to serve as useful reactions to the appropriation of the border's resources for the benefit of either Beijing or Hanoi.

The followers of Nùng Trí Cao could play a role in advancing regional solidarity over national unity, although, given the points made above, that trend does not seem imminent. If public commemorations of Trí Cao in Guangxi should gain rapid popularity in the border region, or if regional efforts to reconstruct local history should cause the image of Trí Cao to slip from its officially sanctioned nationalist moorings, the Beijing government might see such attempts as signs of a potential "splittist" threat. As the very recent efforts of the Cao Bằng cultural bureau demonstrate, there is a desire for Hanoi to reappropriate powerful local symbols such as Nùng Trí Cao to act instead as supports for a centralized image of national unity. In fact, such attempts at reinterpretation have been under way for some time. In 1972, the leading Vietnamese ethnographer Đặng Nghiêm Vạn expressed his desire that "the horizon of the ethnic minority [would expand] until it merged with that of the nation."[74] Despite these efforts to fit his deeds into a nationalist context, Trí Cao's potency is expressed most vividly during the festivals in his honor and rituals practiced in his name. The figure of Trí Cao as the Great King of the Nùng People draws on his localized reputation for prowess, and not on a court- or nation-based reputation.

Today, the descendants of Nùng Trí Cao live in communities divided by the borders of modern nation-states. The communities that honor Trí Cao straddle the border between the Socialist Republic of Vietnam and the People's Republic of China, a region that also contains many sites of bloody confrontation between Chinese and Vietnamese armies. However, these communities still share a common thread of identity, preserved in part by a devotion to the figure of Nùng Trí Cao. Their reverence for this eleventh-century rebel leader is a sentiment that transcends modern political demarcation.

8

Conclusion

This book was constructed as a series of related case studies, connected by the theme of political language. The political language and the political authority this language evoked carried clout in the dynamic but inherently unstable Sino-Vietnamese frontier region. Political actors who chose to employ this language either accepted titles from greater powers from outside the region or created titles that enhanced or transformed their local political standing among their immediate followers. Both scenarios apply to the militia leaders who eventually established an independent Vietnamese kingdom as well as to the upland chieftains who sought to overcome local competition and expand the territories under their control.

My first argument is that the Sinic leadership titles adopted by the Nùng clan in the eleventh century provided a basis for enhanced political authority and that the temple names used by modern inhabitants of the Sino-Vietnamese border region continue to provide a point of unity for communities divided by modern political boundaries. In both cases, individuals in the shadows of powerful neighbors and distant rulers sought to enhance their own political standing by borrowing symbols of power from those neighbors.

My second argument is that Sino-Vietnamese relations were deeply affected by developments involving the Tai-speaking communities along the frontier. At the beginning of the time period covered in this book, Song founders were content to allow Vietnamese rulers to take control of the frontier region when disturbances arose. Following the tradition of tributary protocol, Song rulers, who saw no direct interest in the frontier region, delegated its administration to the local vassal authority, in this case, the Vietnamese court that had emerged with Đinh Bộ Lĩnh's reign. Through the 1040s, the peoples of the frontier region dwelled on the outer edges of territorial concerns for both the Chinese and Vietnamese authorities.

In a related point, I argue that Song court interest in both the Vietnamese kingdom and chieftains along the southern frontier changed with the political visions and individual interests of the Song emperors themselves. The Song founder Zhao Kuangyin's focus on northern territories, as well as his court's hands-off approach toward the management of its southern frontier, stemmed from his desire to complete the state-building and territorial-merging efforts of his mentor and former lord, the Later Zhou ruler Chai Rong. Subsequently, competition with and territorial losses to northern kingdoms generated irredentist yearnings for politically ambitious Northern Song rulers who followed Zhao Kuangyin. These rulers would turn south to attempt territorial gain as well.

The second emperor Song Taizong pursued a more aggressive southern policy that peaked with his failed 980 invasion of the Đại Cồ Việt kingdom (then ruled by Lê Hoàn). This attack followed by one year Taizong's conquest of the Northern Han kingdom and the first (failed) assault on the Liao. The reader may, of course, note Wang Anshi's "positive policy" in the 1060s. However, this Song minister served the young emperor Shenzong, whose irredentist desires focused chiefly on lands lost to the Liao and Xi Xia kingdoms. Shenzong's irredentist activities to the north had encouraged local officials in the south to call for direct rule in the region along the Sino-Vietnamese frontier that had once been controlled indirectly as *jimi* prefectures. Wang Anshi certainly advocated a general policy of securing resources found along the Song's periphery for the economic benefit of the empire, but he was much less interested in territorial control than were Shenzong and the emperor's more zealous advisers.

Issues involving Sino-Vietnamese relations and that relationship's effect on the two countries' shared frontier have modern echoes. Today, as China aspires once again to become a world power, many wonder whether it will be an aggressive or a peaceful force in the community of nations. The historical example of China's interaction with Vietnam over the past thousand years would suggest that China typically identifies its national interest not in strictly military terms but in many far more nuanced ways by seeking to influence its neighbors through cultural, diplomatic, economic, and social exchanges.[1] If this is the case, then fears in U.S. media and policy circles of China's growing threat as an economic and military colossus are misplaced and exaggerated. Likely, China's future goals do not include the territorial domination of its immediate neighbors, but, rather, the Chinese leadership will instead strive for global consensus when China again claims to act as the regional arbitrator of peace and harmony among East and Southeast Asian nation-states.

For neighbors of China who feel its presence most acutely — namely, Korea, Taiwan, and Vietnam — resistance to Chinese influence often came about through the outward acceptance of Chinese cultural norms and political practices. Rulers often followed customs of exchange established by distant Chinese rulers in order to buy time for domestic expansion and consolidation of control. The appearance of a commonly held web of relations maintained within the bounds of the tribute system was often more a product of the historiographical spin of Chinese court chroniclers than a reflection of relations between specific kingdoms and the Chinese court. However, as is evident in the case of Vietnamese rulers and frontier chieftains, the political opportunities created by the acceptance of Chinese titles and acquiescence to Chinese norms gave many non-Han leaders the room they required to take control and consolidate power and legitimacy in their home regions.

In the scenario described above, the modern nations of East and Southeast Asia may one day appear to turn diplomatically to China, and away from the United States, for regional stability, while these same countries' leaders will continue to resist any compromise in domestic affairs with their newly powerful Chinese neighbor. Although I have presented one aspect of a fairly complex picture of the region, exploring such possibilities through the lens of history could well be beneficial. Only researchers actively engaged in the tracking of East Asia's future may finally be able to reveal the fullest dimensions of this picture, for which history has provided only a sketch.

Appendix 1

Figure A. Inscriptions from the Kỳ Sầm Temple, Cao Bằng, Vietnam, purported to be the site of Nùng Trí Cao's tomb, 1997 (James Anderson)

1. Temple entrance:
    A. Pillar inscription to the left of front entrance:
    案山前鳳舞灼文章:
    "Upon the opposing mountain peak, a phoenix dances, and its appearance elucidates the texts [that tell of the arrival of our sage ruler]."

    B. Pillar inscription to the right of front entrance:
    砂外象迫舒權印:
    "Beyond the sands [of this river valley], signs of his arrival will soon be revealed in this seal of his authority."

Appendix 1 187

2. Temple altar space:
    A. Inscriptions on front columns:
        i. Right: 雷洞降神赫赫大名垂宇宙:
        "The god [Trí Cao] descended to the Lôi Huýnh aboriginal region. His great reputation and powers became known throughout the universe."

        ii. Left: 岑山怡聖生至德漬乾坤:
        "The serene saint came to Mount Sầm. Having achieved such a life full of *de* potency that he affected heaven and earth."

    B. Former inscription on the face of the altar (removed circa December 1998):
        塞外高標獨立旗.
        儂王事業世間稀.
        邕衡豈近歸南土?
        王侵安能打宗帥?
        半夜無情開下战.
        千秋追限嶺頭碑.
        神兵龍馬金如在.
        願措王兄一指輝.

        Outside his stronghold, he raised high the banner proclaiming independence. Achievements such as those of King Nùng have rarely been found throughout the ages.

        Are not the prefectures of Yong and Heng close enough to be returned to "the southern territory"?

        When the Chinese king's army invaded, how was it able to defeat our ancestor's troops?

        It was because at midnight, the Chinese king's troops mercilessly launched their attack.

        Generations have recalled these events [and the resulting restrictions?][1], as recorded in the stelae upon this peak.

But the spirits of divine troops, aged but strong and durable, like gold are preserved here.

And remain loyal to the command of the king's kinsmen.

3. Tomb space:
    A. Inscriptions on columns leading into tomb area:
        i. Right: 帝業末成人已老:
            "The work of the emperor has yet to be accomplished, while the people have already grown old."

        ii. Left: 王封申錫國同:
            "The king [ruler] extends his patronage evenly across the kingdom to unify all in his blessing."

Appendix 2

Figure B. Left-hand altar inscriptions from the Nùng Trí Cao Temple, Quảng Hoà Commune, Quảng Uyên County, Cao Bằng, Vietnam (James Anderson)

人安物阜: "The people are at peace and with abundance"

Front colophon:
五福壽為光: "The five blessings [longevity, wealth, health, virtue, and completing one's allotted fates] should be known by all."

Central text:
敬公神靈一材住,兩本廟靈王農志高大土將君之位,賜我福祿幾姓人:
"Raise a joss stick to worship our Patriarch Nùng Trí Cao as a god. This is the temple of the Spirit King Nùng Trí Cao, the Great Native General. Give us common people blessings and prosperity."

Concluding colophon:
四時春在吐:
"Of the Four Seasons, spring with its good luck always near."

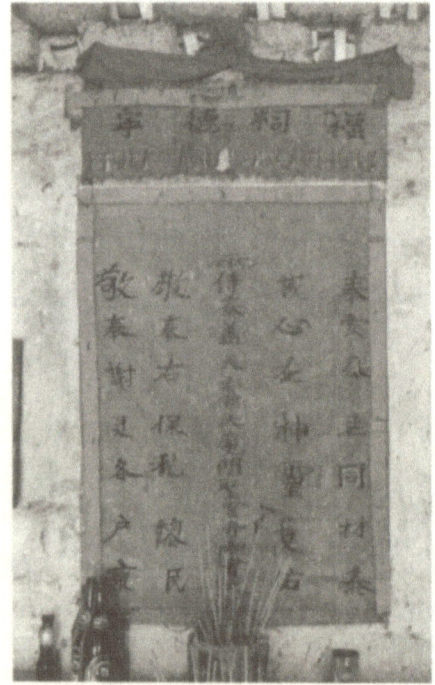

Figure C. Center altar inscription from the Nùng Trí Cao Temple, Quảng Hoà Commune, Quảng Uyên County, Cao Bằng, Vietnam (James Anderson)

福祠德寧: "The Auspicious Temple Brings Virtue and Peace."

Appendix 2

Front colophon:
奉安公老同材泰: "If we worship Duke An, the elders together will find abundance."

Central text:
誠心左神靈護右,兩侍奉盖天右佛伏魔關聖官奇帝君之位,敬奉右保私?黎?民.: "If we act sincerely, the Divine Spirit will protect us. Two attending spirits guard the heavens. Help conceal us from demons while bringing to us wise officials who revere the proper observance of lord-vassal relations. We respectfully welcome your protection and blessings of the people."

Concluding colophon:
敬奉謝灵各户康: "Please worship and give thanks to the Spirit, so that each household may remain in good health."

Figure D. Right-hand altar inscription from the Nùng Trí Cao Temple, Quảng Hoà Commune, Quảng Uyên County, Cao Bằng, Vietnam (James Anderson)

國泰民安: "The country is calm and the people are at peace."

Front colophon:
福地來新奧美玉: "To this prosperous land comes the new, marvelous, and beautiful jade."

Central text:
申奉神靈安且吉,兩本街城惶二地大王之位,誠求福德熾而昌: "Request in prayer that the Spirit bring you peace and good fortune. The rains on our town streets are due to the interventions of our city god together with the Great King. By sincerely seeking blessing and virtue, and by recognizing the Spirit, one will prosper."

Concluding colophon:
神牌安位旺兼金: "May this spirit tablet mark you as both prosperous and one with merit."

Notes

CHAPTER 1

1. Amy Turner Bushnell, "Gates, Patterns, and Peripheries: The Field of Frontier Latin America," in *Negotiated Empires: Centers and Peripheries in the Americas, 1500–1820*, ed. Christine Daniels and Michael V. Kennedy (New York: Routledge, 2002), 16.
2. Edmund Leach, *Political Systems of Highland Burma: A Study of Kachin Social Structure* (London: Athlone Press, 1970). Cited also in Stephen Hugh-Jones and James Laidlaw, eds., *The Essential Edmund Leach*, vol. 1, *Anthropology and Society* (New Haven, Conn.: Yale University Press, 2000), 157.
3. For a clear description of this type of individual prowess, refer to the definition of "soul stuff" in O. W. Wolters, *History, Culture, and Region in Southeast Asian Perspectives*, rev. ed. (Ithaca, N.Y.: Cornell Southeast Asia Program, 1999), 94–95.
4. Huang Xianfan, *Nong Zhigao* (Nong Zhigao) (Nanning: Guangxi Renmin, 1983), 8–10.
5. Toghto et al., *Songshi* (Official history of the Song dynasty) (hereafter *Songshi*) (Beijing: Zhonghua, 1983), 495: 14215.
6. James A. Anderson, "Frontier Management and Tribute Relations along the Empire's Southern Border: China and Vietnam in the 10th and 11th Centuries," PhD diss., University of Washington, 1999, 273–74. The Đại Cồ Việt kingdom was renamed the Đại Việt kingdom in 1054.
7. David Kertzer, *Ritual, Politics, and Power* (New Haven, Conn.: Yale University Press, 1988), 5.
8. *Encyclopedia Britannica Online*, s.v. "Tai," http://search.eb.com/eb/article?eu=72775 (accessed November 26, 2002).
9. United Nations Development Programme Viet Nam, s.v. "Ethnic Minorities Populations in Viet Nam: 1979, 1989 and 1999," http://www.undp.org.vn/projects/vie96010/cemma/vie96010/populations.htm (accessed November 27, 2002).
10. Frank M. LeBar et al., eds., *Ethnic Groups of Mainland Southeast Asia* (New Haven, Conn.: Human Relations Area Files Press, 1964), 232.

11. Li Xiangping, *An Outline of Zhuang History and Culture* (Nanning: Guangxi Minzu, 1995), 1.
12. Material on China was found in Cheng Kejie et al., eds., *Zhuangzu baike cidian* (Zhuang encyclopedic dictionary) (Nanning: Nanning Renmin, 1993), 1. Material on Vietnam was found in Dàng Nghiêm Văn, *Ethnic Minorities in Vietnam* (Hanoi: Thê Giới, 1993), 111–23.
13. K. W. Taylor, "On Being Muonged," *Asian Ethnicity* 2, no. 1 (2001): 29.
14. Stevan Harrell, *Ways of Being Ethnic in Southwest China* (Seattle: University of Washington Press, 2001), 26.
15. Stevan Harrell, ed., *Cultural Encounters on China's Ethnic Frontiers* (Seattle: University of Washington Press, 1995), 23–24.
16. Stevan Harrell, *Ways of Being Ethnic*, 12.

CHAPTER 2

1. Li Tao, *Xu "Zizhi tongjian" changbian* (Draft for a continuation of *The comprehensive mirror for aid in government*) (hereafter *XZZTJCB*) (Beijing: Zhonghua, 1985), 115 *juan*.
2. *Songshi*, 488: 14067.
3. *XZZTJCB*, 114: 2677–78.
4. Ibid.
5. My discussion of world order includes mention of the "nine zone" model found in the *Tribute of Yu* (Yugong) from the *Book of History* (Shangshu) as well as the "five zone" model found, for example, in *Records of the Historian* (Shiji), by Sima Qian (ca. 145–ca. 86 BCE). See Okada Koji, *Studies on the Ethnical and Social History of Southern China* (Zhongguo huanan minzu shehui shi yanjiu), trans. Zhao Lingzhi and Li Delong (Beijing: Minzu Chubanshe, 2002), 1–5.
6. David Schaberg, *A Patterned Past: Form and Thought in Early Chinese Historiography* (Cambridge, Mass.: Harvard University Asia Center, 2001), 125.
7. Okada Koji, *Studies on the Ethnical and Social History*, 2.
8. Véra Dorofeeva-Lichtman, "Mapping a 'Spiritual' Landscape: Representation of Terrestrial Space in the *Shanhaijing*," in *Political Frontiers, Ethnic Boundaries and Human Geographies in Chinese History*, ed. Don J. Wyatt and Nicola Di Cosmo (London: RoutledgeCurzon, 2003), 42.
9. Donald J. Munro, *The Concept of Man in Early China* (Stanford, Calif.: Stanford University Press, 1969), 162.

10. Benjamin Schwartz, *The World of Thought in Ancient China* (Cambridge: Belknap Press of Harvard University, 1985), 301.
11. David Schaberg, *A Patterned Past*, 125.
12. For a wealth of detail regarding the Chinese tribute system, please refer to Herbert Franke, "Diplomatic Missions of the Sung State: 960–1276," lecture, Australian National University, Canberra, March 25, 1981; and James L. Hevia, "A Multitude of Lords: Qing Court Ritual and the Macartney Embassy of 1793," *Late Imperial China* 10, no. 2 (December 1989): 72–105.
13. Ying-shih Yu, *Trade and Expansion in Han China: A Study in the Structure of Sino-Barbarian Economic Relations* (Berkeley: University of California Press, 1967), 38.
14. *"Zhouli" jinzhu jinyi* ... (Modern commentary and translation of the *Rites of Zhou*), trans. and ed. Lin Yin (Taipei: Shangwu Yinshuguan, 1972), 344.
15. For a short study of the significance of spatial arrangement in ancient Chinese political thought, please refer to Véra Dorofeeva-Lichtmann, "Political Concept behind an Interplay of Spatial 'Positions,'" *Extrême-Orient, Extrême-Occident* 18 (1996): 9–33.
16. *"Zhouli" jinzhu jinyi* ..., 345.
17. Pan Yihong, *Son of Heaven and Heavenly Qaghan: Sui-Tang China and Its Neighbors* (Bellingham: Western Washington University Center for East Asia Studies, 1997), 21.
18. Henri J. M. Claessen and Jarich G. Oosten, *Ideology and the Formation of Early States* (New York: E. J. Brill, 1996), 3.
19. James L. Hevia, *Cherishing Men from Afar: Qing Guest Ritual and the Macartney Embassy of 1793* (Durham, N.C.: Duke University Press, 1995), 126.
20. Pan Yihong, *Son of Heaven and Heavenly Qaghan*, 5.
21. John K. Fairbank, ed., *The Chinese World Order: Traditional China's Foreign Relations* (Cambridge: Harvard University Press, 1968), 2.
22. Pan Yihong, *Son of Heaven and Heavenly Qaghan*, 5.
23. Geoff Wade, "Some Topoi in Southern Border Historiography," in *China and Her Neighbors: Borders, Visions of the Other, Foreign Policy, 10th to 19th Century*, ed. Sabrine Dabringhaus and Roderich Ptak (Wiesbaden, Germany: Harrassowitz Verlag, 1997), 150.
24. Wang Gungwu makes a similar point in "The Rhetoric of a Lesser Empire: Early Sung's Relations with Its Neighbors," in *China among Equals:*

The Middle Kingdom and Its Neighbors, 10th–14th Centuries, ed. Morris Rossabi (Berkeley: University of California, 1983), 62.
25. Pan Yihong, *Son of Heaven and Heavenly Qaghan*, 22.
26. Liu Xu, *Jiutang shu* (Old history of the Tang dynasty) (hereafter *JTS*) (Beijing: Zhonghua, 1975), 194: 5162.
27. Pan Yihong, *Son of Heaven and Heavenly Qaghan*, 186.
28. Guolou An, *Songchao zhoubian minzu zhengce yanjiu* (A study of minority border policy during the Song dynasty) (Taipei: Wenjin, 1997), 54.
29. Okada Koji, *Studies on the Ethnical and Social History*, 20.
30. John E. Herman, "The Mu'ege Kingdom: A Brief History of a Frontier Empire in Southwest China," in *Political Frontiers, Ethnic Boundaries and Human Geographies in Chinese History*, ed. Don J. Wyatt and Nicola Di Cosmo (London: RoutledgeCurzon, 2003), 251.
31. Jeffrey Barlow, "The Tang-Song Interregnum," in *The Zhuang*, http://mcel.pacificu.edu/as/resources/zhuang/zhuang8.htm (accessed on December 4, 2001).
32. *Songshi*, 3: 41.
33. *XZZTJCB*, 15: 321.
34. Ganfen Li, *Zhuangzu baike cidian* (Zhuang encyclopedic dictionary) (Nanning: Nanning Renmin, 1993), 650.
35. *XZZTJCB*, 17: 382.
36. *Songshi*, 494: 14199.
37. Nguyễn Ngọc Huy, "Limits on State Power in Traditional China and Vietnam," *Vietnam Forum* 6 (Summer–Fall, 1985): 26. See also Thomas Hodgkin, *Vietnam: The Revolutionary Path* (London: Macmillan Press, 1981), 35.
38. Stevan Harrell, ed., *Cultural Encounters on China's Ethnic Frontiers* (Seattle: University of Washington Press, 1995), 3n.
39. Fan Zuyu, *Tangjian* (Mirror for aid in government of the Tang) (Shanghai: Guji, 1984), 312.
40. Ibid., 71. Reference to Fan's point is found in Jing-shen Tao, "Barbarians or Northerners: Northern Sung Images of the Khitans," in *China among Equals*, ed. Rossabi, 80.

CHAPTER 3

I explored this period in Sino-Vietnamese relations in "Frontier Management and Tribute Relations along the Empire's Southern Border: China and Vietnam in the 10th and 11th Centuries" (PhD diss., University of Washington 1999).

1. For a discussion of the Zhou model of diplomatic interaction, see Liu Boji, *Chunqiu Huimeng zhengzhi* (The politics of the "Peace Covenant" during the Spring and Autumn Period) (Taipei: Zhonghua Congshu, 1962). A specific reference to the Zhou model may be found in *Songshi*, 119: 2795. For a conventional account of China's tribute system, see John K. Fairbank, ed., *The Chinese World Order: Traditional China's Foreign Relations* (Cambridge: Harvard University Press, 1968), 2.
2. Kenneth Hall and John Whitmore, eds., "Economic History of Early Southeast Asia," in *The Cambridge History of Southeast Asia*, vol. 1, part 1, *From Early Times to c. 1500*, ed. Nicholas Tarling (Cambridge: Cambridge University Press, 1999), 261.
3. Alexander Woodside, "Vietnamese History: Confucianism, Colonialism and the Struggle for Independence," *Vietnam: Essays on History, Culture, and Society* (1985): 1–20. Asia Society "Ask Asia," http://www.askasia.org/teachers/Instructional_Resources/Materials/Readings/Vietnam/R_vietnam_4.htm (accessed September 25, 2004).
4. Sima Guang, *Zizhi tongjian* (The comprehensive mirror for aid in government) (hereafter *ZZTJ*) (Taipei: Shijie, 1969), 12: 394; and Ngô Si Liễn, *Đại Việt sử ký toan thư* (The complete history of the Great Viet), ed. Chen Jinghe, in *Daietsu shiki zensho: Kogobon* (Tokyo: Tokyo Daigaku Toyo Bunko Kenkyujo Fuzoku Toyogaku Bunken Senta, 1984, 1986) (hereafter *DVSKTT* [Bunko edition]), BK 2: 107–8.
5. *ZZTJ*, 158: 4908.
6. *DVSKTT* (Bunko edition), BK 4: 148. Sima Guang's account of Lý Bí's actions in *ZZTJ* is somewhat different: Lý Bí takes the title Yuedi and adopts the reign title Đại Đức (Great Virtue). This is likely a transcription error. *ZZTJ* 158: 4920.
7. Keith W. Taylor, *The Birth of Vietnam* (Berkeley: University of California Press, 1983), 150.
8. Fan Zuyu, *Tangjian* (Mirror for aid in government of the Tang), vol. 2 (Taipei: Shangwu, 1977), 595.
9. Pan Yihong, *Son of Heaven and Heavenly Qaghan*, 150–56.
10. *ZZTJ*, 250: 8117. Fan assisted Sima Guang in the compilation of the *ZZTJ*, and one may also find a reference in Fan Zuyu, *Tangjian*, 595. Sima Guang used the term "defense command" in an explanatory note following this passage.
11. Here, we should take a closer look at the official titles granted by the Tang court, specifically, the title "Army of the Peaceful Sea." The term "military commissioner" referred through the mid-Tang dynasty to a specific area

of command, located between today's Shandong, Hebei, and Liaoning provinces. After 880, this title was an honorific designation for military commissioners in South China, and between 880 and 901, it appears that no one was granted this title. Between 901 and 905, three men were granted the title, only one of whom, Zhu Quanzheng's older brother Zhu Quanyu, allegedly took his post in West Lingnan on the border with An Nam, although evidence for this point is not clear.

12. Paul Jakov Smith, introduction to *The Sung Dynasty and Its Precursors, 906–1279*, ed. Denis Twitchett and Paul Jakov Smith, vol. 5, part 1 of *The Cambridge History of China* (Cambridge: Cambridge University Press, forthcoming), 3.
13. Paul Jakov Smith, introduction, 8.
14. Paul Smith refers to this point in Hugh Clark's forthcoming chapter; see Paul Jakov Smith, introduction, 5.
15. Wang Gungwu, *The Structure of Power in North China during the Five Dynasties* (Kuala Lumpur: University of Malaya Press, 1963), 3.
16. Paul Jakov Smith, introduction, 11.
17. Timothy Earle, ed., *Chiefdoms: Power, Economy and Ideology* (Cambridge: Cambridge University Press, 1991), 5.
18. Xie Qikun, *Guangxi tongzhi* (Guangxi gazetteer), vol. 565, Jiaqing edition (Taipei: Wenhai, 1966), 804.
19. This alternate name for the northern Vietnamese region emerged after the decline of the Nam Việt kingdom, a period that was immediately followed by a policy of tighter Han control. The Han court assigned new administrative regions to the south: Giao Chỉ, in the Red River delta; Cưu Chân, to the south of the delta region; and Nhật Nam, to the south of Cưu Chân. "Giao Chỉ" remained the region's administrative title from 111 BCE to 203 CE, and it was reintroduced by the early Song court to describe the entire region under Vietnamese control. "Giao Chỉ" was a pre-Tang title, but the Song court insisted on using it, even after the Việt rulers had adopted the name "Đại Cồ Việt" for their kingdom.
20. *ZZTJ*, 281: 9193.
21. Taylor, *Birth of Vietnam*, 270.
22. Ibid., 280.
23. Ibid., 280–81.
24. *DVSKTT* (Bunko edition), BK 1: 180.
25. Ibid., BK 1: 181.
26. Robert M. Hartwell, *Tribute Missions to China, 960–1126* (Philadelphia: R. M. Hartwell, 1983), 120.

27. *Songshi*, 488: 14058.
28. Ibid., 489: 14079. Xu Song (1781–1848), *Songhuiyao jiben* (Draft of documents pertaining to Song official matters), 1809 edition (hereafter *SHY*) (Taipei: Shijie, 1964), *fanyi* section 4: 62b.
29. *Songshi*, 489: 14080.
30. Ibid., 489: 14088.
31. *DVSKTT* (Bunko edition), BK 1: 181.
32. Ibid., BK 1: 181.
33. According to the Confucian classic *The Book of Ceremony* (Yili), there was the convention among the feudal lords by which a visiting official from one kingdom would use the title *waichen* when speaking to his hosts from another kingdom. This title supported a distinction between the officials of the Warring States period (475–221 BCE) while maintaining the collective identity of the officialdom in the region.
34. The term "Nine Regions" (Jiuzhou) refers to the location of Central Plains societies identified with Chinese culture through the end of the Warring States period. The Five Peaks (Wuling) are the range of mountains that made up China's southern border after the consolidation of the Qin empire in 221 BCE.
35. During the summer of 975, the prefect at Guangzhou made the following report: "Persons involved in theft or bribes that exceed the amount of five thousand cash should be put to death. To gain an announcement of this regulation, I am sending this memorial for the court's decision. Lingbiao is a distant region. Therefore, as for plans to look into obstacles in the region, I request that you do not wait for further reports before making your decision." Li Tao, *Xu "Zizhi tongjian" changbian* (Draft for a continuation of *The comprehensive mirror for aid in government*) (hereafter *XZZTJCB*), (Beijing: Zhonghua, 1985), 16: 338.
36. The authority of a *fan* official or agency was broadly defined, but it ultimately emanated from the central authority of the Chinese court. See Charles O. Hucker, *A Dictionary of Official Titles in Imperial China* (Palo Alto, Calif.: Stanford University Press, 1985), 207.
37. *Songshi*, 488: 14058.
38. Ibid.
39. *XZZTJCB*, 23: 531.
40. Anthony Reid, *Charting the Shape of Early Modern Southeast Asia* (Singapore: Institute of Southeast Asian Studies, 2000), 44.
41. *Songshi*, 488: 14060.
42. *XZZTJCB*, 24: 553.

43. Hall and Whitmore, "Economic History of Early Southeast Asia," 265.
44. Hucker, *Dictionary of Official Titles*, 144.
45. *Songshi*, 488: 14060.
46. Hoàng Xuân Hãn, *Lý Thường Kiệt* (Lý Thường Kiệt), trans. Li Guo, *Nanya yu Dongnanya ziliao* 79, no. 2 (1988): 183.
47. *Songshi*, 488: 14063.
48. Ibid., 488: 14062.
49. *DVSKTT*, 1:194.
50. *Songshi*, 488: 14063.
51. Ibid., 488: 14063.
52. *DVSKTT*, 1: 194.
53. *Songshi*, 488: 14063.
54. The seven-jewel motif was the insignia of the Tantric Buddhist Chakravartin (Lunwang), or Wheel-Turning King, and such an image of universal rule appealed greatly to Song rulers.
55. Although the *Official History of the Song Dynasty* reported that Lê Hoàn died in 1006 and passed the throne on to his son Long Việt at this time, Vietnamese sources claim that Lê Hoàn died one year earlier.
56. *Songshi*, 488: 14065.
57. Hucker, *Dictionary of Official Titles*, 485.
58. *Songshi*, 488: 14064.
59. Edward L. Davis, *Society and the Supernatural in Song China* (Honolulu: University of Hawaii Press, 2001), 67.
60. *XZZTJCB*, 27: 1518.
61. The term "Eastern Fiefs" refers to the ancestral rites Zhenzong practiced to honor Song Taizu and Song Taizong at Fen Yuan on September 3, 1008. See *Songshi*, 7: 137.
62. In the accounts of this episode found in *SHY*, 4: 28, and *XZZTJCB*, *juan* 71, the place-name "Qinzhou" was not included.
63. *Songshi*, 488: 14066.
64. Ibid.
65. *Songshi*, 103: 2506 and 104: 2535.
66. According to Charles Hucker, the position of administrative assistant to the military commissioner was an ad hoc assignment for officials appointed to another position. See Hucker, *Dictionary of Official Titles*, 144.
67. *Songshi*, 488: 14066.
68. Ibid. *DVSKTT* (Bunko edition), BK 2: 111. The *Songshi* account refers to the envoy as Đào Thạc.

69. In its official documents, the Song court referred to Lý Phật Mã as Lý Đức Chính.
70. Keith Taylor, "The Early Kingdoms," in *The Cambridge History of Southeast Asia*, vol. 1, *From Early Times to c. 1500*, ed. Nicholas Tarling, 143.
71. Thongchai Winichakul, *Siam Mapped: A History of the Geo-Body of a Nation* (Honolulu: University of Hawaii Press, 1994), 83.
72. John K. Whitmore, "Elephants Can Actually Swim: Contemporary Chinese Views of Late Ly Dai Viet," in *Southeast Asia in the 9th to 14th Centuries*, ed. David Marr and A. C. Milner (Singapore: Institute of Southeast Asian Studies, 1986), 127.

CHAPTER 4

1. There are references to both Nùng Tôn Phúc and Toàn Phúc. A comparison of relevant passages from a variety of sources leads me to conclude that these two names refer to the same individual, and that Tôn Phúc is the correct name.
2. Ngô Sĩ Liên, *Đại Việt sử ký toàn thư* (The complete history of the great Viet), 1697 woodblock edition (hereafter *DVSKTT* [1993]) (Hanoi: Nhà Xuất Bản Khoa Học Xã Hội, 1993), vol. 4, 25b, 121.
3. Sima Guang (1019–1086), *Sushui jiwen* (Notes from Su River) (Beijing: Xinhua, 1989), 3: 270.
4. Han Xiaorong, "Who Invented the Bronze Drum? Nationalism, Politics, and a Sino-Vietnamese Archeological Debate of the 1970s and 1980s," *Asian Perspectives* 43, no. 1 (Spring 2004): 7.
5. A Mao, "Zhuangzu qingwa tuteng tanmi youzong" (The search for evidence of the Zhuang frog totem), May 4, 2003, Dahuaguang Luyou Wang (Dahuaguang Tourism Website), http://new.gxbcts.com/ReadArt.asp?Art_ID=398 (accessed July 30, 2004).
6. Oscar Chapius, *A History of Vietnam: From Hong Bang to Tu Duc* (Westport, Conn.: Greenwood Press, 1995), 33.
7. Harold Wiens, *Han Chinese Expansion in South China* (Hamden, Conn.: Shoe String Press, 1967), 11–15, cited in Ella Laffey, *Relations between Chinese Provincial Officials and the Black Flag Army, 1883–1885* (PhD diss., Cornell University, 1971), 14.
8. This information was cited in a conference paper by Vương Hùng, "Thái bảo Nông Trí Cao: Sử sách, bia miệng, chứng tích và suy nghĩ" (The grand guardian Nùng Trí Cao: Historical texts, public opinion, physical evidence, and thoughts), presented in *Nùng Trí Cao: Kỷ yếu hội thảo*

khoa học (Nùng Trí Cao: Annals of a meeting for scientific study), ed. Trần Văn Phượng et al. (Cao Bằng: Sở Văn Hóa Thông Tin, 1995), 12–13.
9. David K. Wyatt, *Thailand: A Short History* (New Haven, Conn.: Yale University Press, 1984), 7–9.
10. See Ann Maxwell Hill, *Merchants and Migrants: Ethnicity and Trade among Yunnanese Chinese in Southeast Asia* (New Haven, Conn.: Yale University Southeast Asia Studies, 1998), 65.
11. David Wyatt, *Thailand: A Short History*, 7.
12. Hill, *Merchants and Migrants*, 65.
13. *Songshi*, 495: 14214–15.
14. Hoàng Xuân Hãn, *Lý Thường Kiệt* (Lý Thường Kiệt), trans. Li Guo, cited in *Nanya yu Dongnanya ziliao* (South and Southeast Asian materials) 79, no. 2 (1988) (Beijing: CASS South and Southeast Asian Research Institute), 185.
15. Leo K. Shin, "Contracting Chieftaincy: Political Tribalization of the Southwest in Ming China" (paper presented at the symposium "Empire, Nation, and Region: The Chinese World Order Reconsidered," Berkeley, Calif., 1995), 16.
16. Fang Tie, ed., *Xinan tongshi* (A survey history of the Southwest) (Zhengzhou: Zhongzhou Guji Chubanshe, 2003), 383.
17. Masahiro Kawahara, "Nong Zhigao de panluan he Jiaozhi de guanxi" (The Nùng Trí Cao rebellion and relations with Giao Chỉ), trans. Li Rongcun, *Guoli biance guankan* 1, no. 4 (December 1972): 136.
18. *Songshi*, 495: 14214.
19. An Guolou, *Songchao zhoubian minzu zhengce yanjiu* (A study of minority border policy during the Song dynasty) (Taipei: Wenjin, 1997), 11.
20. Okada Koji, *Studies on the Ethnical and Social History of Southern China* (Zhongguo huanan minzu shehui shi yanjiu), trans. Zhao Lingzhi and Li Delong (Beijing: Minzu Chubanshe, 2002), 135.
21. Okada, *Studies on the Ethnical and Social History*, 132.
22. Li Tao, *Xu "Zizhi tongjian" changbian* (Draft for a continuation of *The comprehensive mirror for aid in government*) (hereafter *XZZTJCB*) (Beijing: Zhonghua, 1985), 18: 395.
23. Fang, ed., *Xinan tongshi*, 383.
24. Huang Xianfan, *Nong Zhigao* (Nong Zhigao) (Nanning: Guangxi Renmin, 1983), 7. The *Songshi* account (4: 55) also includes the titles "censor-in-chief" (*youshi daifu*) and "supreme pillar of the state" (*shangzhuguo*).

25. Zhang Shengzhen and Qin Cailuan, eds., *Zhuangzu shi* (History for the Zhuang people) (Guangzhou: Guangdong Renmin, 2002), 344. Many Vietnamese scholars argue that the prefecture was actually located in the northwest corner of modern-day Cao Bằng.
26. Anonymous, *Việt sử lược* (hereafter *VSL*) (Shanghai: Shangwu, 1936), 1: 30. In the *Songshi* account, Vạn Nhai is referred to as Quảng Nhai prefecture. The *Xu tongjian* account refers to the region as Vạn Nhai.
27. Sima Guang, *Sushui jiwen*, 13: 256–57.
28. *DVSKTT*, 1993, 3: 121.
29. Vương Hùng, "Grand Guardian Nùng Trí Cao," 13.
30. Hill, *Merchants and Migrants*, 54.
31. Xie Qikun, *Guangxi tongzhi* (Guangxi gazetteer), Jiaqing edition (Taipei: Wenhai, 1966), 4950. See Jeffrey Barlow, *The Zhuang*, http://mcel.pacificu.edu/as/resources/zhuang/zhuang8.htm (accessed July 4, 2001).
32. *VSL, juan* 2: 29. See also Tatsuro Yamamoto, Masahiro Kawahara, et al., *Betonamu Chūgoku kankei shi: Kyoku-shi no taitō kara Shin-Futsu Sensō made* (The history of international relations between Vietnam and China: From the rise of the Khuc family to the Sino-French War) (Tokyo: Yamakawa Shuppansha, 1975), 34.
33. *DVSKTT* (Bunko edition), BK 2: 223.
34. Ibid., BK 2: 224.
35. *VSL*, 2: 29.
36. Cited in Ngô Thì Sî, *Đại Việt sử ký tiên biên* (A preliminary compilation of the history of Đại Việt) (hereafter *DVSKTB*), Cảnh Thịnh 8 (1800), from the Viên Hán Nôm holdings #A. 2/1-7, 30A–30B.
37. *DVSKTB*, 30B. Also in *DVSKTT* (1993), 3: 121.
38. *XZZTJCB*, 122: 2887.
39. Ibid., 122: 2886.
40. Cited in *Tho Van Lý-Tran*, vol. 1 (Hanoi: Nhà Xuất Bản Khoa Học Xã Hội, 1977), 245.
41. Sima Guang, *Sushui jiwen*, 13: 256–57.
42. Thongchai Winichakul, *Siam Mapped: A History of the Geo-Body of a Nation* (Honolulu: University of Hawaii Press, 1994), 164.
43. Bunnag Piyanart, "Kinship and Patron-Client Systems in Thai Politics during the Early Ratankosin Period," in *Proceedings of the 4th International Conference on Thai Studies*, vol. 4 (Kunming: Institute of Southeast Asian Studies, 1990), 309.
44. David Wyatt, *Thailand*, 9.
45. Piyanart, "Kinship and Patron-Client Systems," 309.

46. Hill, *Merchants and Migrants*, 65. Also see David Wyatt, *Thailand*, 7.
47. Vương Hùng, "Thái bảo Nông Trí Cao," 13.
48. Shin, "Contracting Chieftaincy," 16.
49. George Condominas, *From Lawa to Mon, from Saa' to Thai: Historical and Anthropological Aspects of Southeast Asian Spaces*, an Occasional Paper of the Department of Anthropology (in association with the Thai-Yunnan Project) (Canberra: ANU Research School of Pacific Studies, 1990), 40.
50. Barlow, *The Zhuang*. http://mcel.pacificu.edu/as/resources/zhuang/zhuang8.htm (accessed July 4, 2001).
51. Sima Guang, *Sushui jiwen, juan* 13.

CHAPTER 5

1. *DVSKTT*, 3: 123.
2. *Songshi*, 495: 14215.
3. Ibid.
4. Ibid.
5. Jeffrey Barlow, "The Zhuang Minority Peoples of the Sino-Vietnamese Frontier in the Song Period," *Journal of Southeast Asian Studies* 18, no. 2 (September 1987): 256.
6. F. M. Savina, *Dictionnaire Étymologique Français-Nùng-Chinois* (Hong Kong: La Société des Missions Étrangères, 1924), 470–71.
7. *DVSKTT* (1993), 3: 124.
8. Ibid., 3: 125.
9. See Charles O. Hucker, *A Dictionary of Official Titles in Imperial China* (Palo Alto, Calif.: Stanford University Press, 1985), 480.
10. See ibid., 401.
11. Xu Lianda, *Zhongguo lidai guangzhi cidian* (Dictionary of Chinese historical official titles) (Anhui: Anhui Jiaoyu, 1991), 140.
12. *DVSKTT* (1993), 3: 116.
13. *DVSKTT* (Bunko edition), BK 3: 1220.
14. Zhang Shengzhen and Qin Cailuan, eds., *Zhuangzu shi* (History for the Zhuang people) (Guangzhou: Guangdong Renmin Chubanshe, 2002), 345.
15. *Songshi*, 495: 14215.
16. John C. Eade, *The Calendrical Systems of Mainland South-East Asia* (New York: E. J. Brill, 1995).
17. Sima Guang, *Sushui jiwen* (Notes from Su River) (Beijing: Xinhua, 1989), 13: 270.

18. Bi Yuan (1730–1797) *Xu "Zizhi tongjian"* (Continuation of *The comprehensive mirror for aid in government*) (hereafter *XZZTJ*) (Shanghai: Guji Chubanshe, 1987), 51: 252.
19. *Songshi*, 196: 4898.
20. *XZZTJCB*, 157: 3848.
21. Ibid., 157: 3848–49.
22. *Songshi*, 495: 14215.
23. *XZZTJCB*, 170: 4084.
24. *Songshi*, 12: 231.
25. Lü Shipeng, "Songdai Zhong-Yue guanxi nianbiao" (A chronicle of Sino-Vietnamese relations during the Song dynasty), *Donghai xuebao* 2, no. 1 (June 1960): 102.
26. *XZZTJCB*, 170: 4078.
27. *Songshi*, 495: 14215.
28. Ibid.
29. Lü Shipeng, "Songdai Zhong-Yue guanxi nianbiao," 102.
30. Ibid.
31. *Songshi*, 495: 14215.
32. Araki Toshikazu, "Nung Chih-kao and the K'o-chü Examinations," *Acta Asiatica* (Tokyo), no. 50 (1986): 92.
33. *Songshi*, 495: 14215. *XZZTJ* 52: 259.
34. *XZZTJ* 52: 259.
35. *Songshi*, 495: 14215.
36. Ibid.
37. A modern fictionalized account of Trí Cao's life makes this claim. Wei Yifan, *Zhuangzu yingxiong Nong Zhigao* (The Zhuang hero Nong Zhigao) (Guangxi: Jili Chubanshe, 1994), 57.
38. *XZZTJCB*, 172: 4142.
39. Ibid.
40. *XZZTJ* 52: 259.
41. *Songshi*, 495: 14216. *XZZTJ* 52: 259.
42. *Songshi*, 495: 14216.
43. Huang Tirong, *Guangxi lishi dili* (The historical geography of Guangxi) (Nanning: Guangxi Minzu Chuban She, 1985), 93.
44. *Songshi*, 495: 14216.
45. Cited in Đỗ Đức Hùng, "Lực lượng quân sự trong cuộc nổi dậy của Nùng Trí Cao hồi giữa thế kỷ XI" (The military strength of the rebel forces assembled by Nùng Trí Cao in the eleventh century), in *Nùng Trí Cao: Kỷ yếu hội thảo khoa học* (Nùng Trí Cao: Annals of a meeting for

scientific study), ed. Trần Văn Phương et al. (Cao Bằng: Sở Văn Hóa Thông Tin, 1995), 135–36. However, the *Songshi* account contains no such suggestion.

46. *Songshi*, 495: 14216.
47. Ibid.
48. Jin Hong, *Guangxi tongzhi* (Guangxi gazetteer), in *Yinying Wenyuan Siku Quanshu*, ed. Qian Yuanchang et al. (Taipei: Taiwan Shangwu, 1983), 443.
49. *Songshi*, 495: 14216.
50. Ibid.
51. According to the thirteenth-century exiled Vietnamese author Lê Tắc, Trí Cao took the title "king of the southern heavens" (*nantian wang*) during the founding of his second kingdom. In this case, there was no third attempt to found a kingdom. Instead, in 1052, Lê Tắc writes that Trí Cao, "without sanction," announced the founding of the Kingdom of the Southern Heavens and proclaimed himself emperor. While unlikely, this alternative account of Trí Cao's claims may illustrate the local leader's efforts to raise the political stakes of his call for independence. See Lê Tắc, *An Nam chí lược* (A survey of the annals of Annam) (Huế: Viện Đại-Học Huế, 1961), 149.
52. *Songshi*, 495: 14216.
53. Ibid.
54. Ibid.
55. Li Tao, *Xu "Zizhi tongjian" changbian* (Draft for a continuation of *The comprehensive mirror for aid in government*) (Taipei: Shijie, 1961), 172: 14a–14b.
56. Ibid., 172: 14b–15a.
57. *Songshi*, 495: 14217.
58. Ibid.
59. Ibid.
60. Ibid., 495: 14216.
61. *DVSKTT* (Bunko edition), BK 2: 237.
62. *Songshi*, 67: 1485.
63. *DVSKTT* (Bunko edition), BK 2: 237.
64. Zhang and Qin, *Zhuangzu shi*, 347.
65. *Songshi*, 495: 14216.
66. Ibid.
67. Ibid.

68. Ibid., 12: 232. Su Jian later committed suicide when he was the Yongzhou prefect during the Vietnamese attack on Yongzhou in 1075.
69. Ibid., 495: 14216.
70. Ibid.
71. Ibid.
72. Huang Tirong, *Guangxi lishi dili*, 95.
73. Zhang and Qin, *Zhuangzu shi*, 347.
74. *Songshi*, 495: 14216–17.
75. Ibid., 495: 14217.
76. Ibid.
77. *XZZTJCB*, 173: 4174.
78. *Songshi*, 11: 227.
79. Ibid., 495: 14217.
80. *XZZTJCB*, 173: 4182–83.
81. *DVSKTT* (Bunko edition), BK 2: 238.
82. Ibid.
83. *XZZTJCB*, 173: 19.
84. *Songshi*, 262: 9075.
85. Ibid., 495: 14217.
86. Wolfram Eberhard, *The Local Cultures of South and East China* (Leiden, Netherlands: E. J. Brill, 1968), 330, 372. Eberhard cites the references made to Di Qing's bronze mask in *Songshi*, 290: 9718, and Wang Bizhi (*jinshi* 1068), *Mianshui yantan lu*, 2: 2b, 4a.
87. Eberhard, *Local Cultures*, 330. More recently, Jeffrey Barlow has argued that Di Qing wore his mask to cover a tattoo scar he had received as a young man. See Jeffrey Barlow, *The Zhuang*, http://mcel.pacificu.edu/as/resources/zhuang/zhuang8.htm (accessed June 1, 2005).
88. *Songshi*, 495: 14217.
89. Ibid., 262: 9075.
90. Ibid., 495: 14217.
91. Jin Hong, *Guangxi tongzhi*, 443.
92. *Songshi*, 495: 14217.
93. Ibid.
94. *DVSKTT* (1993), 3: 127.
95. *Songshi*, 495: 14217.
96. *XZZTJCB*, 175: 18a.
97. Wang Cheng (fl. early twelfth century), *Dongdu shilue* (Account of events in the eastern metropolis), in *Ershiwu bieshi* (The twenty-five unofficial histories), ed. Liu Shaodong et al. (Jinan: Jilu Shushe, 2000), 507.

98. *Songshi*, 495: 14218.
99. *Beijing Portal*, "Ancient Chinese Highway: Tea Horse Road," July 1, 2004, http://www.beijingportal.com.cn/7838/2004/07/01/207@2140238.htm (accessed July 29, 2004).
100. *Zhongguo Chengshiwang* (Cities of China Web), "Major Historical Events in Yaan City" (Yaan lishi dashi), http://www.chinacsw.com/cszx/yaan/lishi.htm (accessed July 29, 2004).
101. *Songshi*, 495: 14218.
102. Ibid.
103. *Songshi*, 495: 14217.
104. *XZZTJCB*, 223: 1a.
105. Peter Bol, "Government, Society and State: On the Political Visions of Ssu-ma Kuang and Wang An-shih," in *Ordering the World: Approaches to State and Society in Sung Dynasty China*, ed. Robert P. Hymes and Conrad Schirokauer (Berkeley: University of California Press, 1993), 154.
106. Ibid., 156.
107. Sima Guang, *Sushui jiwen*, 13: 257.
108. Ibid., 13: 259.
109. Araki Toshikazu, "Nung Chih-kao and the K'o-chü Examinations," 73–94.
110. Ibid., 89–90.
111. Zhou Qufei, *Lingwai daida* (A categorical description of the Lingwai region) (Shanghai: Guji, 1993), 4: 426.
112. Ibid., 4: 426.
113. Ibid., 5: 433.
114. Ibid., 6: 435.
115. Huang Xianfan, *Nong Zhigao* (Nong Zhigao) (Nanning: Guangxi Renmin, 1983), 24.
116. Ibid., 23–24.
117. Barlow, *The Zhuang.* http://mcel.pacificu.edu/as/resources/zhuang/zhuang8.htm (accessed July 4, 2001).
118. *Songshi*, 196: 4898.
119. Ibid., 495: 14217.

CHAPTER 6

1. Đinh Bộ Lĩnh (923–980) founded his independent Vietnamese kingdom with the title Đại Cồ Việt (968–1054). The Lý dynasty ruler Lý Nhật Tôn (b. 1023) later renamed the kingdom Đại Việt (1054–1400). This title would remain in use until the end of the Trần dynasty (1225–1400).

2. Patricia Pelley, "'Barbarians' and 'Younger Brothers': The Remaking of Race in Postcolonial Vietnam," *Journal of Southeast Asian Studies* 29, no. 2 (September 1998): 376.
3. Ibid.
4. Hoàng Xuân Hãn, *Lý Thường Kiệt: Lịch sử ngoại giao và Tông giáo trều Lý* (Lý Thường Kiệt: A history of Song-Lý foreign relations) (Hanoi: Sông Nhị, 1949), 94.
5. Ibid., 260.
6. Ibid., 122.
7. Trần Trọng Kim, *Việt Nam sử lược* (A record of Vietnamese history), vol. 1, reprint (Glendale, Calif.: Đại Nam, 1982), 103. Kim gives the name of the local chieftain as Tôn Đản, providing the characters 尊亶.
8. Nguyen Ngoc Huy et al., *The Le Code: Law in Traditional Vietnam: A Comparative Sino-Vietnamese Legal Study with Historical-Juridical Analysis and Annotations*, vol. 1 (Athens: Ohio University Press, 1987), 10.
9. Le Thanh Khoi, *Histoire du Viet Nam* (Paris: Sudestasie, 1981), 158, 160.
10. Phan Huy Lê, "Nùng Trí Cao nhân vật lịch sử và biểu tương văn hóa" (Nùng Trí Cao as historical figure and cultural phenomenon), in *Nùng Trí Cao: Kỷ yếu hội thảo khoa học* (Nùng Trí Cao: Annals of a meeting for scientific study), ed. Trần Văn Phượng et al. (Cao Bằng: Sở Văn Hóa Thông Tin, 1995), 178. See also Hoàng Xuân Hãn, *Lý Thường Kiệt*, 81–97.
11. Lê Đình Sỹ, *Kế sách giữ nước thời Lý-Trần* (Means of national defense in the Ly-Tran period) (Hanoi: Chính Trị Quốc Gia, 1994), 9.
12. Hà Văn Thư and Lã Văn Lô, *Văn hóa Tày Nùng* (Tay Nung culture) (Hanoi: Nhà Xuất Bản Văn Hóa, 1984), 9.
13. Bế Viết Đẳng, *Các dân tộc Tây, Nùng ở Việt Nam* (The Tay and Nung nationalities in Vietnam) (Hanoi: Viên Khoa Học Xã Hội Việt Nam, Viên Dân Tộc Học 1992), 54.
14. Jeffrey Barlow, *The Zhuang*, http://mcel.pacificu.edu/as/resources/zhuang/zhuang8.htm (accessed July 16, 2001).
15. Ibid.
16. *XZZTJCB*, 22: 490–91.
17. *Songshi*, 191: 4746.
18. Nguyễn Hữu Cung, *Cao Bằng thực lục* (Record of affairs in Cao Bằng), Gia Long 9 (1810). Manuscript Text #A.1129 (Hanoi: Viên Hán Nôm Collection), 13b–16a.
19. Ibid., 15b.
20. *Songshi*, 12: 241.
21. Ibid., 312: 10244.

22. Ibid., 12: 247.
23. Xu Song, *Songhuiyao jiben* (Draft of documents pertaining to Song official matters), 1809 edition (hereafter *SHY*) (Taipei: Shijie, 1964), 198: 7799.
24. Ibid. An interesting ambiguity is whether or not these Nùng leaders were expressing personal loyalty to the Yingzong emperor. The *SHY* account does not provide a clear answer to this question.
25. The *SHY* account mistakenly conflates the names of Lư Báo and Lê Mạo as "Lu Mao." See Shen Kua's account in *Mengxi bitan quanyi* for the proper listing of names.
26. *Songshi*, 191: 4746.
27. See Charles O. Hucker, *A Dictionary of Official Titles in Imperial China* (Palo Alto, Calif.: Stanford University Press, 1985), 137. Hucker contends that the leaders of "tithings" were known as "tithing chiefs" (*jiachang*) or "tithing heads" (*jiatou*), while the *Songshi* account uses the older Han period title "guard commander."
28. The Taiping Xingguo period figures may be found in Yue Shi, *Taiping huan yu ji* (A record of the empire's borders and dimensions during the Taiping period); the Yuanfeng period figures may be found in Wang Cun, *Yuanfeng jiu yu ji* (Gazetteer of the Nine Regions during the Yuanfeng period). For both, see Huang Xianfan, *Nong Zhigao* (Nong Zhigao) (Nanning: Guangxi Renmin, 1983), 91.
29. These regional figures were cited in Huang Xianfan, *Zhuangzu tongshi* (A survey of Zhuang history) (Nanning: Guangxi Minzu, 1988), 52. The Song number was found in Wang Cun's *Yuanfeng jiu yu ji*, while the Tang figure was found in the "geography" (*dili*) section of Ouyang Xiu's *Xintang shu* (New history of the Tang) (Beijing: Zhonghua, 1975). A graph in Huang's book (p. 53) gives the Song population figure as 387,723 households, which appears to be a mistake.
30. Fengshan county in this gazetteer entry was composed of today's Donglan and Fengshan counties, located in northwestern Guangxi. This information is cited in Huang Xianfan, *Nong Zhigao*, 91–92.
31. Li Wenxiong may have been mistaken about Zhao Ding's participation. Zhao was a Song official, but his dates were 1085 to 1147.
32. Li Wenxiong, *Longjin xianzhi* (A record of Longjin county), Minguo 35 (1946), hand-etched reprint (Nanning: Guangxi #2 Provincial Library, 1960), 39. Longjin county was the early-twentieth-century name for today's Longzhou county.

33. Wang Xiangzhi (d. after 1221), *Yudi jisheng* (A record of this region's merits), in Huang Xianfan, *Zhuangzu tongshi*, 50.
34. Keith W. Taylor, "Madagascar in the Ancient Malayo-Polynesian Myths," in *Explorations in Early Southeast Asian History: The Origins of Southeast Asian Statecraft*, ed. Kenneth Hall and John Whitmore (Ann Arbor: Michigan Papers on South and Southeast Asia, 11, 1976), 179.
35. Ngô Si Liên, *Đai Việt sử ký ton a thú* (The complete history of the Great Viet), 1697 edition, trans. Phan Huy Lê, Ngô Đức Tho and Hà Văn Tân (Hanoi: Khoa Học Xã Hội, 1993) (hereafter *DVSKTT* [1993]), 129.
36. Phan Huy Chụ (1782–1840), *Lịch triầu hiến chương loại chí* (An encyclopedia of institutions from successive courts), Tập 4, Binh Che Chi (Hanoi: Vien Su Hoc Viet Nam, 1960–61), 5. *DVSKTT* (1993), 3: 2b.
37. O. W. Wolters, *History, Culture, and Region in Southeast Asian Perspectives*, rev. ed. (Ithaca, N.Y.: Cornell Southeast Asia Program, 1999), 113–14.
38. Ngô Si Liễn, *Đại Việt sử ký toan thư* (The complete history of the Great Viet), ed. Chen Jinghe, in *Daietsu shiki zensho: Kogobon* (Tokyo: Tokyo Daigaku Toyo Bunko Kenkyujo Fuzoku Toyogaku Bunken Senta, 1984, 1986) (hereafter *DVSKTT* [Bunko edition]), BK 3: 242.
39. Ibid.
40. Yi Xingguang, *Yu Jing pu zhuan zhilue* (A biographical chronology of Yu Jing) (Guangzhou: Jinan Daxue, 1993), 78. Officers with the rank of military inspector were often used to patrol frontier regions, and these officials (including Yang) may have been in the area to train the local militia.
41. *Songshi*, 288: 14068.
42. *DVSKTT* (Bunko edition), BK 3: 242.
43. *SHY*, 197: 7730.
44. *DVSKTT* (Bunko edition), BK 3: 242.
45. *SHY*, 197: 7730.
46. During the Tang and Song dynasties, the Chinese court granted this title to high officials at court who participated in decision making as grand councilors in addition to their official duties. See Hucker, *Dictionary of Official Titles*, 554.
47. *Songshi*, 488: 14068. Hucker, *Dictionary of Official Titles*, notes that, during the Song, the title of administrative aide was granted to palace eunuchs assigned to special tasks outside the imperial household. Lý Kế Tiên had earlier traveled to Kaifeng with Mai Cảnh Tiện, who had

also been labeled with a title commonly granted to eunuchs at the Song court. The Vietnamese court in this period was not known to have employed eunuchs, and so this title reflects perhaps a Song scholarly inclination to label as eunuchs any rogue officials who misappropriated court authority.

48. *Songshi*, 488: 14068.
49. *XZZTJCB*, 203: 4923.
50. Ibid.
51. *Songshi*, 495: 14218.
52. Shen Kua, *Mengxi bitan* (Notes from Mengxi), trans. Li Wenze and Wu Hongze, in *Wenbai duizhao "Mengxi bitan" quanyi* (A complete classical-colloquial rendition of *Mengxi bitan*) (Chengdu: Ba Shu, 1996), 347.
53. *SHY*, 197: 7730.
54. Ibid., 197: 7730–31.
55. Shen Kua, *Mengxi bitan*, 347.
56. *Songshi*, 14: 272.
57. *XZZTJCB*, 228.
58. Ibid.
59. *SHY*, 197: 7731.
60. Anon. (ca. thirteenth century), *Việt sử lược* (A survey of the history of the Việt kingdom), anno. Chen Chinghe (Tokyo: Soka University, 1987), 2: 61.
61. *Việt sử lược* (A survey of the history of the Việt kingdom), anno. Qian Xizuo (Taipei: Guangwen, 1968), 38.
62. Peter K. Bol, "Government, Society and State," in *Ordering the World: Approaches to State and Society in Sung Dynasty China*, ed. Robert P. Hymes and Conrad Schirokauer (Berkeley: University of California Press, 1993), 186.
63. Paul Jakov Smith, introduction to *The Sung Dynasty and Its Precursors, 906–1279*, ed. Denis Twitchett and Paul Jakov Smith, vol. 5, part 1 of *The Cambridge History of China* (Cambridge: Cambridge University Press, forthcoming), 24.
64. Huang Xianfan, *Nong Zhigao*, 101.
65. *Songshi*, 471: 13712; 494: 14189–90. See Paul Jakov Smith, introduction, 22–23.
66. Paul J. Smith, "State Power and Economic Activism during the New Policies, 1068–1085: The Tea and Horse Trade and the 'Green Sprouts'

Loan Policy," in *Ordering the World*, ed. Robert P. Hymes and Conrad Schirokauer, 110.
67. Bol, "Government, Society and State," 168.
68. Wang Anshi, "Chibang Jiaozhi" (An official statement concerning Jiaozhi), in *Wang Wengong wenji* (The writings of Wang Anshi), vol. 1 (Shanghai: Shanghai Renmin Chubanshe, 1974), 108–9.
69. *Songshi*, 15: 288.
70. The Five Clans were the Long Fan, Fang Fan, Zhang Fan, Shi Fan, and the Luo Fan. Their home region was located near modern-day Guilin. Cited in *Songshi*, 496: 14241.
71. Ibid.
72. *DVSKTT* (1993), 3: 8a. *Songshi*, 334: 10728. Shen had experience in training frontier militia elsewhere in the empire, and Liu, the *jinshi* scholar, was known to the court for his book *Zheng su fang* (Methods of distinguishing the orthodox from the heterodox), in which he described a strategy for encouraging common people to turn from local practices to court-sanctioned ways.
73. Le Thanh Khoi, *Histoire du Viet Nam* (Paris: Sudestasie, 1981), 159.
74. It is not easy to determine the location of Guwan prefecture. The Taiping garrison was located in Thất Khê prefecture in modern-day northern Cao Bằng. The Yongping garrison was located between Siming prefecture and Môn Châu, or modern-day Na Cham. The Qianlong garrison was located at modern-day Shangsi county in southern Guangxi.
75. *DVSKTT* (1993), 3: 8b.
76. Le Thanh Khoi, *Histoire du Viet Nam*, 159.
77. Phan Huy Chú, *Lịch triều hiến chương loại chí* (An encyclopedia of institutions from successive courts), Tập 2, Nhân Vật Chí, 2b.
78. *Songshi*, 446: 13157.
79. *DVSKTT* (1993), 3: 8b.
80. *Songshi*, 15: 290.
81. Phan Huy Chú, *Lịch triều hiến chương loại chí*, 2b. See also *Songshi*, 15: 290. The compilers of the *Songshi*'s "Basic Annals" appear to have believed that Thường Kiệt's name was Lý Hiến.
82. *Songshi*, 303: 10051.
83. Ibid., 334: 10736.
84. *XZZTJCB*, 279: 6831.
85. Ibid., 279: 6843.
86. Hoàng Xuân Hãn, *Lý Thường Kiệt*, 285.

87. Ibid.
88. The Vietnamese text reads: "Nam quốc sơn hà Nam đế cư, Tiệt nhiên định phân tại thiên thư, Như hà ngịch lỗ lai xâm pham, Nhữ đẳng hành khan thủ bại hư." Cited in Editorial Board of the Institute of Literature in the Committee for the Social Sciences of Vietnam, *Tho van Lý Trần* (The literature of the Lý-Trần period) (Hanoi: Khoa Hoc Xa Hoi, 1977–88), 321.
89. *DVSKTT* (1993), 3: 9b.
90. Hoàng Xuân Hãn, *Lý Thường Kiệt*, 291.
91. *Songshi*, 334: 10736.
92. Li Tao, *Xu "Zizhi tongjian" changbian* (Draft for a continuation of *The comprehensive mirror for aid in government*) (Taipei: Shijie, 1961), 297: 15a.
93. *DVSKTT* (Bunko edition), BK 3: 251.
94. *Songshi*, 15: 297.
95. *DVSKTT* (1993), 3: 11a.
96. Lê Văn Huru. *Đại Việt sử ký* (History of the Dai Viet kingdom) (Hanoi: Han Nom Institute), A. 1272/1, 140a.
97. Hoàng Xuân Hãn, *Lý Thường Kiệt*, 338.
98. *Songshi*, 334: 10732.
99. Ibid., 488: 14069.
100. Ibid.
101. *Benchao huawai zhoujun tu* (An illustration of prefectures and commanderies beyond the influence of our dynasty), in *Songben lidai dili zhichang tu* (Song period edition historical atlas), Toyo Bunko ed. (Shanghai: Guji, 1989), 80–81.
102. For a useful source on Vietnamese historical geography, see Nguyễn Văn Siêu (1799–1872), *Đại Việt địa dư toàn biên* (The complete atlas of the Đại Việt kingdom) (Hanoi: Viên Sử Học, Văn Hóa, 1997).
103. Le Thanh Khoi, *Histoire du Viet Nam*, 158.
104. Okada Koji, *Chukoku kanan minzoku shakaishi kenkyu* (Studies on the ethnic and social history of South China) (Tokyo: Kyuko Shoin, 1993), 246.
105. Ibid., 249.
106. Ibid., 20.
107. Ibid.
108. Ibid.
109. *Songshi*, 488: 14069.

110. Ibid., 488: 14070.
111. Ibid.

CHAPTER 7

1. Jin Hong, *Guangxi tongzhi* (Guangxi gazetteer), in *Yinying wenyuan siku quanshu*, ed. Qian Yuanchang et al. (Taipei: Taiwan Shangwu, 1983), 293.
2. Diana Lary, *Region and Nation: The Kwangsi Clique in Chinese Politics, 1925–1937* (London and New York: Cambridge University Press, 1974), 7.
3. Jin Hong, *Guangxi tongzhi*, 293.
4. For studies, please refer to Valerie Hansen, *Changing Gods in Medieval China, 1127–1276* (Princeton, N.J.: Princeton University Press, 1990), and Patricia Ebrey and Peter Gregory, eds., *Religion and Society in T'ang and Sung Society* (Honolulu: University of Hawaii Press, 1993).
5. Wang Cheng (fl. early twelfth century), *Dongdu shilue* (Account of events in the eastern metropolis), in *Ershiwu Bieshi* (The twenty-five unofficial histories), ed. Liu Shaodong et al. (Jinan: Jilu Shushe, 2000), 951.
6. Jin Hong, *Guangxi tongzhi*, 379–80.
7. Ibid., 443.
8. Gu Yanwu (1613–1682), *Tianxia junguo libing shu: Yunnan*, section 2, Zongqiuerlinzhaizangban lithograph ed. (Beijing: Beitu Jichengju, Guangxu 27 [1901]), 8.
9. Guangxi Institute of Ethnology (Guangxi Minzu Yanjiusuo), *Guangxi shaoshu minzu diqu shike beiwen ji* (A collection of inscriptional materials from the minority regions of Guangxi) (Guilin: Guangxi Xin Hua Shu Dian Fa Xing, 1982), 113.
10. Pamela Kyle Crossley, *The Translucent Mirror: History and Identity in Qing Imperial Ideology* (Berkeley: University of California Press, 1999), 337–38.
11. Prasenjit Duara, "Sovereignty and Citizenship in a Decentered China," foreword, in *China Off Center: Mapping the Margins of the Middle Kingdom*, ed. Susan Blum and Lionel Jensen (Honolulu: University of Hawaii Press, 2002), xiv–xv.
12. Dru C. Gladney, *Muslim Chinese: Ethnic Nationalism in the People's Republic* (Cambridge: Harvard University Press, 1991, 1996), 87.
13. Lary, *Region and Nation*, 21.
14. Katherine Palmer Kaup, *Creating the Zhuang: Ethnic Politics in China* (Boulder, Colo.: L. Rienner, 2000), 34.

15. Ibid., 37.
16. Lary, *Region and Nation*, 211.
17. Stevan Harrell, *Ways of Being Ethnic in Southwest China* (Seattle: University of Washington Press, 2001), 31.
18. Gladney, *Muslim Chinese*, 66.
19. Harrell, *Ways of Being Ethnic*, 32, 35.
20. Kaup, *Creating the Zhuang*, 77.
21. Ibid., 101. Here, I would also include my personal observations of this festival in April 1997.
22. Lillian Craig Harris, "Xinjiang, Central Asia and the Implications for China's Policy in the Islamic World," *China Quarterly*, no. 133 (March 1993): 115.
23. Kaup, *Creating the Zhuang*, 106.
24. Louisa Schein, *Minority Rules: The Miao and the Feminine in China's Cultural Politics* (Durham, N.C.: Duke University Press, 2000), 24.
25. Ibid., 130.
26. Kaup, *Creating the Zhuang*, 144.
27. Ibid., 165–66.
28. For example, see Nan Yue, "A Discussion of the Nature of Nong Zhigao's Revolt," *Minzu yanjiu* 8 (1959): 41.
29. See Huang Xianfan, *Nong Zhigao* (Nong Zhigao) (Nanning: Guangxi Renmin, 1983), 10.
30. Georges Condominas, "Aspects of a Minority Problem in Indochina," *Pacific Affairs* 24 (1951): 78–79.
31. Lã Văn Lô, "Bước đầu nghiên cứu về chế độ xã hội Tày, Nùng, Thái dưới thời Pháp thuộc" (First step in the research on the social system of the Tay, Nung, and Thai areas during the French occupation)," *Nghiên cứu lịch sử* (Historical research), no. 68 (1964): 38. Cited in the translator's forward to Chu Văn Tấn, *Reminiscences on the Army for National Salvation: Memoir of General Chu Van Tan*, trans. Mai Elliott (Ithaca, N.Y.: Cornell University Press, 1974).
32. Nguyễn Tuấn Liệu, "May nét tình hình và nhận xét về chế độ quang trong dân tộc Tày ở Hà Giang" (A few aspects and observations on the *quang* system among the Tay minority in Ha Giang province), *Nghiên cứu lịch sử* (Historical research), no. 44 (1962): 21. Cited in the translator's forward to Chu Văn Tấn, *Reminiscences on the Army for National Salvation*.
33. Nguyễn Hự Cung, *Cao Bằng thực lục* (Record of affairs in Cao Bằng), Gia Long 9 (1810), manuscript text #A.1129 (Hanoi: Viện Hán Nôm Collection), 49b–50a.

34. Mark W. McLeod, "Indigenous Peoples and the Vietnamese Revolution," *Journal of World History* 10, no. 2 (Fall 1999): 359–60 and accompanying footnote.
35. Le Thanh Khoi, *Histoire du Viet Nam* (Paris: Sudestasie, 1981), 382–83. See Anon. (mid-nineteenth century), *Cao Bằng thành hãm sự ký* (An account of the sacking of the city of Cao Bằng), manuscript text #A.1379 (Hanoi: Viện Hán Nôm Collection). See also Zhao Erxun (1844–1927) et al., eds. *Qing shi gao* (Beijing: Zhonghua Shu Ju, 1976–77), 364: 11423.
36. "The Fierce Resistance of Our People," *Nhân dân* (The people), December 1, 2001, http://www.nhandan.org.vn/english/history/20011201.html (accessed June 30, 2004).
37. Nguyên Thi Giang et al., eds., *Liệt Tĩnh Vật Phù* (Rhapsodies describing provincial practices and personages), manuscript text #A.1173 (Hanoi: Viện Hán Nôm Collection), 35a.
38. Nguyễn Đức Nha, *Cao Bằng sự tích* (Historical artifacts of Cao Bằng), manuscript text #A.89 (Hanoi: Viện Hán Nôm Collection), 2a.
39. Ibid., 2a.
40. I find it interesting that in the Nguyễn period court gazetteer *Đại Nam nhất thống chí* (The complete annals of Dai Nam), there is no mention of these temples, about which local officials had written so much at around the same time the court project was being compiled.
41. Anonymous, *Notice sur le 2ème territoire militaire et la région de Cao-Bang* (Hanoi: Thư Viên Quốc Gia Collection, 1932), 6–7.
42. McLeod, "Indigenous Peoples," 360–61.
43. Wu's given name was Wu Yuanqing, although he used the nickname "Big-Bellied Number Four" (Changyao Si). Zhang Shengzhen and Qin Cailuan, eds., *Zhuangzu shi* (History for the Zhuang people) (Guangzhou: Guangdong Renmin Chubanshe, 2002), 848–52.
44. Ibid., 866–67.
45. Ella Laffey, *Relations between Chinese Provincial Officials and the Black Flag Army, 1883–1885* (PhD diss., Cornell University, 1971), 111.
46. Ibid., 113–14.
47. Laffey notes that Deo Van Long, the first president of the French-supported Tai Federation (1984) in the border region, was proud of his own Black Flags family ties. Ibid., 272–73.
48. Auguste Pavie, *A la conquête des coeurs* (Paris: Presses Universitaires de France, 1947), 99. Cited in Jean Michaud, "A Historical Panorama of the Montagnards in Northern Vietnam under French Rule," in *Turbulent*

Times and Enduring Peoples: Mountain Minorities in the South-east Asian Massif (London: Curzon Press, 2000), 59.
49. Michaud, "A Historical Panorama," 59–60.
50. Ibid., 61.
51. Alfred McCoy, *The Politics of Heroin: CIA Complicity in the Global Drug Trade*, rev. 2nd ed. (New York: Lawrence Hill Books, 1991), 121.
52. Ibid., 121.
53. McLeod, "Indigenous Peoples and the Vietnamese Revolution," 362.
54. Stein Tønnesson, *The Vietnamese Revolution of 1945: Roosevelt, Ho Chi Minh and de Gaulle in a World at War* (London: Sage Publications, 1991), 124–25. Cited in McLeod, "Indigenous Peoples and the Vietnamese Revolution," 362–63.
55. David Marr, Emeritus Professor, Division of Pacific and Asian History, RSPAS, Australian National University, in discussion with the author, June 2001.
56. Comment overheard during visit to the Pác Bó Cave revolutionary landmark in March 2001.
57. Liêu Ngọc, interview by author during visit to the Quảng Nguyên commune, February 26, 1997.
58. William J. Duiker, *The Communist Road to Power in Vietnam*, 2nd ed. (Boulder, Colo.: Westview Press, 1996), 138.
59. Andrew Hardy, in a recent article, makes this argument for state sponsorship of the supposedly spontaneous migration to upland areas. However, Hardy does not specifically refer to the local impact on areas closest to the Sino-Vietnamese border. See Andrew Hardy, "Strategies of Migration to Upland Areas in Contemporary Vietnam," *Asia Pacific Viewpoint* 41, no. 1 (April 2000): 25.
60. Andrew Turton, introduction, in *Civility and Savagery: Social Identity in Tai States* (Richmond, Surrey: Curzon Press, 2000), 25.
61. Cited in Sima Qian, *Shiji* (Records of the historian) (Beijing: Zhonghua, 1959), *juan* 12, 478.
62. A stela found at Sóc Hà referred to the temple as the Bama Temple. Jin Hong's Qing period *Guangxi tongzhi* refers to a Bama Temple located to the north of Sizhou native prefecture on a cliff beside a hot spring. From this reference, it is difficult to tell whether or not Jin was describing the same site. Cited in Jin Hong, *Guangxi tongzhi*, 450.
63. Đinh Ngọc Hải, "Bàn Về Bảo Vệ Và Phát Huy Tác Dụng Di Tích Nùng Trí Cao Tại Cao Bằng," in *Nùng Trí Cao: Kỷ Yếu Hội Thảo Khoa Học* (Cao Bằng: Sở Văn Hòa Thông Tin, 1995), 167.

64. Vương Hùng, former vice-director of the Cao Bằng cultural bureau, interview with the author, February 1997.
65. The Kỳ Sầm Temple is officially located in the village of Ngần, within the district of Hòa An in Cao Bằng province.
66. The grandson of the current temple keeper provided this bit of information during my visit to the Cao Bằng region, February 23–26, 1997.
67. For a study of such government-sponsored uses of Vietnamese historical landmarks in recent years, see Ian Glover, "Letting the Past Serve the Present — Some Contemporary Uses of Archaeology in Viet Nam," *Antiquity* 73, no. 281 (September 1999): 594.
68. Lary, *Region and Nation*, 6.
69. Asian Development Bank, *Asian Development Bank Country Operational Strategy Study: Vietnam*, December 1995, http://www.adb.org/Documents/COSSs/vie.pdf, ii.
70. "Tourism Belt Forming along China-Vietnam Border," *People's Daily Online*, October 15, 2002, http://english.people.com.cn/202210/eng_20021015_105102.shtml.
71. "Guangxi Cleans Up Cross-Border Tourism," Xinhua News Agency, September 10, 2002 (Beijing: COMTEX News Network), 1008253h2132.
72. Haimin Huang and Thanh van Thai, "Roundup: Vietnamese Border Gate Economy Blossoms," Xinhua News Agency, May 22, 2003 (Beijing: COMTEX News Network), 1008141h6707.
73. Carolyn L. Cartier, *Globalizing South China* (Oxford: Blackwell Publishers, 2001), 260.
74. Đặng Nghiêm Vạn, "An Outline: The Thai in Vietnam," *Vietnam Studies* 32 (1972): 194–96. Cited in Patricia Pelley, "'Barbarians' and 'Younger Brothers': The Remaking of Race in Postcolonial Vietnam," *Journal of Southeast Asian Studies* 29, no. 2 (September 1998): 383.

CHAPTER 8

1. Professor Alan Wood (University of Washington, Bothell), e-mail to author, December 31, 2004.

APPENDIX 1

1. This character could be 恨 (*hen* [hate]), which would change the reading of this line to the following: "Generations have recalled these events with acrimony, as they were recorded in the stelae upon this peak."

BIBLIOGRAPHY

1. Endymion Porter Wilkinson, *Chinese History: A Manual* (Cambridge: Harvard University Asia Center, 1998), 491.
2. See Günter Lewin's notice in Etienne Balazs and Yves Hervouet, eds., *A Sung Bibliography* (Hong Kong: The Chinese University Press, 1978), 69. Lewin's notes appear to be at least partially a paraphrasing of commentary from the *Songshi* (Official history of the Song dynasty) and other later Chinese collections.

Glossary of Chinese Characters

A Nùng	阿儂
Ái	愛
Ai Châu	愛州
An Dương Vương	安陽王
An Lushan	安祿山
An Nam	安南
Andezhou	安德州
anfushi	安撫使
anfusi	安撫司
Annan duhu	安南都護
Annan Duhufu	安南都護府
Annan jinghaijun	安南靜海軍
Annandao zhaotaoshi	安南道招討使
Araki Toshikazu	荒木敏一
Âu Lạc	甌駱
Bạch Đằng	白藤
Bai Tian	白田
baidie	白氎
Bảo Lạc	保樂
Bảo Thắng	保勝
baojie shouzheng gongchen	保節守正功臣
Bát Ải	八隘
Bế Khắc Thiệu	閉可紹
Benchao huawai zhoujun tu	本朝化外州郡圖
benji	本紀
Bi Gia Dụ	費嘉祐
Bi Juzheng	薛居正
bingfu	兵服
bingma dujian	兵馬都監
bingxing	丙型

Bình	平
Bình An	平安
binh bộ thị lang	兵部侍郎
Bình Dương	平陽
Bình Nguyên	平原
Bình Nùng Chiếu	平儂詔
Binli	賓禮
Binzhou	賓州
Binzhou	邠州
Bộ Thiệu Kham	章紹欽
Bộ Thiệu Tư	章紹嗣
Bộ Văn Dũng	卜文勇
Bổng Thánh	桻聖
Bose	白色
bu	部
buxie	布燮
Cai Qi	蔡齊
caifu	采服
Cầm	笒
Cần Vương	謹王
Cảnh	景
Cao Jin	曹覲
Cao Xiu	曹脩
caoci	漕司
Chai Rong	柴榮
chang	場
Changsha	長沙
chaogong zhidu	朝貢制度
Chaotian	朝天
Chen	陳
Chen Gong	陳珙
Chen Shaogui	陳紹規
Chen Shu	陳曙
Chen Yaosou	陳堯叟
Cheng Zhuo	成卓
Chengdu	成都

Glossary

Chenzhou	郴州
chibang Jiaozhi	敕勝交趾
Chiêu Thánh Hoàng Đế	昭聖皇帝
chongning	崇寧
Chu	周
Chu	楚
Chukoku kanan minzoku shakaishi kenkyu	中国華南民族社会史爱究
cishi	刺史
Cơ Lang	機郎
Cổ Loa	古螺
Cửu Chân	九真
Daan	大安
đại bảo	太保
Đại Cồ Việt	大瞿越
Đại Đức	大德
Đại La	大羅
Đại Phát	大發
Đại Thắng Vương	大勝王
Đại Việt	大越
Đại Việt Sử Ký Toan Thư	大越史記全書
dajiangjun wei youqianniu	大將軍為右千牛
Dali	大理
dali cheng	大理丞
Dali Guo	大歷國
dali sicheng	大理寺丞
Đan Ba	丹波
Đãn Nãi Giáp	甲但乃
Danan Guo	大南國
Danzhou	儋州
dao	道
Đào Thạc Phụ	陶碩輔
dashi	大食
Datong	大同
Daxin	大新
dazhong xiangfu	大中祥符
Dazuo Weijiangjun	大左衞將軍

de 德
Deqing 德慶
Di 狄
Di Qing 狄青
dianfu 甸服
Địch Lão 狄獠
Diễn 演
Điền 田
dili 地理
Đinh 丁
Đinh Bộ Lĩnh 丁部領
Đinh Liễn 丁璉
Định Nguyên Châu 定源州
Đinh Tuệ 丁璿
Đỗ Hanh 杜亭
đô hộ phủ 都護府
Đô Kim 都金
dong 洞
Dong Ou 東歐
Dong Zhongshu 董仲舒
Dongfeng 東封
dongjiang 洞將
Donglan 東蘭
Du Qi 杜杞
Duanzhou 端州
duda tiju chama si 都大提舉茶馬司
dudu 都督
dudu fu 都督府
duhu fushi 都護副使
dujian 都監
Dujuncun 都軍村
Duobuzhai 咄步砦
Dương Cảnh Thông 楊景通
Đường Châu 唐州
dutou 都頭
duxunjian 都巡檢

Glossary

duzhihuishi	都指揮使
fan	藩
Fan Zuyu	范祖禹
fanfu	藩服
Fang Fan	方蕃
Fengshan	鳳山
Fengshan	封禪
Fengshan xianzhi	鳳山縣志
Fengzhou	封州
Fenyin	汾隱
fu	府
fu	服
Fujian	福建
Fuliang	富良
fushi	副使
gan	贛
gang	崗
Gao Pian	高駢
Gao Shian	高士安
Gaoyao	高要
Giao	交
Giao Chỉ (Jiaozhi)	交趾
Giáp Đồng	甲峒
Gongzhou	龔州
Gu Yanwu	顧炎武
guancha xunguan	觀察巡官
guangaoshi	官誥使
Guangnan xilu	廣南西路
Guangzhou	廣州
guanke	官客
Guanmen	館門
Guigang	貴港
Guihua	歸化
Guijiang	桂江
Guilin	桂林
Guiping	桂平

Guiren Pu	歸仁舖
Guixian	貴縣
Guizhou	桂州
Guizhou	貴州
Guo Kui	郭逵
Guo Wei	郭威
Guoyu	國語
Guwan	古萬
Guwu	古勿
Hà Dương	河陽
Hà Giang	河江
Hà Khánh Thường	何慶常
Hạ Lang	下琅
Ha Văn	何文
Haikang	海康
Hainan	海南
Han	漢
Hanyuan	漢源
Hao Lư	華閭
heiqijun	黑旗軍
Hejiang	合江
Hengshan	橫山
Hengshanzhai	橫山砦
Hengzhou	橫州
heqin	和親
Hezhou	賀州
Hiệu Thành Tràng	效誠場
Hoa Lư	華閭
Hoàn	環
Hoan	驩
Hoan Châu	驩州
Hoàng	黃
Hoàng Khánh Tập	黃慶集
Hoàng Thành Nhã	黃成雅
Hoàng Trọng Khanh	黃仲卿
Hoàng Tú man	黃秀蠻

Hồng Liên Công Vương Phụ Mã Hộ Quốc Công	紅蓮公王駙馬護國公
Hou Zhou	後周
houfu	侯服
houtu	後土
Hua Xia	華夏
Huang Chao zhi luan	黃巢之亂
Huang Fen	黃汾
Huang Lingde	黃令德
Huang Shifu	黃師宓
Huang Wei	黃瑋
Huang Xiangui	黃獻珪
huangdi	黃帝
huangfu	荒服
huanglu daochang	黃籙道場
Hunan	湖南
Hùng Lược	雄略
Hurun	湖潤
Jaya Indravarman I (Shili Yintaman)	釋利因嗒蠻
jia	甲
jiachang	甲長
Jiang Jie	蔣偕
Jiang Jieshi	蔣介石
Jiangnan	江南
Jiangxi	江西
jianjiao taishi	檢校太師
jianjiao taiwei	檢校太尉
Jiaozhi junwang	交趾郡王
jiatou	甲頭
jidianshi	祭奠使
jiedu panguan	節度判官
jiedufushi	節度副使
jiedushi	節度使
jie-e	解額
jieshi	解試
jiezhen	節鎮
jiezhengzhen	節政鎮

jimi	羈縻
Jin	金
Jincheng	金城
Jinghaijun	靜海軍
Jinghaijun jiedushi	靜海軍節度使
Jinghu lu	荊湖路
Jingjiangfu	靜江府
jinglue anfushi	經略安撫使
jinglueshi	經略使
Jingrui	景瑞
Jingxi	靖西
jinshi	進士
jinzi guanglu daifu	金紫光祿大夫
jinzoushi	進奏使
Jiufu	九服
Jiuzhou	九州
jizhuanti	紀傳體
junwang	郡王
Kaifeng	開封
kaifu yitong sansi	開府義同三司
Kangzhou	康州
Kế Thành	計誠
Kejiaren	客家人
keju	科舉
Khai Hoàng	開皇
Khai Quốc	開國
Khuất Liệu	屈獠
Khúc Thừa Mỹ	曲承美
Kunlun Guan	崑崙關
Kỳ Sầm đại vương miếu	邱岑大王廟
laihua	來化
Laiyuan	來遠
Lâm	林
Lâm Tây	臨西
Lạng Châu	諒州
Lào Cai	老街

Lê	黎
Lê Hoàn	黎桓
Lê Lợi	黎利
Lê Long Đĩnh	黎龍廷
Lê Long Toàn	黎龍全
Lê Long Việt	黎龍戉
Lê Mạo	黎貌
Lê Minh Hộ	黎明護
Lê Ngọc Triệu	黎臥朝
Lê Tái Nghiêm	黎再嚴
Lê Thiệu	黎紹
Lê Văn Hưu	黎文修
Lê Văn Thịnh	黎文盛
Leizhou	雷州
li	禮
lị	理
Li Jianzhong	李建中
Li Ruozhuo	李若拙
Li Shun	黎順
Li Tao	李燾
Li Wenxiong	李文雄
Li Wenzhu	李文著
Li Xiao	李肅
Li Zhuo	李琢
Liang Shi	梁適
Lianzhou	廉州
Liao	遼
Lịch triều hiến chương loại chí	歷朝憲章類誌
Liệu Thông	廖通
lịk	歷
ling	令
Ling Ce	凌策
Ling Piao	嶺表
Lingnan	嶺南
Linxian	彬縣
Liu Gong	劉龑

Liu Hongcao	劉弘操
Liu Ji	劉凡
Liu Yan	劉䶮
Liu Yi	劉彝
Liu Yin	劉隱
Liuzhou	柳州
Lizhou	黎州
Lôi Hỏa	雷火
Lợi Nhân	利人
Long Dực	龍翼
Long Fan	龍蕃
Long Yanyao	龍彥瑤
Longjin xianzhi	龍津縣志
longnao	龍腦
Longzhou	龍州
Lư Báo	盧豹
Lu Shen	陸詵
Lục	陸
Lunwang	輪王
Luo Fan	羅蕃
Lương Châu	梁珠
Lương Nhâm Văn	梁任文
Lưu Ký	劉紀
Lưu Vinh Phúc	劉永福
Luzhou	綠洲
Lý	李
Lý Ac Thuyên	李偓佺
Lý Bí	李賁
Lý Can Đức	李乾德
Lý Công Hiển	李公顯
Lý Công Uẩn	李公蘊
Lý Hiến	李憲
Lý Hữu Vinh	李幼榮
Lý Kế Tiên	李繼先
Lý Khoan Thái	李寬泰
Lý Nhân Mỹ	李仁美

Lý Nhân Tông	李仁宗
Lý Nhật Tôn	李日尊
Lý Phật Mã	李佛瑪
Lý Phật Tử	李佛子
Lý Thái Tông	李太宗
Lý Thướng Kiệt	李常傑
Ma Gui	馬貴
Ma Hoàng	麻黃
Man	蠻
manfu	蠻服
manqiu	蠻酋
manyi	蠻夷
manzei	蠻賊
Mengxi bitan	夢溪筆談
Miao	苗
min	閩
Minh Đức Hoàng Hậu	明德皇后
minzu shibie	民族識別
mo	貊
Mo Hongyan	莫洪燕
Môn Châu	門州
Mu Zhongying	穆重穎
Nam Việt (Nanyue)	南越
Nam Việt Đế	南越帝
Nan Han	南漢
Nanbei chao	南北朝
Nandan	南丹
Nandu	南度
Nanjiao	南交
Nanliang	南梁
nanping wang	南平王
Nantang	南唐
Nantian Guo	南天國
Nanyue wang	南越王
Nanyue wuwang	南越武王
Nanzhao	南詔

nei	內
nei chen	內臣
neifu	內附
neijun	內郡
neiluan waihuan	內亂外患
Nghệ An	義安
Nghiêm	嚴
Ngô Hoài Tự	吳懷嗣
Ngô Quyền	吳權
Ngô Sĩ Liên	吳士連
Ngự Long	馭龍
Ngụy Trọng Hòa	魏仲和
Ngụy Trưng	魏徵
Nguyễn Bá Trâm	阮伯簪
Nguyễn Đức Nha	阮德雅
Nguyễn Thiệu Cung	阮紹恭
Nguyễn Thủ Cương	阮守疆
Nhật Nam	日南
Như Nguyệt	如月
Nhương	瀼
Ninglang	寧蒗
Nong Dalingshen Dianxia	儂大靈神殿下
Nông Tú Diệp	農秀葉
Nùng	儂
Nùng Binh	儂兵
Nùng Chí Trung	儂志忠
Nùng Dân Phú	儂民富
Nùng Hạ Khanh	儂夏卿
Nùng Kế Phong	儂繼封
Nùng Kế Tông	儂繼宗
Nùng Kiến Hậu	儂建侯
Nùng Lượng	儂亮
Nùng Nhật Tân	儂日新
Nùng Toàn Lộc	儂全祿
Nùng Tôn Phúc	儂存福
Nùng Tông Đán	儂宗旦

Glossary

Nùng Trí Cao (Nong Zhigao)	儂智高
Nùng Trí Hội	儂智會
Nùng Trí Quang	儂智光
Nùng Trí Thông	儂智聰
Nùng Trí Xuân	儂智春
Nùng Văn Vân	農文雲
Okada Koji	岡田宏二
Ôn	溫
Pan Mei	潘美
Pan Qixu	潘其旭
Panyu	番禺
Phan Huy Chụ	潘輝注
Phong	峰
Phong Châu	峰州
Phù Lan Trại	扶蘭砦
Phúc Lộc	福祿
Phụng Kiền	奉乾
Pin Jiaozhi xiang, que shi Guangyuan jin	貧交趾象,卻失廣源金
Pingle	平樂
pingman	平蠻
Pingnan	平南
Pu Luo-e	蒲羅過
Puzhou	蒲州
qi	乞
qi bao	七寶
qiangjie	強界
Qianlong	乾隆
Qianlong	遷隆
qianxia	鈐轄
Qianzhou	虔州
qihao	旗號
Qili	啟曆
Qin	秦
Qingyuan	清遠
Qinzhou	欽州
Qiu Qing	秋情

Quan Triêu	觀朝
Quang Lang	桄榔
Quảng Nguyên	廣淵
Quảng Nguyên	廣源
quanzhi liuhoushi	權知留後事
qumiyuan	樞密院
Quyết Lý	決裡
Renhui Huangdi	仁惠皇帝
Renzong	仁宗
Rong	戎
Rongan	融安
Ronghe	榮河
Rongzhou	榮州
Rongzhou	融州
Rongzhou	容州
Ruan Yuan	阮元
Ruhongzhai	如洪寨
Ruxizhai	如昔寨
Sanfoqi	三佛齊
sanong	三公
sanshi	三師
Santang	三塘
Sanyuesan	三月三
Shandong	山東
Shangshu	尚書
Shangsi	上思
Shanxi	陝西
Shao Hua	邵曄
Shen Qi	沈起
shengshi	省試
shengzu	聖祖
Shenzong	神宗
Shi Fan	石蕃
Shi Jian	石鑑
shi feng	實封
shiguan	史館

Shiji	史記
Shixi	石西
Shu	蜀
shubing	戍兵
shumishi	樞密使
Shun	順
Shun'an Zhou	順安州
Shunzhou	順州
Si En	思恩
Sichuan	四川
Sigong	司空
Siling	思陵
sima	司馬
Sima Guang	司馬光
Sima Qian	司馬遷
Sima Tan	司馬談
Siming	思明
Sơn	山
Song	宋
Song Huizong	宋徽宗
Song Renzong	宋仁宗
Song Shenzong	宋神宗
Song Zhenzong	宋真宗
Song Zhezong	宋哲宗
Songhuiyao jiben	宋會要輯本
Songshi	宋史
su	俗
Su Jian	蘇緘
Sui	隋
Sun Jie	孫節
Sun Mian	孫沔
Sun Pu	孫抃
Susang	宿桑
taibao	太保
taifu	太傅
Taiping	太平

Taiping huanyuji	太平寰宇記
Taishan	泰山
taishi	太師
taizi zhongyun	太子中允
Taizong	太宗
Taizu	太祖
Tần Bà	頻婆
tanchuo	坦綽
Tang	唐
Tang Xuanzong	唐玄宗
Tang Yizong	唐懿宗
Tangjian	唐鑑
Tao Bi	陶弼
Temo	特磨
Tengzhou	藤州
Thạch Lâm	石林
thái bảo	太保
Thái Bình	太平
thái úy	太尉
Thàn	申
Thần Điện	神電
Thàn Thiệu Thái	申紹泰
Thàn Thừa Quý	申承貴
Thảng Do	黨猶
Thăng Long	升龍
Thành Châu	誠州
Thanh Minh	清明
Thất Khê	七源
Thiên Cảm	天感
Thiên Đức	天德
thiên hạ	天下
Thiên Tử Quân	天子軍
thông thụy	通瑞
Thuận Châu	順州
Thượng Lang	上琅
Thường Tân	常新

Tiandeng	天等
Tiandi Hui	天地會
tiangan dizhi	天干地支
Tianjing	天井
tianshu	天書
Tianyang	田陽
Tianzhou	田州
Tianzi	天子
Tô Mậu Châu	蘇茂州
Toàn Phúc	全福
Toghto	脫脫
tongban	通判
tongping zhangshi	同平章事
tongzhong shumen xiaping zhangshi	同中書門下平章事
tou Nanchao	投南朝
Trân Châu	珍州
Trần Cồng Vĩnh	陳公尤
Trần Huy Phác	陳輝樸
Trần Ứng Ky	陳應機
Trệ Nguyên Châu	毳源州
Triệu	趙
Triệu Đà (Zhao Tuo)	趙佗
triều đình	朝廷
Triều Dương	潮陽
Triệu Hoài Đức	趙懷德
Trịnh Tú	鄭琇
Trùng Châu	澄州
Trường	長
Trường Bà Khán	張婆看
Trương Châu	長州
Trương Hâi	漲海
Trương Hát	張喝
Trường Sanh Quốc	長生國
Trường Thiệu Phùng	張紹馮
tù	囚
Tự Châu	驩州

Tư Lạng	思浪
Tư Lang Châu	思琅州
Tư Thành	資成
tuding	土丁
tugong	土貢
tusi	土司
tuteng	圖騰
Vạn Tiệp	萬捷
Văn Xuân	萬春
Vi	韋
Việt	越
Việt sử lược	越史略
Vĩnh An	永安
Vĩnh Phong	永豐
Võ Nhị	武珥
Vũ An	武安
Vũ Lặc	武勒
Vũ Thắng	武勝
Vương Duy Khánh	王惟慶
Vương Thiệu Tộ	王紹祚
wai	外
waichen	外臣
waiyi	外夷
Wang Anshi	王安石
Wang Cheng	王稱
Wang Han	王罕
Wang Qiangyou	王乾祐
Wang Qinruo	王欽若
Wang Sui	王遂
Wang Weizheng	王惟正
Wang Wengong wen ji	王文公文集
Wang Xiangzhi	王象之
Wang Yanfu	王彥符
Wang Zhenglun	王正倫
wang zhi ru huo	望之如火
wangji	王畿

wangming	亡命
wansui	萬歲
Wansuidian	萬歲殿
Wei Guan	魏瓘
Wei Zhaomei	衛昭美
weide	威德
weifu	衛服
Wen Yanbo	溫彥博
Wenbai duizhao mengxi bitan quanyi	文白對照夢溪筆談全譯
Wenmen	溫悶
Wenshan	文山
Wu Ji	武吉
Wu Lingyun	吳淩雲
Wu Wuju	吳舞舉
Wu Xingfan	五姓蕃
Wudai	五代
Wudi	武帝
Wufu Zhizhi	五服之制
wuling	五嶺
Wuming	武鳴
Wuyang	勿陽
Wuzhou	梧州
wuzong jiangjun	武總將軍
Xi Xia	西夏
xia fang	下放
Xia Lei	下雷
xian	縣
xiang	湘
Xiangzhou	象州
Xiao Gu	蕭固
Xiao Zhu	蕭注
Xiao Zi	蕭諮
xiaochang	校長
Xiaohai	小海
xiashui	夏稅
Xichuan	西川

xidong	溪洞
xidong qiushuai	溪洞酋帥
Xijiang	西江
xinfa	新法
xingbu langzhong	刑部郎中
xingjun sima	行軍司馬
Xinning	新寧
Xintangshu	新唐史
Xiong Ben	熊本
Xiping	西平
Xu Dao	徐道
Xu Shen	徐申
Xu Song	徐松
Xu zizhi tongjian changbian	續資治通鑒長編
xuanfushi	宣撫使
Xuất Nhật Tân	帥日新
Xun Kuang	荀況
xunjian	巡檢
Xunjiang	潯江
Xunzhou	潯州
Xunzi	荀子
Ỷ Lan	倚蘭
Yaan	雅安
yajiao	牙校
Yang Baocai	楊保材
Yang Tian	楊畋
Yang Wenguang	楊文廣
Yang Wenjie	楊文傑
Yangguang Tang	陽廣堂
Yanling	延陵
yaofu	要服
Yazhou	雅州
Yi	夷
yi	義
yi	驛
yi man zhi man	以蠻治蠻

yidai gongchen	翊戴功臣
yifu	夷服
Yili	儀禮
Yin	陰
Yingde	英德
Yingzhou	英州
Yingzong	英宗
Yizhou	宜州
Yizhou	益州
Yizu zizhixian	彝族自治縣
Yong	邕
Yongguan	邕管
Yongjiang	邕江
Yongping	永平
Yongzhou	邕州
you qianniu weijiangjun	右千牛衛將軍
Youjiang	右江
Yu Jing	余靖
Yu Jing pu zhuan zhilue	余靖譜傳誌略
Yuan Yong	袁用
Yuan Yun	元贇
Yuanfeng jiuyu zhi	元豐九域志
Yuanhai anfushi	緣海安撫使
Yuanshi Tianzun	元始天尊
Yudi jisheng	輿地紀勝
yue	粵
yue	粵
Yue Shi	樂史
Yuedi	越帝
Yugong	禹貢
Yujiang	鬱江
Yujiang	郁江
yushi zhongcheng	御史中丞
zaixiang	宰相
Zhancheng	占城
Zhang Fan	張蕃

Zhang Fangping	張方平
Zhang Guan	張觀
Zhang Li	張立
Zhang Shoujie	張守節
Zhang Tian	張田
Zhang Zhong	張忠
zhangshi	張史
Zhanguo Shidai	戰國時代
Zhao Dechang	趙德昌
Zhao Di	趙締
Zhao Ding	趙鼎
Zhao Gui	趙炅
Zhao Kuangyin	趙匡胤
Zhao Shidan	趙師旦
Zhao Shu	趙署
Zhao Xu	趙頊
Zhao Zhen	趙禎
Zhaozhou	昭州
zhenfu	鎮服
Zheng San	鄭三
zhengshi	正史
zhengsu fang	正俗方
Zhennan	鎮南
zhidujian	權都監
zhihuishi	指揮使
zhiqu miyuanshi	知樞密院事
zhishi	指使
zhixi	支繫
zhizhong	至忠
Zhong Jian	仲簡
Zhonghua minzu	中華民族
Zhongxiu Dujunshen Miao	重修都軍神廟
Zhongyuan	中原
Zhou	周
zhou	州
Zhou li	周禮

zhouguan	周官
zhoushu	周書
Zhuang	壯
Zhuangzu tongshi	狀族通史
zhuanyunshi	轉運使
Zhuanyunsi	轉運司
Zhujiang	珠江
Zijin	紫金
zizhi tongjian	資治通鑑
zuo qianniu weijiangjun	左千牛衛將軍
zuo you jiang	左右江
Zuojiang	左江

Bibliography

Notes

The Chinese and Vietnamese sources examined for this book are by no means purely objective, contextless accounts of relations between the two courts. While Song period records of Sino-Vietnamese tributary activity are still available today, the earliest extant Vietnamese accounts of tenth-century historical events date from the fourteenth century. These accounts, compiled and edited under Trần dynastic (1225–1400) patronage, reflect intellectual concerns that were quite different from the concerns of tenth- and eleventh-century Vietnamese leaders. Therefore, I include an introduction to these accounts in the following brief discussion of the variety of historical sources used in this book. I also indicate the historiographical emphases and orientations modern Chinese and Vietnamese historians inherited from their scholarly predecessors.

The twenty-four imperial "standard histories" (*zhengshi*) make up the core of premodern Chinese historical learning and are the foundation upon which subsequent generations of scholars formed their understanding of peoples along the frontiers. The organization of these histories owes its origins to Sima Qian's (154–86 BCE) *Records of the Historian* (*Shiji*), a project started by the author's father, Sima Tan (d. 110 BCE), and completed around 87 BCE. The "annals-biography" (*jizhuanti*) arrangement of materials, in which a court-centered chronological history is presented first and is followed by biographical sketches and short monographs that illustrate previous points, became the model for all subsequent projects deemed standard histories.[1]

Methods for compiling these histories did not remain constant. Prior to 630, works later designated standard histories were efforts of a single individual or, at most, two or three scholars. Following the early Tang reorganization of the "historiography bureau" (*shiguan*), standard histories gradually became court-sanctioned group projects that reflected the aims and aspirations of the subsequent dynasty under which they were compiled. Often assembled quite rapidly by teams of scholars at the outset of a new dynastic order, the bulk of the sources for these histories were documents collected by the historiography bureau of the previous dynasty. Materials that did not support and illustrate court-centered annals sections were often eliminated or deemphasized. Although standard histories had become ponderously detailed records of court institutions and practices by the time the *Official History of the Song Dynasty* (Songshi) was compiled, they reflected the central court's interest in clarifying its actions for others and did not attempt to elucidate the perspectives of officials on the periphery.

While efforts at fairness and editorial objectivity had been notable elements of Chinese historiography since Sima Qian's precedent-setting enterprise, so, too, were the practices of moral commentary and "teaching by example." The most influential of such histories after the early Song is *The Comprehensive Mirror for Aid in Government* (Zizhi tongjian), by Sima Guang (1019–1086). This project was completed between the years 1067 and 1084 and arguably began with an order from the Song emperor Yingzong (r. 1064–67).[2] Sima Guang has often been labeled a political conservative, owing to his opposition to the implementation of Wang Anshi's new policies, and the professed purpose for this history's compilation certainly supports a politically conservative outlook. Sima Guang and his assistants produced their history to serve as a guide for central court policy and the moral training of its leadership. His historical narrative has been described as "a history book of practical lessons," using recorded examples of statecraft to guide the behavior of contemporary rulers and officials. As an early proponent of the ideology later termed "Neo-Confucianism," Sima Guang sought to read into past court events moral portents for the empire's fortunes.

Another important Song source for this project is the *Draft for a Continuation of "The Comprehensive Mirror for Aid in Government"* (Xu Zizhi tongjian changbian), by Li Tao (1115–1184). An admirer of Sima Guang's work, Li Tao sought to continue his project into the Northern Song. However, he was as concerned about presenting a complete and unprejudiced picture of the historical records as he was interested in extracting moral lessons from these events. Therefore, Li Tao and his staff often included full drafts of memorials and court edicts, rather than the short excerpts more common to histories compiled in his day. Li Tao's efforts ensured that a greater amount of primary sources would be available for future study. Although commentary by this Song historian often ended with moralistic judgments, his method of study provided subsequent generations with a greater array of materials with which to begin similar studies.

As mentioned above, premodern Vietnamese annalist histories did not appear until the fourteenth century, and compilers of these court-based histories largely followed the examples of their Chinese counterparts. The most prominent Vietnamese text describing Sino-Vietnamese relations in the tenth and eleventh centuries is *The Complete History of the Great Viet* (Đại Việt sử ký toan thư), compiled in 1479 under the direction of Ngô Sĩ Liên (fl. 1442–79). This history was commissioned by the Trần emperor to express the independent nature of the Vietnamese kingdom in the shadow of its looming northern neighbor. It was written two centuries after one of its main sources, the no longer extant *History of the Great Viet Kingdom* (Đại Việt sử ký) of Lê Văn Hưu (1230–1322), which was completed in 1272. Lê Văn Hưu's account recorded the history of the Vietnamese kingdom through the end of the Lý dynasty in 1224. For this reason, and because Ngô Sĩ Liên used the work of the Song scholar Sima Guang as his historiographical model, the Vietnamese text contains many of the same stylistic characteristics found in the earlier Chinese works. Differences between these texts reflect differing perspectives rather than alternative sources.

Primary Sources

Chinese

Ban Gu 班固. *Hanshu* 漢書 (History of the Han). Beijing: Zhonghua, 1962.

Bi Yuan 畢沅. *Xu "Zizhi tongjian"* 續資治通鑑 (Continuation of *The comprehensive mirror for aid in government*). Shanghai: Guji Chubanshe, 1987.

Chen Jun 陳均. *Huangchao piannian gangmu beiyao* 皇朝編年綱目備要 (Essential outline year by year of the events of the dynasty). Taipei: Chengwen, 1966.

Chen Shou 陳壽. *Sanguozhi* 三國志 (Chronicle of the Three Kingdoms). Beijing: Zhonghua, 1959.

Fan Chengda 范成大. *Guihai yuheng zhi* 桂海虞衡志 (A description of the forests and peaks across the South Seas region). Shanghai: Guji, 1993.

Fan Ye 范曄. *Houhanshu* 後漢書 (History of the Latter Han). Taipei: Dingwen, 1994.

Fan Zuyu 范祖禹. *Tangjian* 唐鑑 (Mirror for aid in government of the Tang). Taipei: Shangwu, 1977; Shanghai: Guji, 1984.

Gu Yanwu 顧炎武. *Tianxia junguo libing shu: Yunnan.* Section 2. Zongqiuerlinzhaizangban lithograph edition. Beijing: Beitu Jichengju, Guangxu 27 (1901).

Hu Wei 胡渭. *"Yugong" zhuizhi* 禹貢錐指 (A quick study of the *Tribute of Yu*). Shanghai: Guji, 1996.

Li Fang 李昉. *Wenyuan yinghua* 文苑英華 (Beauty of literature). Taipei: Shangwu, 1983.

Li Tao 李燾. *Xu "Zizhi tongjian" changbian* 續資治通鑑長編 (Draft for a continuation of *The comprehensive mirror for aid in government*). Taipei: Shijie, 1961; Beijing: Zhonghua, 1985.

Li Wenxiong 李文雄. *Longjin xianzhi* 龍津縣志 (A record of Longjin county), Minguo 35 (1946). Hand-etched reprint. Nanning: Guangxi #2 Provincial Library, 1960.

Liu Xin 劉歆. *Xijing zaji* 西京雜記 (Miscellaneous records of the Western Capital). Taipei: Shangwu, 1979.

Liu Xu 劉昫. *Jiutang shu* 舊唐書 (Old history of the Tang dynasty). Beijing: Zhonghua, 1975.

Ma Duanlin 馬端臨. *Wenxian tongkao* 文獻通考 (General investigation on important writings). Taipei: Xinxing, 1963.

Ouyang Xiu 歐陽修. *Xin tangshi* 新唐書 (New history of the Tang). Beijing: Zhonghua, 1975.

Shen Kua 沈括. *Mengxi bitan quanyi* 夢溪筆談全譯 (A complete colloquial translation of notes taken at Mengxi). Translated and edited by Li Wenze 李文澤 and Wu Hongze. In *Baiwen duizhao "Mengxi bitan" quanyi* 文白對照夢溪筆談全譯 (A complete classical-colloquial rendition of *Mengxi bitan*). Chengdu: Bashu, 1996.

Sima Guang 司馬廣. *Sushui jiwen* 涑水記文 (Notes from Su River). Beijing: Xinhua, 1989.

———. *Zizhi tongjian* 資治通鑑 (The comprehensive mirror for aid in government). Taipei: Shijie, 1969.

Sima Qian 司馬遷. *Shiji* 史記 (Records of the historian). Beijing: Zhonghua, 1959.

Song da zhaoling ji. (A collection of the Song imperial edicts). Beijing: Zhonghua, 1962.

Toghto 脫脫 et al. *Songshi* 宋史 (Official history of the Song dynasty). Beijing: Zhonghua, 1983.

Wang Anshi 王安石. "Chibang Jiaozhi" 敕牓交趾 (An official statement concerning Jiaozhi). In *Wang Wengong wenji* 王文公文集 (The writings of Wang Anshi), vol. 1. Shanghai: Shanghai Renmin Chubanshe, 1974.

Wang Cheng 王稱. *Dongdu shilue* 東都事略 (Account of events in the eastern metropolis). Taipei: Guoli Zhongyang Tushuguan, 1991.

———. *Dongdu shilue* 東都事略 (Account of events in the eastern metropolis). In *Ershiwu bieshi* 二十五別史 (The twenty-five unofficial histories), ed. Liu Shaodong et al. Jinan: Jilu Shushe, 2000.

Wang Dayuan. *"Daoyi zhilue" jiaoshi* (Annotated edition of *The account of island barbarians*). Beijing: Zhonghua, 1981.

Wang Qinru 王欽若 et al. *Cefu yuangui* 冊府元龜 (The magic mirror in the Palace of Books). Ming Chongzhen 15 (1642) edition. Hong Kong: Zhonghua, 1960.

———. *Songben "Cefu yuangui"* 宋本冊府元龜 (The Song edition of *The magic mirror in the Palace of Books*). Beijing: Zhonghua, 1989.

Wei Zheng 魏征. *Suishu* 隋書 (History of the Sui). Beijing: Zhonghua, 1973.

Xu, Song 徐鬆. *Songhuiyao jiben* 宋會要輯稿 (Draft of documents pertaining to Song official matters). 1809 edition. Taipei: Shijie, 1964.

Yue Shi 樂史. *Taiping huanyuji* 太平寰宇記 (A record of the empire's borders and dimensions during the Taiping period).

Zeng Zaozhuang 曾棗莊 and Liu Lin 劉琳, eds. *Quan Songwen* 全宋文 (The complete literature of the Song). Chengdu: Bashu, 1988.

Zhao Rugua 趙汝適. *Zhufan zhi jiaozhu* (An annotated edition of the chronicles of various barbarians) 諸蕃志校注. Collated by Feng Chengjun 馮承鈞. Shanghai: Shangwu, 1940.

Zheng Qiao 鄭樵. *Tongzhi* 通志 (Comprehensive treaty). Beijing: Zhonghua, 1995.

Zhou Qufei 周去非. *Lingwai daida* 嶺外代答 (A categorical description of the region beyond the passes). *Siku juanshu* edition from the premodern collection *Nanfang caomu zhuang*. Shanghai: Guji, 1993.

Zhu Mu 祝穆. *Gujin shiwen leiju* 古今事文類聚 (A classified collection of facts and texts from antiquity to the present). Shanghai: Guji, 1992.

Vietnamese

Anonymous. *Việt sử lược* 越史略 (A survey of the history of the Việt kingdom). Shanghai: Shangwu, 1936.

Anonymous. *Cao Bằng thành hãm sự ký* (An account of the sacking of the city of Cao Bằng). Mid-nineteenth century. Manuscript text #A.1379. Hanoi: Viện Hán Nôm Collection.

Anonymous. *Việt sử lược* 越史略 (A survey of the history of the Việt kingdom). Ca. thirteenth century. Annotated by Chen Jinghe. Tokyo: Soka University, 1987.

Anonymous. *Đại Việt sử ký* 大越史記 (History of the great Viet). Viên Hán Nôm Manuscript #A.1272/1.

Giang, Nguyên Thi 江元詩 et al., eds. *Liệt tỉnh vật phù* 列省風物賦 (Rhapsodies describing provincial practices and personages). Manuscript Text #A.1173. Hanoi: Viện Hán Nôm Collection.

Lê Tắc. *An Nam chí lược* 安南志略 (A survey of the annals of An Nam). Hue: Viện Đại Học Huế, 1961.

———. *An Nam chí lược* 安南志略 (A survey of the annals of An Nam). Beijing: Zhonghua, 1995.

Ngô Si Liễn. *Đại Việt sử ký toan thư* 大越史記全書 (The complete history of the Great Viet). Edited by Chen Jinghe. In *Daietsu shiki zensho: Kogobon*. Tokyo: Tokyo Daigaku Toyo Bunko Kenkyujo Fuzoku Toyogaku Bunken Senta, 1984, 1986.

———. *Đại Việt sử ký toan thư* 大越史記全書 (The complete history of the Great Viet). 1697 woodblock edition. Translated by Phan Huy Lê, Ngô Đức Tho, and Hà Văn Tân. Hanoi: Nhà Xuất Bản Khoa Học Xã Hội, 1993.

Ngô Thì Sĩ. *Đại Việt sử ký tiền biên* 大越史記前編 (A preliminary compilation of the history of Great Viet). Cảnh Thịnh 8 (1800) edition. Viện Hán Nôm Manuscript #A.2/1-7.

Nguyễn Đức Nha 阮德雅. *Cao Bằng sự tích* 高平事跡 (Historical artifacts of Cao Bang). Manuscript text #A.89. Hanoi: Viện Hán Nôm Collection.

Nguyễn Hựu Cung 阮祐恭. *Cao Bằng thực lục* 高平實錄 (Record of affairs in Cao Bằng). Gia Long 9 (1810). Manuscript Text #A.1129. Hanoi: Viên Hán Nôm Collection.

Phan Thanh Giản. *Khâm Định Việt sử thông giám cương mục* 欽定越史通鑑綱目 (Outline by imperial decree of the mirror for the history of the Great Viet). 1881 edition. Viện Hán Nôm Manuscript # A.1/1-9.

Thiền Uyển tập anh 禪苑集英 (Outstanding figures of the Zen community). Microfilm text #1267. Hanoi: Viện Hán Nôm Collection.

Việt sử lược 越史略 (A survey of the history of the Việt kingdom). Annotated by Qian Xizuo 錢熙祚. Taipei: Guangwen, 1968.

Secondary Sources

A Mao 阿毛. "Zhuangzu qingwa tuteng tanmi youzong" 壯族青蛙圖騰探秘游踪 (The search for evidence of the Zhuang frog totem). May 4, 2003, Dahuaguang Luyou Wang 大華光旅游網 (Dahuaguang Tourism Website), http://new.gxbcts.com/ReadArt.asp?Art_ID=398 (accessed July 30, 2004).

Abadie, Maurice. *Minorities of the Sino-Vietnamese Borderland with Special Reference to Thai Tribes*. Translated by Walter E. J. Tips. Bangkok: White Lotus Press, 2001.

An Guolou 安國樓. *Songchao zhoubian minzu zhengce yanjiu* 宋朝周邊民族政策研究 (A study of minority border policy during the Song dynasty). Taipei: Wenjin, 1997.

Anderson, James A. "Frontier Management and Tribute Relations along the Empire's Southern Border: China and Vietnam in the 10th and 11th Centuries." PhD diss., University of Washington, 1999.

Anonymous. *Notice sur le 2ème territoire militaire et la région de Cao-Bang*. Hanoi: Thư Viện Quốc Gia Collection, 1932.

Araki Toshikazu. "Nung Chih-kao and the K'o-chü Examinations." *Acta Asiatica* (Tokyo), no. 50 (1986): 73–94.

Armstrong, John A. *Nations before Nationalism*. Chapel Hill: University of North Carolina Press, 1982.

Asian Development Bank. *Asian Development Bank Country Operational Strategy Study: Vietnam*. December 1995. http://www.adb.org/Documents/COSSs/vie.pdf, ii.

Aung-Thwin, Michael. "The 'Classical' in Southeast Asia: The Present in the Past." *Journal of Southeast Asian Studies* 26, no. 1 (March 1995): 75–92.

———. "Jambudipa: Classical Burma's Camelot." In *Essays on Burma*, edited by John P. Ferguson. Leiden, Netherlands: E. J. Brill, 1981.

Backus, Charles. "The Nan-Chao Kingdom and Frontier Policy in Southwest China during the Sui and T'ang Periods." PhD diss., Princeton University, 1978.

Bai, Yaotian. *Nong Zhigao: lishi de xingyun er yu qi er* 儂智高: 歷史的幸運兒與棄兒 (Nong Zhigao: History's Fortunate Son or Abandoned Son). Beijing: Minzu Pub., 2006.

Balazs, Etienne, and Yves Hervouet, eds. *A Sung Bibliography*. Hong Kong: The Chinese University Press, 1978.

Barfield, Thomas. *The Perilous Frontier: Nomadic Empires and China*. Cambridge: Basil Blackwell, 1989.

Barlow, Jeffrey. *The Zhuang*. http://mcel.pacificu.edu/as/resources/zhuang/.

———. "The Zhuang Minority Peoples of the Sino-Vietnamese Frontier in the Song Period." *Journal of Southeast Asian Studies* 18, no. 2 (September 1987): 250–69.

Bế Viết Đẳng. *Các dân tộc Tây, Nùng ở Việt Nam* (The Tay and Nung nationalities in Viet Nam). Hanoi: Viên Khoa Học Xã Hội Việt Nam, Viện Dân Tộc Học, 1992.

Beasley, W. G., and E. G. Pulleyblank. *Historians of China and Japan*. London: Oxford University Press, 1961.

Beijing Portal. "Ancient Chinese Highway: Tea Horse Road." July 1, 2004. http://www.beijingportal.com.cn/7838/2004/07/01/207@2140238.htm (accessed July 29, 2004).

Bell, Catherine. *Ritual Theory, Ritual Practice*. New York: Oxford University Press, 1992.

Benchao huawai zhoujun tu 本朝化外州郡圖 (An illustration of prefectures and commanderies beyond the influence of our dynasty). In *Songben lidai dili zhichang tu* 宋本歷代地理指掌圖 (Song period edition historical atlas). Toyo Bunko edition. Shanghai: Guji, 1989.

Bui Quang Tung and Nguyen Huong. *Le Dai-viet et ses voisins* (The Dai Viet kingdom and its neighbors). Paris: Editions L'Harmattan, 1990.

Bushnell, Amy Turner. "Gates, Patterns, and Peripheries: The Field of Frontier Latin America." In *Negotiated Empires: Centers and Peripheries in the Americas, 1500–1820*, edited by Christine Daniels and Michael V. Kennedy. New York: Routledge, 2002.

Cadiere, L., and Paul Pelliot. "Premier étude sur les sources Annamites de l'histoire d'Annam" (An initial study of Annamite sources for the history of Annam). *Bulletin de l'Ecole Française d'Extrême-Orient* 4 (1904): 617–71.

Cartier, Carolyn L. *Globalizing South China*. Oxford: Blackwell Publishers, 2001.

Chinese Academy of Social Sciences. *Gudai Zhong-Yue guanxi shi ziliao xuanpian* 古代中越關係史資料選篇 (Selected historical materials regarding ancient Sino-Vietnamese relations). Beijing: Shekeyuan, 1982.

Chan, Hok-lam. *Legitimation in Imperial China: Discussions under the Jurchen-Chin Dynasty (1115–1234)*. Seattle: University of Washington Press, 1984.

Chang Hewen. *Yuenan Huaqiao shihua* (A discussion of the history of Overseas Chinese in Vietnam). Taipei: Li Ming Cultural Enterprises, 1971.

Chapius, Oscar. *A History of Vietnam: From Hong Bang to Tu Duc*. Westport, Conn.: Greenwood Press, 1995.

Chen Zhichao. "Yi er wu ba nian qianhou Song Meng Zhen sanchao jian de guanxi" 1258 年前後送蒙真三朝的關係 (Song-Mongol-Jurchen relations around 1258). In *Songshi yanjiu lunwen ji* 宋史研究論文集 (Selected essays on research in Song history). Shanghai: Shanghai Guji, 1982.

Cheng Kejie et al., eds. *Zhuangzu baike cidian* (Zhuang encyclopedic dictionary). Nanning: Nanning Renmin, 1993.

Chu Văn Tấn. *Reminiscences on the Army for National Salvation: Memoir of General Chu Van Tan*. Translated by Mai Elliott. Ithaca, N.Y.: Cornell University Press, 1974.

Claessen, Henri J. M., and Jarich G. Oosten. *Ideology and the Formation of Early States*. New York: E. J. Brill, 1996.

Condominas, George. "Aspects of a Minority Problem in Indochina." *Pacific Affairs* 24 (1951): 77–82.

———. *From Lawa to Mon, From Saa' to Thai: Historical and Anthropological Aspects of Southeast Asian Spaces*. An Occasional Paper of the Department of Anthropology (in association with the Thai-Yunnan Project). Canberra, Australia: ANU Research School of Pacific Studies, 1990.

Crossley, Pamela Kyle. *The Translucent Mirror: History and Identity in Qing Imperial Ideology*. Berkeley: University of California Press, 1999.

Đặng Nghiêm Vạn. "An Outline: The Thai in Vietnam." *Vietnam Studies* 32 (1972): 143–196.

———. *Ethnic Minorities in Vietnam*. Hanoi: Thê Giới, 1993.

Daniels, Christine, and Michael V. Kennedy, eds. *Negotiated Empires: Centers and Peripheries in the Americas, 1500–1820*. New York: Routledge, 2002.

Davis, Edward L. *Society and the Supernatural in Song China*. Honolulu: University of Hawaii Press, 2001.

Đỗ Đức Hùng. "Lực lượng quân sự trong cuộc nổi dậy của Nùng Trí Cao hồi giữa thế kỷ XI" (The military strength of the rebel forces assembled by Nùng Trí Cao in the eleventh century). In *Nùng Trí Cao: Kỷ yếu hội thảo khoa học* (Nùng Trí Cao: Annals of a meeting for scientific study), edited by Trần Văn Phương et al. Cao Bằng: Sở Văn Hóa Thông Tin, 1995.

Dorofeeva-Lichtmann, Véra. "Mapping a 'Spiritual' Landscape: Representation of Terrestrial Space in the *Shanhaijing*." In *Political Frontiers, Ethnic Boundaries and Human Geographies in Chinese History*, edited by Don J. Wyatt and Nicola Di Cosmo. London: RoutledgeCurzon, 2003.

———. "Political Concept behind an Interplay of Spatial 'Positions.'" *Extrême-Orient, Extrême-Occident* 18 (1996): 9–33.

Duara, Prasenjit. "Sovereignty and Citizenship in a Decentered China," foreword. In *China Off Center: Mapping the Margins of the Middle Kingdom*, edited by Susan Blum and Lionel Jensen. Honolulu: University of Hawaii Press, 2002.

Dumont, Louis. *Homo Hierarchicus: The Caste System and Its Implications*. Chicago: University of Chicago Press, 1970.

Duiker, William J. *The Communist Road to Power in Vietnam*. 2nd edition. Boulder, Colo.: Westview Press, 1996.

Eade, John C. *The Calendrical Systems of Mainland South-East Asia*. New York: E. J. Brill, 1995.

Earle, Timothy, ed. *Chiefdoms: Power, Economy and Ideology*. Cambridge: Cambridge University Press, 1991.

Eberhard, Wolfram. *The Local Cultures of South and East China*. Leiden, Netherlands: E. J. Brill, 1968.

Ebrey, Patricia, and Peter Gregory, eds. *Religion and Society in T'ang and Sung Society*. Honolulu: University of Hawaii Press, 1993.

Editorial Board of the Institute of Literature in the Committee for the Social Sciences of Vietnam. *Tho van Lý Trần* (The literature of the Lý-Trần period). Hanoi: Khoa Hoc Xa Hoi, 1977–88.

Encyclopedia Britannica Online. "Tai." http://search.eb.com/eb/article?eu=72775.

Fairbank, John K., ed. *The Chinese World Order: Traditional China's Foreign Relations*. Cambridge: Harvard University Press, 1968.

Fang, Tie, ed. *Xinan tongshi* 西南通史 (A survey history of the Southwest). Zhengzhou: Zhongzhou Guji Chubanshe, 2003.

Ferrand, Gabriel. *Kunlun ji Nanhai gudai hangxing kao* 昆侖及南海古代船行考 (A study of Kunlun and ancient South Seas navigation). Translated by Feng Chengjun. Beijing: Zhonghua, 1957.

"The Fierce Resistance of Our People." *Nhân dân* (The people), December 1, 2001. http://www.nhandan.org.vn/english/history/20011201.html (accessed June 30, 2004).

FitzGerald, C. P. *The Chinese View of Their Place in the World*. London: Oxford University Press. 1964.

―――. *The Southern Expansion of the Chinese People*. New York: Praeger, 1972.

Franke, Herbert. "Diplomatic Missions of the Sung State: 960–1276." Public lecture, Australian National University, Canberra, Australian Capitol Territory, March 25, 1981.

―――, ed. *Sung Biographies*. Wiesbaden, Germany: Steiner, 1976.

Gaspardone, Emile. "Bibliographie annamite." *Bulletin de l'Ecole Française d'Extrême-Orient* 34 (1934): 1–172.

Gernet, Jacques. *A History of Chinese Civilization*. 2nd edition. Cambridge: Cambridge University Press, 1996.

Gladney, Dru C. *Muslim Chinese: Ethnic Nationalism in the People's Republic*. Cambridge: Harvard University Press, 1991, 1996.

Glover, Ian. "Letting the Past Serve the Present — Some Contemporary Uses of Archaeology in Viet Nam." *Antiquity* 73, no. 281 (September 1999): 594–602.

Guan Fuchuan. *Songdai Guangzhou de haiwai maoyi* 宋代廣州的海外貿易 (Song dynasty overseas trade from Canton). Guangzhou: Guangdong Renmin, 1987.

"Guangxi cleans up cross-border tourism." Xinhua News Agency, September 10, 2002. Beijing: COMTEX News Network.

Guangxi Institute of Ethnology (Guangxi Minzu Yanjiusuo 廣西民族研究所). *Guangxi shaoshu minzu diqu shike beiwen ji* 廣西少數民族地區碑文集 (A collection of inscriptional materials from the minority regions of Guangxi). Guilin: Guangxi Xin Hua Shu Dian Fa Xing, 1982.

Guangxi tongzu wenxue 廣西童族文學 (Zhuang literature from Guangxi). Nanning: Guangxi Tongzu Zizhi Chu Renmin, 1961.

Guo Tingyi et al. *Zhong-Yue wenhua lunji* 中越文化論集 (A collection of essays on Sino-Vietnamese culture). Taipei: Zhonghua Wenhua, 1956.

Hà Văn Thư and Lã Văn Lô. *Văn hóa Tày Nùng* (Tay Nung culture). Hanoi: Nhà Xuất Bản Văn Hóa, 1984.

Hagesteijn, Renee. *Circles of Kings: Political Dynamics in Early Continental Southeast Asia*. Dordrecht, Holland; Providence, R.I.: Foris Publications, 1989.

Hall, Kenneth, and John Whitmore, eds. "Economic History of Early Southeast Asia." In *The Cambridge History of Southeast Asia*. Vol. 1, part 1, *From Early Times to c. 1500*, edited by Nicholas Tarling. Cambridge: Cambridge University Press, 1999.

―――. *Explorations in Early Southeast Asian History: The Origins of Southeast Asian Statecraft*. Michigan Papers on South and Southeast Asia, 11. Ann Arbor: University of Michigan, 1976.

Han Xiaorong. "Who Invented the Bronze Drum? Nationalism, Politics, and a Sino-Vietnamese Archeological Debate of the 1970s and 1980s." *Asian Perspectives* 43, no. 1 (Spring 2004).

Hansen, Valerie. *Changing Gods in Medieval China, 1127–1276*. Princeton, N.J.: Princeton University Press, 1990.

Hanyu da zidian 漢語大字典 (Great Han character dictionary). Chengdu: Sichuan Cishu, 1988.

Hardy, Andrew. "Strategies of Migration to Upland Areas in Contemporary Vietnam." *Asia Pacific Viewpoint* 41, no. 1 (April 2000): 23–34.

Harrell, Stevan. *Ways of Being Ethnic in Southwest China*. Seattle: University of Washington Press, 2001.

———, ed. *Cultural Encounters on China's Ethnic Frontiers*. Seattle: University of Washington Press, 1995.

Harris, Lillian Craig. "Xinjiang, Central Asia and the Implications for China's Policy in the Islamic World." *China Quarterly*, no. 133 (March 1993): 111–29.

Hartwell, Robert M. *Tribute Missions to China, 960–1126*. Philadelphia: R. M. Hartwell, 1983.

Helms, Mary W. *Craft and the Kingly Ideal: Art, Trade, and Power*. Austin: University of Texas Press, 1993.

Henderson, John B. *The Development and Decline of Chinese Cosmology*. New York: Columbia University Press, 1984.

Herman, John E. "The Mu'ege Kingdom: A Brief History of a Frontier Empire in Southwest China." In *Political Frontiers, Ethnic Boundaries and Human Geographies in Chinese History*, edited by Don J. Wyatt and Nicola Di Cosmo. London: RoutledgeCurzon, 2003.

Hevia, James L. "A Multitude of Lords: Qing Court Ritual and the Macartney Embassy of 1793." *Late Imperial China* 10, no. 2 (December 1989): 72–105.

———. *Cherishing Men from Afar: Qing Guest Ritual and the Macartney Embassy of 1793*. Durham, N.C.: Duke University Press, 1995.

Hill, Ann Maxwell. *Merchants and Migrants: Ethnicity and Trade among Yunnanese Chinese in Southeast Asia*. New Haven, Conn.: Yale University Southeast Asia Studies, 1998.

Hoàng Văn Lâu. "A Poem from the Tenth Century" (Về bài tư ở thế kỷ X). In *Several Issues regarding the Study of Han Nom* (Một số văn đề bạn học Hán Nôm). Hanoi: Khoa Học Xã Hội, 1983.

Hoàng Xuân Hãn. *Lý Thương Kiệt* (Lý Thương Kiệt). Translated by Li Guo 利國. *Nanya yu Dongnanya ziliao* 南亞與東南亞資料 (South Asian and

Southeast Asian materials) 79, no. 2 (1988); 36 (1989). Beijing: CASS South and Southeast Asian Research Institute.

———. *Lý Thương Kiệt: Lịch sử ngoại giao và Tông giáo triầu Lý* (Lý Thương Kiệt: A history of Song-Lý foreign relations). Hanoi: Sông Nhị, 1949.

Hodgkin, Thomas. *Vietnam: The Revolutionary Path*. London: Macmillan Press, 1981.

Holcombe, Charles. *The Genesis of East Asia: 221 B.C.–A.D. 907*. Honolulu: University of Hawaii Press, 2001.

Holmgren, Jennifer. *Chinese Colonisation of Northern Vietnam: Administrative Geography and Political Development in the Tongking Delta, First to Sixth Centuries A.D.* Oriental Monograph Series no. 27. Canberra: Australian National University, Faculty of Asian Studies, 1980.

Hsieh, Shih-chung. "On the Dynamics of Tai/Dai-Lue Ethnicity: An Ethnohistorical Analysis." In *Cultural Encounters on China's Ethnic Frontiers*, edited by Stevan Harrell. Seattle: University of Washington Press, 1995.

Huang, Haimin, and Thanh van Thai. "Roundup: Vietnamese Border Gate Economy Blossoms." *Xinhua News Agency*, May 22, 2003. Beijing: COMTEX News Network.

Huang Xianfan. *Zhuangzu tongshi* 壯族通史 (A survey of Zhuang history). Nanning: Guangxi Minzu, 1988.

———. *Nong Zhigao* 儂智高 (Nong Zhigao). Nanning: Guangxi Renmin, 1983.

Huang Xiurong. *Guangxi lidai dili* 廣西歷代地理 (The history and geography of the Guangxi region). Nanning: Guangxi Minzu, 1985.

Huang Zhilian. *Yazhou de hua xia zhixu: Zhongguo yu Yazhou guojia guanxi xingtai lun* 亞洲的華夏秩序：中國與亞洲國家關係形態論 (Asia's Sinic order: A discussion of the nature of Sino-Asian relations). Beijing: Zhongguo Renmin Daxue, 1992.

Hucker, Charles O. *A Dictionary of Official Titles in Imperial China*. Palo Alto, Calif.: Stanford University Press, 1985.

Hugh-Jones, Stephen, and James Laidlaw, eds. *The Essential Edmund Leach*. Vol. 1, *Anthropology and Society*. New Haven, Conn.: Yale University Press, 2000.

Hymes, Robert P., and Conrad Schirokauer, eds. *Ordering the World: Approaches to State and Society in Sung Dynasty China*. Berkeley: University of California Press, 1993.

Jiang, Shaoyu. *Songchao shi shi leifan* 宋朝史事類凡 (A collection of various matters from the Song dynasty). Shanghai: Guji, 1981.

Jin Hong. *Guangxi tongzhi* (Guangxi gazetteer). In *Yinying wenyuan siku quanshu*, ed. Qian Yuanchang et al. Taipei: Taiwan Shangwu, 1983.

Kaup, Katherine Palmer. *Creating the Zhuang: Ethnic Politics in China.* Boulder, Colo.: L. Rienner, 2000.

Kawahara, Masahiro. "Nong Zhigao de panluan he Jiaozhi de guanxi" 儂智高的叛亂和交趾的關係 (The Nùng Trí Cao rebellion and relations with Giao Chi). Translated by Li Rongcun. *Guoli biance guankan* 國立編冊館刊 1, no. 4 (December 1972): 83–100.

Kertzer, David. *Ritual, Politics, and Power.* New Haven, Conn.: Yale University Press, 1988.

Lã Văn Lô. "Bước đầu nghiên cứu về chế độ xã hội Tày, Nùng, Thái dưới thời Pháp thuộc" (First step in the research on the social system of the Tay, Nung, and Thai areas during the French occupation). *Nghiên cứu lịch sử* (Historical research), no. 68 (1964).

LaFont, Pierre-Bernard. *Les frontières du Vietnam: Histoire des frontières de la peninsule indochinoise* (The frontiers of Vietnam: History of the frontiers of the Indochinese peninsula). Paris: L'Harmattan, 1989.

Laffey, Ella. *Relations between Chinese Provincial Officials and the Black Flag Army, 1883–1885.* PhD diss., Cornell University, 1971.

Lary, Diana. *Region and Nation: The Kwangsi Clique in Chinese Politics, 1925–1937.* London and New York: Cambridge University Press, 1974.

Lattimore, Owen. *Studies in Frontier History: Collected Papers 1928–1958.* Paris: Mouton & Company, 1962.

Lê Đình Sỹ. *Kế sách giữ nước thời Lý-Trần* (Means of national defense in the Ly-Tran period). Hanoi: Chính Trị Quốc Gia, 1994.

Le Thanh Khoi. *Histoire du Viet Nam.* Paris: Sudestasie, 1981.

LeBar, Frank M., et al., eds. *Ethnic Groups of Mainland Southeast Asia.* New Haven, Conn.: Human Relations Area Files Press, 1964.

Leach, Edmund. *Political Systems of Highland Burma: A Study of Kachin Social Structure.* London: Athlone Press, 1970.

Leonard, Jane Kate. *Wei Yuan and China's Rediscovery of the Maritime World.* Cambridge: Harvard University Press, 1984.

Li Ganfen. *Zhuangzu baike cidian* 壯族百科辭典 (Zhuang encyclopedic dictionary). Nanning: Nanning Renmin, 1993.

Li Xiangping. *An Outline of Zhuang History and Culture.* Nanning: Guangxi Minzu, 1995.

Li Yutang 李雨堂 et al. *Wuhu pingnan yanyi* 五虎平南演義 (The tale of pacifiying the southern Wuhu barbarians). Taipei: Fengyun Shidai, 1987.

Lin Tianwai. *Songdai xiangyao maoyi shigao* 宋代香藥貿易史 (A history of the perfume trade of the Song dynasty). Taipei: Zhongguo Wenhua Daxue, 1986.

Liu Boji. *Chunqiu Huimeng zhengzhi* 春秋會盟政治 (The politics of the "Peace Covenant" during the Spring and Autumn Period). Taipei: Zhonghua Congshu, 1962.

Lü Shipeng. *Bei shu shiqi de Yuenan* 北屬時期的越南 (Vietnam during the period of Chinese rule: 3rd century BCE to the 10th century). Monograph Series no. 3. Hong Kong: Chinese University of Hong Kong, New Asia Research Institute, 1964.

———. "Songdai Zhong-Yue guanxi nianbiao" 宋代中越關係年表 (A chronicle of Sino-Vietnamese relations during the Song dynasty). *Donghai xuebao* 東海學報 2, no. 1 (June 1960).

Marr, David, and A. C. Milner, eds. *Southeast Asia in the 9th to 14th Centuries*. Singapore: Institute of Southeast Asian Studies, 1986.

Maspero, M. Georges. *Le royaume de Champa*. Paris: Les Éditions G. Van Oest, 1928.

Maspero, Henri. "Études d'histoire d'Annam." *Bulletin de l'École Française d'Extrême-Orient* 16 (1916): 1–55; 18 (1918): 1–36.

McCoy, Alfred. *The Politics of Heroin: CIA Complicity in the Global Drug Trade*. Revised 2nd edition. New York: Lawrence Hill Books, 1991.

McLeod, Mark W. "Indigenous Peoples and the Vietnamese Revolution." *Journal of World History* 10, no. 2 (Fall 1999): 353–89.

Michaud, Jean, ed. *Turbulent Times and Enduring Peoples: Mountain Minorities in the South-east Asian Massif*. London: Curzon Press, 2000.

Mote, Frederick W., and Denis Twitchett, eds. *The Cambridge History of China: The Ming Dynasty, 1368–1644*. Vol. 7, part 1. Cambridge: Cambridge University Press, 1988.

Munro, Donald J. *The Concept of Man in Early China*. Stanford, Calif.: Stanford University Press, 1969.

Nan Yue. "A Discussion of the Nature of Nong Zhigao's Revolt." *Minzu yanjiu* 民族研究 (Ethnicity research) 8 (1959).

Nguyễn Huệ Chi. *Thơ Văn Lý-Trần* (Literature of the Lý and Trần dynasties), vol. 1. Hanoi: Nhà Xuất Bản Khoa Học Xã Hội, 1977.

Nguyễn Ngọc Huy. "Limits on State Power in Traditional China and Vietnam." *The Vietnam Forum* 6 (Summer–Fall 1985).

Nguyễn Ngọc Huy et al. *The Le Code: Law in Traditional Vietnam: A Comparative Sino-Vietnamese Legal Study with Historical-Juridical Analysis and Annotations*, vol. 1. Athens: Ohio University Press, 1987.

Nguyễn Quang Hồng, ed. *Văn khắc Hán Nôm Việt Nam* (The Sino-Nom engraved texts of Vietnam). Hanoi: Nhà Xuất Bản Khoa Học Xã Hội, 1992.

Nguyễn Tài Cẩn. "Một vài ý kiền về phương hướng đào tạo cản bộ ngành Hán Nôm" (Several points regarding training orientation for cadres working in Han Nom collections). In *Thư tịch cổ và nhiệm vụ mới: Kỷ yếu hội nghị "Văn đề thư tịch Hán Nôm" ngày 28-4-1978 tại Hà Nội* (Ancient catalogs and their modern mission: Proceedings from the April 28, 1978, Hanoi conference "Problems with Han Nom catalogs"). Hanoi: Nhà Xuất Bản Khoa Học Xã Hội, 1979.

Nguyễn Tuấn Liệu. "May nét tính hính và nhận xét về chế độ quang trong dân tộc Tày ở Hà Giang" (A few aspects and observations on the *quang* system among the Tay minority in Ha Giang province). *Nghiên cứu lịch sử* (Historical research), no. 44 (1962).

Nguyễn Văn Siêu. *Đại Việt địa dư toàn biên* (The complete atlas of the Đại Việt kingdom). Hanoi: Viên Sử Học, Văn Hóa, 1997.

Okada Koji. *Chukoku kanan minzoku shakaishi kenkyu* (Studies on the ethnic and social history of southern China). Tokyo: Kyuko Shoin, 1993.

———. *Studies on the Ethnical and Social History of Southern China* (Zhongguo huanan minzu shehui shi yanjiu 中國華南民族社會史研究). Translated by Zhao Lingzhi 趙令志 and Li Delong 李德龍. Beijing: Minzu Chubanshe, 2002.

Pan Yihong. *Son of Heaven and Heavenly Qaghan: Sui-Tang China and Its Neighbors*. Bellingham: Western Washington University Center for East Asia Studies, 1997.

Pavie, Auguste. *A la conquête des coeurs*. Paris: Presses Universitaires de France, 1947.

Pelley, Patricia. "'Barbarians' and 'Younger Brothers': The Remaking of Race in Postcolonial Vietnam." *Journal of Southeast Asian Studies* 29, no. 2 (September 1998).

Peng Lin. *"Zhouli" zhuti sixiang yu chengshu niandai yanjiu* 周禮主體思想與成書年代研究 (A study of the basic doctrines and the date of completion regarding the *Rites of Zhou*.) Hebei: Zhongguo Shehui Kexue, 1991.

Phan Huy Chu. *Lịch triều hiến chương loại chí* (An encyclopedia of institutions from successive courts). Hanoi: Vien Su Hoc Viet Nam, 1960–61.

Phan Huy Lê. "Nùng Trí Cao nhân vật lịch sử và biểu tượng văn hóa" (Nùng Trí Cao as historical figure and cultural phenomenon). In *Nùng Trí Cao: Kỷ yếu hội thảo khoa học* (Nùng Trí Cao: Annals of a meeting for scientific study), edited by Trần Văn Phượng et al. Cao Bằng: Sở Văn Hóa Thông Tin, 1995.

Phúc Tư Khâm 覆茲欽. *Đại Nam nhất thống du đồ* 大南一統輿圖. Tự Đức 14 (1861) edition. VHN Manuscript.

Piyanart, Bunnag. "Kinship and Patron-Client Systems in Thai Politics during the Early Ratankosin Period." In *Proceedings of the 4th International Conference on Thai Studies*, vol. 4. Kunming: Institute of Southeast Asian Studies, 1990.

Reid, Anthony. *Charting the Shape of Early Modern Southeast Asia*. Singapore: Institute of Southeast Asian Studies, 2000.

Reynolds, Craig J. "A New Look at Old Southeast Asia (Early Southeast Asian Historiography)." *The Journal of Asian Studies* 54, no. 2 (May 1995): 419–47.

Rossabi, Morris, ed. *China among Equals: The Middle Kingdom and Its Neighbors, 10th–14th Centuries*. Berkeley: University of California Press, 1983.

Sariti, Anthony W. "A Note on Foreign Policy Decision Making in the Northern Sung." *Sung Studies Newsletter* (Ithaca) no. 8 (October 1973): 3–11.

Savina, F. M. *Dictionnaire Étymologique Français-Nùng-Chinois*. Hong Kong: La Société des Missions Étrangères, 1924.

Schaberg, David. *A Patterned Past: Form and Thought in Early Chinese Historiography*. Cambridge: Harvard University Asia Center, 2001.

Schafer, Edward H. *The Vermilion Bird: T'ang Images of the South*. Berkeley: University of California Press, 1967.

Schein, Louisa. *Minority Rules: The Miao and the Feminine in China's Cultural Politics*. Durham, N.C.: Duke University Press, 2000.

Schwartz, Benjamin. *The World of Thought in Ancient China*. Cambridge: Belknap Press of Harvard University, 1985.

Shen, Jingfang. "Term Zhao and the Theories in Relation to It." In *Proceedings of the 4th International Conference on Thai Studies*, 2: 211–13. Kunming: Institute of Southeast Asian Studies, 1990.

Shin, Leo K. "Contracting Chieftaincy: Political Tribalization of the Southwest in Ming China." Paper presented at the symposium "Empire, Nation, and Region: The Chinese World Order Reconsidered," at Berkeley, California, 1995.

Sima Qian. *Records of the Grand Historian: Han Dynasty I*. Translated by Burton Watson. Revised edition. New York: Columbia University Press, 1993.

Smith, Paul Jakov. Introduction to *The Sung Dynasty and Its Precursors, 906–1279*, edited by Denis Twitchett and Paul Jakov Smith. Vol. 5, part 1 of *The Cambridge History of China*. Cambridge: Cambridge University Press, forthcoming.

———. "State Power and Economic Activism during the New Policies, 1068–1085: The Tea and Horse Trade and the 'Green Sprouts' Loan Policy." In *Ordering the World: Approaches to State and Society in Sung Dynasty China*, edited by Robert P. Hymes and Conrad Schirokauer. Berkeley: University of California Press, 1993.

Smith, Richard J. *Chinese Maps: Images of All Under Heaven*. Hong Kong: Oxford University Press, 1996.

Somers, Robert Milton. *The Collapse of T'ang Order*. PhD diss., Yale University, 1975.

Tan Qixiang. *Zhonggou lishi ditu ji* 中國歷史地圖集 (The historical atlas of China). Shanghai: China Cartographic Publishing House, 1989.

Tan Phat, Antoine Nguyen. *Mahayana Buddhism and Its Background in India and China*. PhD diss., California Institute of Integral Studies, 1981.

Tao Jing-shen. *Two Sons of Heaven: Studies in Sung-Liao Relations*. Tucson: University of Arizona Press, 1988.

Tarling, Nicholas, ed. *The Cambridge History of Southeast Asia*. Vol. 1, *From Early Times to c. 1800*. Cambridge: Cambridge University Press, 1992.

Taylor, Keith W. "Madagascar in the Ancient Malayo-Polynesian Myths." In *Explorations in Early Southeast Asian History: The Origins of Southeast Asian Statecraft*, edited by Kenneth Hall and John Whitmore. Ann Arbor: Michigan Papers on South and Southeast Asia 11, 1976.

———. *The Birth of Vietnam*. Berkeley: University of California Press, 1983.

———. "The Early Kingdoms." In *The Cambridge History of Southeast Asia*, vol. 1, *From Early Times to c. 1500*, edited by Nicholas Tarling. Cambridge: Cambridge University Press, 1992.

———. "Looking behind the Vietnamese Annals: Lý Phật Mã (1028–54) and Lý Nhật Tôn (1054–72) in the *Việt Sử Lược* and the *Toan Thư*." *The Vietnam Forum* 7 (Winter–Spring 1986).

———. "Notes on the *Việt Điện U Linh Tập*." *The Vietnam Forum* 8 (Summer–Fall 1986).

———. "On Being Muonged." *Asian Ethnicity* 2, no. 1 (2001): 25–34.

Taylor, Keith W., and John K. Whitmore, eds. *Essays into Vietnamese Pasts*. Studies on Southeast Asia no. 19. Cornell Southeast Asian Program, 1995.

Thongchai Winichakul. *Siam Mapped: A History of the Geo-Body of a Nation*. Honolulu: University of Hawaii Press, 1994.

Tønnesson, Stein. *The Vietnamese Revolution of 1945: Roosevelt, Ho Chi Minh and de Gaulle in a World at War*. London: Sage Publications, 1991.

"Tourism belt forming along China-Vietnam border." *People's Daily Online*, October 15, 2002. http://english.people.com.cn/202210/eng_20021015_105102.shtml.

Trần Trọng Kim. *Việt Nam sử lược* (A record of Vietnamese history). Vol. 1. Saigon: Trung Tâm Học Liệu Xuất Bản, 1971; Glendale, Calif.: Đại Nam, 1982.

Trần Văn Phương et al., eds. *Nùng Trí Cao: Kỷ yếu hội thảo khoa học* (Nùng Trí Cao: Annals of a meeting for scientific study). Cao Bằng: Sở Văn Hóa Thông Tin, 1995.

Turton, Andrew, ed. *Civility and Savagery: Social Identity in Tai States*. Richmond, Surrey: Curzon Press, 2000.

United Nations Development Programme Viet Nam. "Ethnic Minorities Populations in Viet Nam: 1979, 1989 and 1999." http://www.undp.org.vn/projects/vie96010/cemma/vie96010/populations.htm.

Xu Lianda. *Zhongguo lidai guangzhi cidian* 中國歷代管制詞典 (Dictionary of Chinese historical official titles). Anhui: Anhui Jiaoyu, 1991.

Wade, Geoff. "Some Topoi in Southern Border Historiography." In *China and Her Neighbors: Borders, Visions of the Other, Foreign Policy, 10th to 19th Century*, edited by Sabine Dabringhaus and Roderich Ptak. Wiesbaden, Germany: Harrassowitz Verlag, 1997.

Walker, Richard L. *The Multi-state System of Ancient China*. Hamden, Conn.: The Shoe String Press, 1953.

Wang Gungwu. *China and the Chinese Overseas*. Singapore: Times Academic Press. 1991.

———. *The Structure of Power in North China during the Five Dynasties*. Kuala Lumpur: University of Malaya Press, 1963.

Wechsler, Howard J. *Offerings of Jade and Silk: Ritual and Symbol in the Legitimation of the Tang Dynasty*. New Haven, Conn.: Yale University Press, 1985.

Wei Yifan. *Zhuangzu yingxiong Nong Zhigao* 壯族英雄儂智高 (The Zhuang hero Nong Zhigao). Guangxi: Jili Chubanshe, 1994.

Weng Dujian. *Zhongguo minzu Guangxi shi gangyao* 中國民族廣西史綱要 (A survey history of Chinese minorities in Guangxi). Beijing: Zhongguo Shehui Kexue, 1990.

Whitmore, John K. *Vietnam, Ho Quy Ly, and the Ming (1371–1421)*. The Lac Viet Series 2. New Haven, Conn.: Yale Center for International and Area Studies, 1985.

Wilkinson, Endymion Porter. *Chinese History: A Manual*. Cambridge: Harvard University Asia Center, 1998.

Wolters, O. W. "Historians and Emperors in Vietnam and China: Comments Arising Out of Le Van Huu's History. Presented to the Tran Court in 1272." In *Perceptions of the Past in Southeast Asia*, edited by Anthony Reid and David Marr. Singapore: Heinemann Educational Books, 1979.

———. *History, Culture, and Region in Southeast Asian Perspectives*. Revised edition. Ithaca, N.Y.: Cornell Southeast Asia Program, 1999.

———. "Possibilities for a Reading of the 1293–1357 Period in the Vietnamese Annals." In *Southeast Asia in the 9th and 14th Centuries*, edited by David Marr and A. C. Milner. Singapore: Institute of Southeast Asian Studies, 1986.

Womack, Brantly. *China and Vietnam: The Politics of Asymmetry*. New York: Cambridge University Press, 2006.

Woodside, Alexander B. "Territorial Order and Collective-Identity Tensions in Confucian Asia: China, Vietnam, Korea." *Daedalus* 127, issue 3 (Summer 1998): 191–220.

———. *Vietnam and the Chinese Model: A Comparative Study of Vietnamese and Chinese Government in the First Half of the Nineteenth Century*. Cambridge: Harvard University Press, 1988.

———. "Vietnamese History: Confucianism, Colonialism and the Struggle for Independence." *Vietnam: Essays on History, Culture, and Society* (1985): 1–20. Asia Society "Ask Asia." http://www.askasia.org/teachers/Instructional_Resources/Materials/Readings/Vietnam/R_vietnam_4.htm (accessed September 25, 2004).

Wyatt, David K. *Thailand: A Short History*. New Haven, Conn.: Yale University Press, 1984.

Wyatt, Don J., and Nicola Di Cosmo, eds. *Political Frontiers, Ethnic Boundaries and Human Geographies in Chinese History*. London: RoutledgeCurzon, 2003.

Xie Qikun. *Guangxi tongzhi* 廣西通志 (Guangxi gazetteer). Jiaqing edition. Taipei: Wenhai, 1966.

Xu Yunqiao. *Annan tongshi* 安南通史 (A survey history of An Nam). Singapore: Shijie, 1957.

Yamamoto, Tatsuro 山本達郎. *Annan shi kenkyu* 安南史研究 (Research in Annamese history). Vol. 1. Tokyo: Yamakawa, 1950.

Yamamoto, Tatsuro 山本達郎, Masahiro Kawahara 河原正博, et al. *Betonamu Chūgoku kankei shi: Kyoku-shi no taitō kara Shin-Futsu Sensō made* ベトナム中国関係史：曲氏の抬頭から清仏戦争まで (The history of international relations between Vietnam and China: From the rise of the Khuc family to the Sino-French War). Tokyo: Yamakawa Shuppansha, 1975.

Yi Xingguang. *Yu Jing pu zhuan zhilue* 余靖譜傳誌略 (A biographical chronology of Yu Jing). Guangzhou: Jinan Daxue, 1993.

Yu, Ying-shih. *Trade and Expansion in Han China: A Study in the Structure of Sino-Barbarian Economic Relations*. Berkeley: University of California Press, 1967.

Yunnan Academy of Social Sciences. *Proceedings of the 4th International Conference on Thai Studies, 11–13 May 1990*. Kunming: Shehuikexueyuan Dongnanyayanjiusuo, 1990.

Zhang Rongfang. *Nanyue guoshi* 南越國史 (History of the Nam Việt kingdom). Guangzhou: Guangdong Renmin, 1995.

Zhang Shengzhen and Qin Cailuan, eds. *Zhuangzu shi* 壯族史 (History for the Zhuang people). Guangzhou: Guangdong Renmin Chubanshe, 2002.

Zhao Erxun (1844–1927) et al., eds. *Qing shi gao* 清史稿 (A draft of Qing History). Beijing: Zhonghua Shu Ju, 1976–77.

Zhongguo Chengshiwang 中國城市網 (Cities of China Web site). "Major Historical Events in Yaan City" (Yaan lishi dashi 雅安歷史大事). http://www.chinacsw.com/cszx/yaan/lishi.htm (accessed July 29, 2004).

Zhou Cheng. *Song Dongjing kao* 宋東京考 (A study of the Song period imperial capital). Taipei: Wenshizhe, 1990.

Zhouli jinzhu jinyi 周禮今注今譯 (Modern commentary and translation of the *Rites of Zhou*). Translated and edited by Lin Yin. Taipei: Shangwu Yinshuguan, 1972.

Index

A Nùng: marriage relationship, 90, 126; A *Official History of the Song Dynasty*, writings on, 89–90; role in Trí Cao's rebellion, 90, 104, 112; temples devoted to, 173, 176*f*; titles granted, 68
An Dương Vương, 44
An Lushan Rebellion (*755–763*), 38
An Nam Protectorate, 38–39
Army of the Peaceful Sea, 38–39
Asian Development Bank, 180
Âu Lạc kingdom, 44

Bản Phân Temple, 173
Barlow, Jeffrey, 28, 77, 91, 117, 123
Battle of Bạch Đằng River, 43, 143
Battle of Fuliang River, 143–44
Bế clan, 164
Bế Khắc Thiệu, 166
Bi Gia Dụ, 131
Bi Juzheng, 28
Bình Dương, princess, 29, 77
Binh Dương, 77
Black Flag Army, 168–69
Bol, Peter, 114, 138
Bộ Thiệu Kham, 96
Bộ Thiệu Tư, 96
Bộ Văn Dũng, 52–53
bronze drum tradition, 70–71
Bushnell, Amy Turner, 6

Cai Qi, 16–17
Cao Jin, 103, 156
Cao Xiu, 107
Cham kingdom, 46, 49–52, 64, 130–31, 142
Chen Gong, 96, 101–2
Cheng Zhuo, 145
Chen Shaogui, 28
Chen Shu, 107, 108, 110
Chen Yaosu, 52, 53
Chiang Kai-shek (Jiang Jieshi), 157
chieftaincy system, 83
Chinese Communist government, 13, 158, 159. *See also* People's Republic of China
Chinese Nationalists, 157–58
Chinese Republic of Five Nationalities, 157
civil service examination exam policy, 115–16
Chu clan, 73, 123
Cổ Loa citadel, 43–44
The Complete History of the Great Viet, writings on: A Nùng, 90; Ai Cau insurrection, 79; Đinh Bộ Lĩnh vs. Đinh Liễn leadership, 46–47; Lê Hoàn attack on aboriginal settlements, 53; tribute mission of Đinh Bộ Lĩnh, 45; tribute mission of Lý dynasty, 61–62

265

Condominas, George, 84
Crossley, Pamela, 156
Cultural Revolution, 159

Đại Việt court, pre- and *11th* century: heavenly right to hegemonic action for the greater good, 80–81; marriage alliances to establish local ties, 29–30, 77–78, 164; *thổ ty* system of administration, 164–65; tribute system, 89; Twelve Lords period, 44
Dali kingdom, 8, 75, 84, 91
Đãn Nãi Giáp, 78
Đào Ngạn Temple, 173
Đảo Thạc Phụ, 61
Defend the Sovereign Royalist Movement, 168
Deng Xiaoping, 160–61
Deo Van Long, 171
Deo Van Tri, 169
Đinh Bộ Lĩnh, 40, 44–48, 65, 81–82
Đinh clan, 39. *See also specific leaders*
Đinh Liễn, 40, 44–48
Đinh Tuệ, 48
Di Qing, 107–12, 124, 128, 129
Đỗ Hanh, 52
Đồng Mu Temple, 173
Dong Zhongshu, 19
Dorofeeva-Lichtman, Vera, 18
Draft for a Continuation of "The Comprehensive Mirror for Aid in Government" (Li Tao), 103
Draft of Documents Pertaining to Song Official Matters (Song Xu), 126
Duan Siping, 75, 91

Du Qi, 64
Dương Cảnh Thông, 137

Eberhard, Wolfram, 110

Fan Zuyu, 31–32
Fenyin temple, 60
First Indochina War, *1946–1954*, 169, 171
Five Clans, 140
Five Dynasties period, 41, 75
Five Zones of Service, 18–19
French colonial administration, 13, 167–71
Fuliang River defense, 143–44

Gao Pian, 38
Gao Shian, 101
Garnier, Francis, 169
Gladney, Dru, 157, 158
Great Unity, 19
Guangxi Gazetteer, 156
Guangxi Zhuang Autonomous Region, China, 160
Guo Kui, 142, 144
Guo Wei, 39
Gu Yanwu, 156

Hà clan, 164
Hà Khánh Thường, 56
Hall, Kenneth, 34
Han community: Chinese nationalism and, 157; frontier settlements, 17, 127–28, 149; home region, 72; *neifu* status requested by, 27–28; present-day, 13; tribute system, obligation under, 20
Han dynasty, 35
Harrell, Stevan, 13, 30, 159

Hartwell, Robert, 45
Hà Văn Thư, 122
Heaven and Earth Society, 168
Hevia, James, 23–24
Hill, Ann Maxwell, 72, 76
History of the Great Viet
  (purportedly by Lê Văn Hưu), 145
Hmông, 170
Hoàng clan, 73, 164. *See also specific leaders*
Hoàng Khánh Tạp, 57–58
Hoàng Thành Nha, 53
Hoàng Trọng Khanh, 126, 133
Hoàng Xuân Hãn, 121–22
Hồ Chí Minh, 171
Hou Zhou, 39
Huang Chao Rebellion, 27
Huang Chongyin, 169
Huang Fen, 112
Huang Lingde, 52–53
Huang Shifu, 100, 102
Huang Wei, 100
Huang Xianfan, 117, 162
Huang Xiangui, 112

An Illustration of Prefectures and Commandaries beyond the Influence of Our Dynasty, 148
Indochinese Communist Party (ICP), 170
Indochinese Wars: First, *1946–1954*, 169, 171; Second, *1955–1976*, 172; Third, *1979*, 162, 172

Jaya Indravarman I, 46
Jiang Jie, 115
Jiang Jieshi (Chiang Kai-shek), 157
jiedushi system, 41–42, 61
jiezhen defense command, 50–51

jimi system: Northern Song period, 149; Song dynasty re-establishment of, 9–10, 27–29, 31, 38–48; Tang dynasty development of, 26–27, 31–32, 41; tributary relations vs., 18

Kaup, Katherine, 159, 160
Kertzer, David, 9
Khitans, 95
Khúc Thừa Mỹ, 123
Kinh, 5, 13, 164, 168, 172
Kublai Khan, 91
Kỳ Sầm Temple, 91, 167, 173, 177–78, 178*f*

Laffey, Ella, 72
Laos, Tai-speakers in, 12
Lary, Diana, 154, 158, 179
Lã Văn Lô, 122
Leach, Edmund, 7
LeBlond, Commandant, 167–68
Lê clan, tributary relations with the Chinese court, 39–40, 65. *See also specific leaders*
Lê Đinh Sỹ, 122
Lê Hoàn, reign of (*980–1009*): Cham invaded under, 49; consolidation of power under, 49; death and succession, 56–57; Luzhou plunder, 52; overthrow of Đinh Tuệ, 48; people submit to Song authority, 56; political and economic consolidation during, 50; Ruhong garrison attack, 52–55; Song invasion defeated, 48–49, 65, 123–24; Song Taizong's recognition of, 53–54; trade controlled under, 50; tribute

missions to Song court, 50–51, 55–56
Lê Lợi, 166–67
Lê Long Đĩnh, 56–57, 59–60
Lê Long Toàn, 56
Lê Long Việt, 56
Lê Mạo, 126, 133
Lê Minh Đế, 56
Lê Minh Hộ, 57
Lê Minh Sương, 60
Lê Tái Nghiêm, 60
Lê Thành Khôi, 122
Lê Thiệu, 56
Lê Văn Hưu, 145
Lê Văn Khôi Rebellion, 164–65
Lê Văn Thịnh, 145–46
Liang Shi, 107
Liêu Ngọc, 171
Liệu Thông, 133
Li Jianzhong, 53
Liao kingdom, 58
Ling Ce, 56–57
Li Ruozhuo, 53
Li Tao, 103
Liu Gong, 43, 123
Liu Hongcao, 43
Liu Ji, 110–11
Liu Yan, 41
Liu Yi, 140
Liu Yin, 123
Li Wenxiong, 128
Li Wenzhu, 59
Li Xiao, 101
Lôi Hỏa, 90–91
Long Yanyao, 27
Lu Jia, 54
Lư Báo, 126, 133–35
Lương Châu, 112
Lương Nhâm Văn, 60

Lưu Ký, 133–36, 140
Lu Shen, 127, 132–33
Lu Yongfu, 168–69
Lý Ac Thuyên, 63
Lý Bí revolt, 35–37
Lý Can Đức, 137, 145
Lý Công Hiển, 63
Lý Công Uẩn, reign of (*1009–1028*), 39, 59–63, 77
Lý dynasty: beginnings, 59–60; political and economic consolidation during, 50, 92; succession, 129; tributary relations through ritual practices, 18–20, 39–40. *See also specific leaders*
Lý Hữu Vinh, 37
Lý Kế Tiên, 131
Lý Khoan Thái, 62
Lý Nhân Mỹ, 61
Lý Nhân Tông, 150
Lý Nhật Tôn, reign of (*1054–1072*), 78–79, 129, 130–31, 134, 136–37
Lý Phật Mã, reign of (*1000–1054*): activist policies in frontier management, 77–82; beginnings, 63; border relations under, 77; Champa invasion, 64; death of, 129; expansionist policy, 29–30, 64, 66, 129–30; frontier population submits to Song, 64, 96; imperial image, 79, 80; internal revolts, suppression of, 78–79; marriage alliances to establish local ties, 29–30, 77–78; Nùng Trí Cao enfeoffment, 91–92, 99; Nùng Trí Cao rebellion during, 91–94, 108–10, 112; Nùng Tôn Phúc revolt, 68–69, 80–84, 124; Song Renzong court relationship,

Index

63–64, 80–81, 85, 96; Trân Cồng Vĩnh insurgency, 15–16, 64
Lý Phật Tử, 37
Lý Thướng Kiệt, 122, 123, 137, 139, 141–42
Lý Thướng Kiệt (Han), 121

Ma clan, 164
Macartney mission, 23–24
Ma Gui, 104
Man barbarians of Qinzhou, 59
McCoy, Alfred, 170
McLeod, Mark, 168, 172
Miao rebellion, 169
Michaud, Jean, 170
Ming period, 83
Mirror for Aid in Government of the Tang (Fan Zuyu), 31
Mo Hongyan (Mo clan), 28–29
müang society, 72–73, 82–83
Myanmar, Tai-speakers in, 12

Nã Lư Temple, 173
Nanning Economic and Technological Development Area, 180
Nanzhao kingdom, 31, 75, 84
Nanzhao War (862–66), 38
negotiation, paradigm of, 6–7
neifu status requests, pre-*11th* century: Champa emissaries, 46; Dinh Bo Linh and the Đại Cồ Việt kingdom, 45; Han frontier communities, 27–28; Mo clan, 28–29
neifu status requests, Song Renzong reign: Nùng Tông Đán, 125–26; Nùng Trí Cao, 93, 96–98, 125–26; Trân Cồng Vĩnh, 15–18, 63–64
Ngô clan, 43–44. *See also specific leaders*

Ngô Hoài Tự, 61
Ngô Quyền, 43–44
Nguyễn Bá Trâm, 50
Nguyễn clan, 164
Nguyễn Đinh Trạc, 164–65
Nguyễn Đức Nha, 167
Nguyễn Ngọc Huy, 122
Nguyễn Thiêu Cung, 55–56, 59
Nguyễn Thủ Cương, 62
Nguyễn Văn Nha, 164–65
Ngụy Trưng, 180*f*
Nine Zones of Service, 18
Nong clan, 158, 164
Nông Tú Diệp, 168
Nong Zhigao, 117
Nong Zhigao (Huang), 162
Notes from Mengxi (Shen Kua), 133
Nùng, origin of term, 13
Nùng Binh, 126
Nùng Chí Trung, 100
Nùng clan: A Nùng's marriage into, 90; anti-French resistance, 167–71; frontier alliances post-Tri Cao rebellion, 125–26, 133–35; home region, 72; imperial privilege granted to leaders of, 163–64; kinship relationships, 73, 76; loyalty relationships, 73–74; post-Second Indochinese War, 172; present-day, 12; recognized by Song Shenzong, 135; rise of, early Song period, 74–77; Sino-Vietnamese border war and, 121–22; temple keepers, 177; tribute system, obligation under, 83; Tri Cao in shaping identity of, 173. *See also specific leaders*; Zhuang clan
Nùng Đanh Đạo, 76

Nùng Dân Phú, 75–76, 83
Nùng Hạ Khanh, 90, 126
Nùng Hạ Thanh, 75
Nùng Ké Phong, 112
Nùng Kế Tông, 112
Nùng Kiến Hậu, 100
Nùng Lương, 126
Nùng Nhật Tân, 125
Nùng Toàn Lộc, 76
Nùng Tông Đán, 121, 122, 125–26, 133–35, 141–42
Nùng Tôn Phúc, rise in power, 76–77
Nùng Tôn Phúc citadel, 173, 175*f*
Nùng Tôn Phúc revolt, 68–69, 80–84, 86–87, 124
Nùng Trí Cao: ambition of, 115–16; death of, 8, 113; early life, 89–94; enfeoffment, 91–92, 99; imperial image, 8; incarcerated at Thăng Long, 7; influence in shaping regional identity, 6–8; *neifu* status requested by, 93, 96–98, 125–26; official image, China and Vietnam, 7, 8, 161–62, 177–78; symbol of, 88
Nùng Trí Cao, commemorations: China's border region, 155–63, 162*f*; conclusions, 152–53, 179–82; festivals, 152, 167; introduction, 152–54; Vietnam's border region, 91, 163–79, 166*f*, 174*f*, 175*f*, 178*f*, 180*f*
Nùng Trí Cao cult, 155, 172
Nùng Trí Cao rebellion: attempts to obtain legitimacy, 6–7, 96–98, 125–26; basis for, 84, 89, 115–18; conclusions, 113–18; first act of (*1041*), 7, 86, 88, 91–95; frontier relations following, 124–25; Huang interpretation, 162; introduction, 88–89; military recruitment and strength, 99–102, 105, 106; overview, 7–8; pacification campaign post-, 11; second act of (*1048*), 7, 93–98; suppression, results of, 119; Vietnamese involvement in, 91–94, 108–10, 112
Nùng Trí Cao rebellion, Song Renzong court and the: court politics in, 69, 96–98; Di Qing counterattack plan, 107–12; family members executed, 112–13; Vietnamese involvement, 108–10, 112; Yizhou defense prepared, 113
Nùng Trí Cao rebellion, third act of (*1052*): Binzhou, attacks on, 106, 110–12; causes of, 98–99; Chen defeat, 108; Chinese chronicle of, 104–5; Di Qing counterattack, 107–12, 124; family members captured, 112–13; first campaign, 101–3; flees to Dali kingdom, 8; Guangzhou, attacks on, 105–7; Hengshan garrison, siege of, 103, 133; Hezhou, attack on, 106; Kingdom of the Great South established, 7, 102; map, 99*f*; military recruitment and strength, 99–102, 105, 106; results to political alliances, 133; trade during, 103–4; Vietnamese depiction of, 105; Yongzhou, attacks on, 52, 59, 94, 96–97, 101–3, 106–12; Zhaozhou, attack on, 106
Nùng Trí Hội, 126, 134, 135, 140

Nùng Trí Quang, 112
Nùng Trí Thông, 69
Nùng Trí Xuân, 145

Official History of the Song Dynasty (Songshi), writings on: A Nùng, 89–90; border negotiations, 147, 150; Đinh Bộ Lĩnh vs. Đinh Liễn leadership, 47–48; Five Clans tribute, 140; Lê Hoàn dynasty, 48; Lê Hoàn's Ruhong Garrison attack, 54–55; Nùng clan, 74; Nùng Tông Đán's political allegiance, 133; Nùng Trí Cao, 107, 113, 145; Nùng Trí Cao rebellion, 51–52, 108, 112–13; Wang-Nhật Tân meeting, 125; Zhang Li's execution, 102
Okada Koji, 149

Pác Bó Cave, 171
Pan Mei, 42
Pan Qixu, 163
Pan Yihong, 25
Pavie, Auguste, 169
Pavilion of Orthodoxy, 58
Pelley, Patricia, 120, 121
People's Republic of China: *1949–1966*, 158–60; *1966–1976*, 160–61; *1978*, era post-, 161; commemorations of Nùng Trí Cao, 155–63, 162*f*; Cultural Revolution, 159; ethnic identification project, 13, 159; minority policy, 161; nationalism movement, 157–58
People's Republic of China, present day: border zone development, 179–81; economic potential, 3–4; ethnic-minority groups in, 12

Phạm Văn Lưu, 164–65
Phan Huy Lê, 122
power, paradigm of, 6
Program of Action, 170
Pu Luo-e, 51

Qin dynasty, 35
Qing dynasty, 76, 157
Quảng Hoà Commune temple, 175*f*
Quảng Nguyên, 75–76, 90–91
Quảng Nguyên Commune temple, 173, 177
Quan Triêu, 124

A Record of Fengshan County, 128
A Record of Longjin County, 128
A Record of the Empire's Borders and Dimensions during the Taiping Period (Yue Shi), 129
A Record of This Region's Merits (Wang Xiangzhi), 129
Reid, Anthony, 49
Rites of Zhou (Zhou li), 19, 22–23
Riviere, Henri, 169
Ruhong garrison incident, 52–55

Schaberg, David, 18, 19
Schein, Lousa, 161
Schwartz, Benjamin, 19
Second Indochina War, *1955–1976*, 172
Sha clan, 158
Shao Hua, 56–57
Shen Kua, 133
Shen Qi, 140
Shi Jian, 112, 114
Sima Guang, 68–69, 81, 93, 114–15, 138
Sima Qian, 18, 173

Sino-Cham relations, Song dynasty, 46, 49–52, 64, 130–31, 142
Sino-French War (*1881–1884*), 169
Sino-Vietnamese border: map, 5*f*, 147*f*; negotiations, 120, 144–48, 163–64
Sip Song Chau Tai, 169–70
Smith, Paul, 39, 41, 138, 139
Sóc Hà Commune, view from, 4*f*
Sóc Ha Commune temple, 173, 174*f*, 177
Socialist Republic of Vietnam: border zone development, 179–81; economic potential, 3–4; Tai-speakers population in, 12–13. *See also* Vietnam
Song-Đại Việt, pre-*11th* century: conclusions, 63–67; *neifu* status requests during, 27–28, 28–29, 45, 46; Zhuang clan, 28–29; periods of encounters defining emergence of autonomous polities, 35; establishment of local political order, 35–37; fall of Tang to founding of Song, 38–48; *jiedushi* system transformation, 37–39; recentralization of Song authority, 27–29, 31, 38–48; trade during, 34, 49–50; Vietnamese expansion curtailed, 64–65. *See also* Le Hoan reign
Song-Đại Việt border region: Han community settlement of, 17, 127–28, 149; identity, factors in shaping, 6–8, 154; post-demarcation relations, 17; present-day, 3–4, 11–12, 179–81
Song-Đại Việt border war (*1075–1077*): basis for, 17, 118, 119, 124, 126–27; conclusions, 148–51; Fuliang River defense, 143–44; Lý Thưóng Kiệt attack in self defense, 141–43; map, 141*f*
Song-Đại Việt frontier relations, *11th* century: contributions to tensions in, 163; Liao frontier conflict defeat, 58; Lingnan Frontier, 36*f*; post-Nùng Trí Cao's defeat, 124–25; Qinzhou attack, 59; Renzong-Lý courts power-sharing relationship, 16–17, 85. *See also specific rulers*; Tai-speaking frontier communities, early Song period
Song-Đại Việt frontier relations, pre-border war: basis for conflicts during, 66; breakdown in, 119; cultural shifts, 128–29; economics of, 31, 138–40; historical scholarship on, 121–23; introduction, 119–23; Song militia reorganization, 126–27, 132–33, 140; Song territorial expansion, 138–40; Thàn Thiệu Thái attacks, 130–32; Việt territorial expansion, 129–30; Yang Baocai kidnapping, 130–31
Song-Đại Việt frontier relations, pre-border war shifting alliances: Han settlements increase, 127–28, 149; Lưu Ký, 135–36; Nùng clan, 125–26, 133–35; population shifts influence on, 127–29; Tai-speaking communities, 121–24
Song-Đại Việt tributary relations, *11th* century: celestial orders impact on, 58; conclusions, 30–32; early Song period, 31;

a hierarchical framework through ritual practices, 9–10, 18–20, 24, 25; historical changes in, 8–9; political context, 17–26. *See also* tribute missions, *11th* century; *under specific emperors*

Song-Đại Việt tributary relations, pre-*11th* century: Đinh ruling family, 44–48, 65; historical changes in, 8–9; *jiedushi* system incorporated, 41–42; *jimi* system re-established, 9–10, 27–29, 31, 38–48; Nanzhao resistance to, 38; trade relations, 59; tribute system, Nùng interpretation of, 83. *See also* Le Hoan reign; tribute missions, pre-*11th* century

Song dynasty: founding of, 38–48; Guest Ritual (Binli), 24; ritual practices defining a hierarchical world order, 9–10

Song dynasty, pre-*11th* century: political power of local leaders, 41, 42; recentralization of authority, 27–29, 31, 38–48

Song Huizong, reign of (*1101–1125*), 149, 150–51

Song Renzong, reign of (*1010–1063*): end of, 131; frontier management, 85, 150; frontier population submits to Song, 15, 16, 64, 96; Lý dynasty relationships, 62–64, 80–81, 85, 96; Nùng Tôn Phúc revolt, response to, 68–69; trade during, 64, 103–4, 140–41; tribute missions during, 80–81, 96–97, 102, 113, 131

Song Renzong, reign of (*1010–1063*), *neifu* status requests received: Nùng Tông Đán, 125–26; Nùng Trí Cao, 93, 96–98, 125–26; Trân Cồng Vĩnh, 15–18, 63–64

Song Renzong, reign of (*1010–1063*), Nùng Trí Cao rebellion: amnesty offered post-, 113; Binzhou counterattack, 110–12; conclusions, 113–18; court politics in, 96–98; Di Qing counterattack plan, 107–12; family members executed, 112–13; Vietnamese involvement in, 108–10, 112; Yizhou defense prepared, 113

Song Shenzong, reign of (*1067–1085*): beginning, 134; expansionist policy, 138–40; military preparedness, southern border, 74–75, 94–95; Nùng clan recognized, 135; political ambitions, 138–39; tribute missions during, 134, 140

Song Taizong, reign of (*939–997*): central control tightened, 43; civil service exam system, 116; frontier management, 28, 32, 75; *jiedushi* system under, 42; Lê Hoàn, military expedition against, 48–49; tribute mission by Mo clan, 28–29

Song Taizu, reign of (*927–976*), 28, 40, 43, 45, 83

Song Yingzong, reign of (*1063–1067*), 131, 134

Song Zhenzong, reign of (*997–1022*), 55–63

Southern Han kingdom, 41, 42–43, 123

Sri Vijaya, 46

Sui dynasty, 37

Su Jian, 105, 142
Sun Jie, 111
Sun Mian, 107, 110
Sun Pu, 113
A Survey of the History of Viet (author unknown), 137

Taiping Rebellion, 158
Tai-speaking communities: anti-French resistance, 168–70; bronze drum people, 70–71; frontier management, freedom in, 30; historically, 70–73; historical scholarship on, 122–23; home region, 70*f*, 71–72; kinship relationships, 72–73; modern day, 71; *müang* (upland) societies, 72–73, 82–83; Nùng Trí Cao, pride in, 152; population, present day, 11–12; post-1949 era, 160; post-border demarcation relations, 164; Sino-Vietnamese border war alliances, 121–24, 164; suppression of, post-Nùng Trí Cao rebellion, 118; tribute system in reclaiming regional independence, 9. *See also specific clans*
Tai-speaking frontier communities, early Song period: border relations, 77–78; chieftaincy system, 83; clan rivalry, 69–74; conclusions, 84–87; Nùng clan, rise of, 74–77; Nùng Tôn Phúc revolt, 68–69, 80–84, 86–87, 124; political geography, 69–74, 70*f*; tribute system, obligation under, 20, 82–83
Tang dynasty: chieftaincy system, 83; fall of, 38–48; Hoàng clan under, 73–74; *jiedushi* system transformed during, 37–39; *jimi* system during, 26–27, 31–32, 74; resistance to tributary ties, 38
Tanguts, 95
Tang Xuanzong, 37–39
Tao Bi, 142, 144
Tày community, 12, 13, 173
Taylor, Keith, 13
Thái clan, 12
Thailand, Tai-speakers in, 12
Than clan, 77
Thăng Long, 99, 121, 144
Thanh Minh Festival, 167
Thân Thiệu Thái, 63, 77, 130, 132
Thân Thừa Quý, 63
Third Indochina War, *1979*, 162, 172
Thongchai Winichakul, 82
Tønnesson, Stein, 170
Toshikazu, Araki, 98, 107, 115–16
trade relations: Huizong reign, 150–51; Lê Hoàn reign, 50; during Nùng Trí Cao rebellion, 103–4; Qing dynasty toll routes, 76; Renzong reign, 64, 103–4, 140–41; at Yongzhou, 59; Zhenzong reign, 59
Trân Cồng Vĩnh, 15–17, 63–64
Trấn Huy Phác, 166
Trần Trọng Kim, 122
Trần Ứng Ky, 64
tribute missions, *11th* century: Five Clans requirement, 140; Lý court, 80–81, 134; Lý Nhật Tôn, 131; Nùng Trí Cao, 96–97, 102; Xiao Gu, 98; Xichuan, 113. *See also* Song-Đại Việt tributary relations, *11th* century
tribute missions, pre-*11th* century: Champa emissaries, 46; Dinh

Bo Linh and the Đại Cồ Việt
  kingdom, 46–47; Lê Hoàn, 50–51,
  55–56; Lý Hữu Vinh, 37;
  Mo clan, 28–29; Sri Vijaya
  emissaries, 46. See also Song-Đại
  Việt tributary relations, pre-*11th*
  century
Tribute of Yu (*Yugong*), 22
tribute system: development of,
  17–26; reciprocity system vs.,
  82–83. See also Song-Đại Việt
  tributary relations; *under specific
  leaders*
Triệu clan, 37
Triệu Đà, 35, 54
Triệu Hoài Đức, 55–56
Trịnh Tú, 45, 46
Trường Bà Khán, 62
Trương Hà Temple, 173
Trường Thiệu Phùng, 50
Tu clan, 158
Turton, Andrew, 172
Twelve Lords period, 44

Uighur communities, 160

Vi/Vy clan, 73, 164
victim, paradigm of the, 6
Việt Minh, 171
Vietnam: French colonial
  administration, 121, 167–71;
  scholarship during *1950s*, 164.
  See also Đại Việt court; Socialist
  Republic of Vietnam
Việt Nam sử lược (Trần Trọng Kim),
  122
Võ Nhị, 112
Vương Duy Khánh, 15–16
Vương Thieu Tộ, 45

Wade, Geoff, 25
Wang Anshi, 9, 31–32, 74, 114, 119,
  137–40
Wang Cheng, 155
Wang Gungwu, 41
Wang Han, 106, 125
Wang Qiangyou, 101
Wang Qinruo, 58
Wang Sui, 156
Wang Weizheng, 63
Wang Xiangzhi, 129
Wang Yanfu, 46
Wang Zhenglun, 106
Warlord Period, 125
Warring States period, 83
Wei Guan, 105
Wei Zhaomei, 52
Wen Yanbo, 26
White Tai, 169–70, 171
Wolters, O. W., 86
Woodside, Alexander, 34
Wudi, 36
Wu Ji, 101
Wu Lingyun, 168
Wu Wuju, 112
Wu Yazhong, 168
Wyatt, David, 72, 82

Xiao Gu, 96–97, 125, 126
Xiao Zhu, 105
Xiao, Zi, 36
Xichuan, 113
Xiong Ben, 145
Xiongnu nomadic people, 19
Xi Xia kingdom, 68–69
Xuân Hoà Temple, 173
Xuất Nhật Tân, 63
Xu Dao, 75
Xun Kuang, 19

Xu Shen, 73

Yang Baocai, 130, 131
Yang Tian, 107
Yang Wenguang, 156
Yang Wenjie, 52
Yao, 95
Yellow Flag Army, 169
Yongzhou, attacks on, 52, 69, 75, 94, 96–97, 101–3, 106–12; trade at, 52, 59
Yongzhou, 71, 75, 96–97
Yuan Yong, 110
Yuan Yun, 98
Yu Jing, 107, 108, 110, 112, 130
Yu Qing, 131
Yu Shi, 129

Zhang Fangping, 94–95
Zhang Guan, 52, 53
Zhang Li, 101, 102
Zhang Shoujie, 142
Zhang Tian, 134
Zhang Zhong, 106
Zhao Di, 142
Zhao Gui, 41–42
Zhao Kuangyin, 39, 41–42
Zhao Shidan, 104
Zhao Tuo, 117
Zheng San, 168
Zhong Jian, 105
Zhongxiu Dujunshen Temple, 156
Zhou dynasty, 18–23, 21*f*, 39
Zhou Qufei, 116
Zhuang clan: anti-French resistance, 168; cultural artifacts of, 70–71; identification, reorganization and indoctrination by CCP, 159–60; *neifu* status requested, 28–29; origin of term, 13; post-1978 reforms, 161; present-day, 12; regional organization, 158–59; scholarship on, 161, 162. *See also* Nùng clan
Zhuang Villages, 158

www.ingramcontent.com/pod-product-compliance
Lightning Source LLC
Chambersburg PA
CBHW030337240426
43661CB00052B/1661